inB1P e 1095

*5 48
HP
MM
5/o

D0077990

# Three Plays

*Nāga-Mandala*
*Hayavadana*
*Tughlaq*

# Three Plays

*Nāga-Mandala*

*Hayavadana*

*Tughlaq*

Girish Karnad

DELHI
OXFORD UNIVERSITY PRESS
CALCUTTA CHENNAI MUMBAI

Oxford University Press, Great Clarendon Street, Oxford OX2 6DP

Oxford   New York
Athens   Auckland   Bangkok   Calcutta
Cape Town   Chennai   Dar es Salaam   Delhi
Florence   Hong Kong   Istanbul   Karachi
Kuala Lumpur   Madrid   Melbourne   Mexico City
Mumbai   Nairobi   Paris   Singapore
Taipei   Tokyo   Toronto

and associates in
Berlin   Ibadan

© Oxford University Press 1994
Oxford India Paperbacks 1995
Third impression 1998

ISBN 0 19 563765 8

No performance or reading of any of these plays may be
given unless a license has been obtained in advance from
Girish Karnad, 697 Fifteenth Cross Road,
J.P. Nagar, Phase II, Bangalore 560078
and no copy of the play or any part thereof may be
reproduced for any purpose whatsoever by any method
without written permission from the publishers.

Typeset by Rastrixi, New Delhi 110070
Printed in India at Rekha Printers Pvt. Ltd., New Delhi 110020
and published by Manzar Khan, Oxford University Press
YMCA Library Building, Jai Singh Road, New Delhi 110001

# Contents

# Author's Introduction*

My generation was the first to come of age after India became independent of British rule. It therefore had to face a situation in which tensions implicit until then had come out in the open and demanded to be resolved without apologia or self-justification: tensions between the cultural past of the country and its colonial past, between the attractions of Western modes of thought and our own traditions, and finally between the various visions of the future that opened up once the common cause of political freedom was achieved. This is the historical context that gave rise to my plays and those of my contemporaries.

In my childhood, in a small town in Karnataka, I was exposed to two theatre forms that seemed to represent irreconcilably different worlds. Father took the entire family to see plays staged by troupes of professional actors called *natak companies* which toured the countryside throughout the year. The plays were staged in semipermanent structures on proscenium stages, with wings and drop curtains, and were illuminated by petromax lamps.

Once the harvest was over, I went with the servants to sit up nights watching the more traditional *Yakshagana* performances. The stage, a platform with a back curtain, was erected in the open air and lit by torches.

By the time I was in my early teens, the *natak companies* had ceased to function and *Yakshagana* had begun to seem quaint, even silly, to me. Soon we moved to a big city. This city had a college and electricity, but no professional theatre.

I saw theatre again only when I went to Bombay for my postgraduate studies. One of the first things I did in Bombay was to go and see a play, which happened to be Strindberg's *Miss Julie* directed by the brilliant young Ebrahim Alkazi.

I have been told since then that it was one of Alkazi's less successful productions. The papers tore it to shreds the next day. But when I walked out of the theatre that evening, I felt as though

---

* This is a considerably revised and expanded version of my paper, 'In Search of a New Theatre', in Carla M. Borden, ed., *Contemporary India* (Delhi: Oxford University Press, 1989).

I had been put through an emotionally or even a physically painful rite of passage. I had read some Western playwrights in college, but nothing had prepared me for the power and violence I experienced that day. By the norms I had been brought up on, the very notion of laying bare the inner recesses of the human psyche like this for public consumption seemed obscene. What impressed me as much as the psychological cannibalism of the play was the way lights faded in and out on stage. Until we moved to the city, we had lived in houses lit by hurricane lamps. Even in the city, electricity was something we switched on and off. The realization that there were instruments called dimmers that could gently fade the lights in or out opened up a whole new world of magical possibilities.

Most of my contemporaries went through some similar experience at some point in their lives. We stepped out of mythological plays lit by torches or petromax lamps straight into Strindberg and dimmers. The new technology could not be divorced from the new psychology. The two together defined a stage that was like nothing we had known or suspected. I have often wondered whether it wasn't that evening that, without being actually aware of it, I decided I wanted to be a playwright.

At the end of my stay in Bombay, I received a scholarship to go abroad for further studies. It is difficult to describe to a modern Indian audience the traumas created by this event. Going abroad was a much rarer occurrence in those days; besides, I came from a large, close-knit family and was the first member of the family ever to go abroad. My parents were worried lest I decide to settle down outside India, and even for me, though there was no need for an immediate decision, the terrible choice was implicit in the very act of going away. Should I at the end of my studies return home for the sake of my family, my people and my country, even at the risk of my abilities and training not being fully utilized in what seemed a stifling, claustrophobic atmosphere, or should I rise above such parochial considerations and go where the world drew me?

While still preparing for the trip, amidst the intense emotional turmoil, I found myself writing a play. This took me by surprise, for I had fancied myself a poet, had written poetry through my teens, and had trained myself to write in English, in preparation for the conquest of the West. But here I was writing a play and in Kannada, too, the language spoken by a few million people in South

India, the language of my childhood. A greater surprise was the theme of the play, for it was taken from ancient Indian mythology from which I had believed myself alienated.

The story of King Yayati that I used occurs in the *Mahabharata*. The king, for a moral transgression he has committed, is cursed to old age in the prime of life. Distraught at losing his youth, he approaches his son, pleading with him to lend him his youth in exchange for old age. The son accepts the exchange and the curse, and thus becomes old, older than his father.* But the old age brings no knowledge, no self-realization, only the senselessness of a punishment meted out for an act in which he had not even participated. The father is left to face the consequences of shirking responsibility for his own actions.

While I was writing the play, I saw it only as an escape from my stressful situation. But looking back, I am amazed at how precisely the myth reflected my anxieties at that moment, my resentment with all those who seemed to demand that I sacrifice my future. By the time I had finished working on *Yayati*—during the three weeks it took the ship to reach England and in the lonely cloisters of the university—the myth had enabled me to articulate to myself a set of values that I had been unable to arrive at rationally. Whether to return home finally seemed the most minor of issues; the myth had nailed me to my past.

Oddly enough the play owed its form not to the innumerable mythological plays I had been brought up on, and which had partly kept these myths alive for me, but to Western playwrights whom until then I had only read in print: Anouilh (his *Antigone* particularly) and also Sartre, O'Neill, and the Greeks. That is, at the most intense moment of self-expression, while my past had come to my aid with a ready-made narrative within which I could contain and explore my insecurities, there had been no dramatic structure in my own tradition to which I could relate myself.

One of the first plays of post-independence India to use myth to make a contemporary statement was Dharamvir Bharati's *Andha Yug* ('The Blind Age'). The play is about the aftermath of the Kurukshetra War, which forms the climax of the epic *Mahabharata*. The

---

* In the *Mahabharata*, King Yayati has five sons; after the elder four refuse their father, the youngest yields to his entreaties.

entire epic is in fact a build-up to this great confrontation between
Good and Evil, in which God himself participated in the form of
Lord Krishna. It was during this war that Krishna expounded the
*Bhagavadgita*, a discourse on the ethics of action and knowledge that
has exercised the most profound influence on Indian thought
through the ages. Yet this fratricidal war left in its wake nothing
but desolation and a sense of futility. No 'new world' emerged from
the wholesale massacre of the youth of the country. Arjuna, the
hero, became impotent. Lord Krishna himself meekly accepted a
curse and died an absurd death. In his play, Bharati used the myth
to give voice to the sense of horror and despair felt in India in the
wake of the partition of the country and the communal bloodbaths
that accompanied it.

Although later Satyadev Dubey's production proved that it was
genuine theatre, *Andha Yug* was actually written for the radio, as a
play for voices. It was as if, at the time of conceiving the play, the
playwright could imagine no stage on which to place it.

Indeed this contradiction haunts most contemporary playwright-
ing and theatre in India. Even to arrive at the heart of one's own
mythology, the writer has to follow signposts planted by the West,
a paradoxical situation for a culture in which the earliest *extant* play
was written in A.D. 200! The explanation lies in the fact that what
is called 'modern Indian theatre' was started by a group of people
who adopted 'cultural amnesia' as a deliberate strategy. It originated
in the second half of the nineteenth century in three cities, Bombay,
Calcutta and Madras. None of these seaports built by the British for
their maritime trade had an Indian past of its own, a history
independent of the British. These places had developed an Indian
middle class that in all outward respects aspired to 'look' like its
British counterpart. The social values of this class were shaped by
the English education it had received and by the need to work with
the British in trade and administration.

Inevitably the theatre it created imitated the British theatre of the
times, as presented by visiting troupes from England. Several new
concepts were introduced, two of which altered the nature of Indian
theatre. One was the separation of the audience from the stage by
the proscenium, underscoring the fact that what was being presented
was a spectacle free of any ritualistic associations and which therefore
expected no direct participation by the audience in it; and the other

was the idea of pure entertainment, whose success would be measured entirely in terms of immediate financial returns and the run of the play.

Until the nineteenth century, the audience had never been expected to pay to see a show. Theatre had depended upon patronage—of kings, ministers, local feudatories, or temples. With the myth-based story line already familiar to the audience, the shape and success of a performance depended on how the actors improvised with the given narrative material each time they came on stage. Actors did not rehearse a play so much as train for particular kinds of roles, a system still followed today in folk and traditional theatre forms. The principle here is the same as in North Indian classical music, where the musician aims to reveal unexpected delights even within the strictly regulated contours of a raga, by continual improvisation. It is the variability, the unpredictable potential of each performance that is its attraction. The audience accepts the risk.

With the new theatre, in conformity with the prevailing laissez-faire philosophy, risk became the producer's responsibility, the factor determining the company's investment policy. The audience paid in cash to see a show guaranteed as a 'success' and in return received as much entertainment as could be competitively fitted within the price of a ticket. A performance became a carefully packaged commodity, to be sold in endless identical replications.*

The proscenium and the box office proclaimed a new philosophy of the theatre: secularism—but a commercially viable secularism.

The secularism was partly necessitated by the ethnic heterogeneity of the new entrepreneurial class. In Bombay, for instance, the enterprises were financed by the Parsis, who spoke Gujarati. But the commonly understood language was Urdu, popularized by the Muslim chieftains who had ruled over most of India since the sixteenth century. Naturally many of the writers employed by the Parsi theatre were Muslim. And the audience was largely Hindu!

---

* Interestingly, although in Bombay ticketing of shows was the logical result of bringing theatre within the free market economy, in Bengal, where the Anglophile landed gentry had immediately made theatre their exclusive privilege, ticketing was the means by which this privilege was attacked and the form made accessible to the middle class.

The consequences of this secularism were that every character on stage, whether a Hindu deity or a Muslim legendary hero, was alienated from his true religious or cultural moorings; and myths and legends, emptied of meaning, were reshaped into tightly constructed melodramas with thundering curtain lines and a searing climax. Unlike traditional performances, which spread out in a slow, leisurely fashion, these plays demanded total attention, but only at the level of plot. Incident was all. Even in *natak* companies run entirely by Hindus, the basic attitude was dictated by this Parsi model.

There was, however, a far more important reason for the superficiality of the fare. The audience that patronized the Parsi theatre professed values it made no effort to realize in ordinary life. Whereas in public it accepted the Western bourgeois notions of secularism, egalitarianism, and individual merit, at home it remained committed to the traditional loyalties of caste, family, and religion. Only a society honest enough to face squarely the implications of this division within itself could have produced meaningful drama out of it. But as the new bourgeoisie claimed to be ashamed of the domestic lifestyle to which it nevertheless adhered tenaciously, the theatre certainly would never be allowed to acknowledge and project these contradictions.

It is possible to argue, as Ashis Nandy has done, that this inner division was not psychologically harmful at all but was a deliberate strategy adopted by this class to ensure that its personality was not totally absorbed and thereby destroyed by the colonial culture. Whatever the case, the effect on drama was to render it sterile. Despite its enormous success as spectacle over nearly seventy years, the Parsi theatre produced no drama of any consequence.

With the advent of 'talking' films in the 1930s the Parsi theatre collapsed without a fight. In the West, movies diminished the importance of theatre but did not destroy it. In India, professional theatre was virtually decimated by the film industry, which had learned most of its tricks from the theatre and could dish out the made-to-order entertainment on a scale much larger than the theatre could afford and at cheaper rates. India has not seen a professional theatre of the same proportions since.

In the process of settling down, the Parsi theatre had absorbed several features of traditional or folk performing arts, such as music, mime, and comic interludes. In Maharashtra, for instance, where this theatre flourished and continues to survive, its greatest contribution was in the field of music, in the form of a rich and varied body of theatre songs. However, to my generation of playwrights, reacting against memories of the Parsi stage in its decadence, music and dance seemed irrelevant to genuine drama. The only legacy left to us then was a lumbering, antiquated style of staging.

Yet there was no other urban tradition to look to, and in my second play, having concluded that Anouilh and Co. were not enough, I tried to make use of the Parsi stagecraft. This time the play was historical and therefore, perhaps inevitably, had a Muslim subject. (I say inevitably, for the Hindus have almost no tradition of history: the Hindu mind, with its belief in the cycle of births and deaths, has found little reason to chronicle or glamorize any particular historical period. Still, independence had made history suddenly important to us; we were acutely conscious of living in a historically important era. Indian history as written by the British was automatically suspect. The Marxist approach offered a more attractive alternative but in fact seemed unable to come to terms with Indian realities. Even today Marxist ideologues are lost when confronted with native categories like caste. It was the Muslims who first introduced history as a positive concept in Indian thought, and the only genuinely Indian methodology available to us for analyzing history was that developed by the Muslim historians in India.)

My subject was the life of Muhammed Tughlaq, a fourteenth century sultan of Delhi, certainly the most brilliant individual ever to ascend the throne of Delhi and also one of the biggest failures. After a reign distinguished for policies that today seem far-sighted to the point of genius, but which in their day earned him the title 'Muhammed the Mad,' the sultan ended his career in bloodshed and political chaos. In a sense, the play reflected the slow disillusionment my generation felt with the new politics of independent India: the gradual erosion of the ethical norms that had guided the movement for independence, and the coming to terms with cynicism and realpolitik.

The stagecraft of the Parsi model demanded a mechanical succession of alternating *shallow* and *deep* scenes. The shallow scenes were played in the foreground of the stage with a painted curtain—normally depicting a street—as the backdrop. These scenes were reserved for the 'lower class' characters with prominence given to comedy. They served as *link* scenes in the development of the plot, but the main purpose was to keep the audience engaged while the deep scenes, which showed interiors of palaces, royal parks, and other such visually opulent sets, were being changed or decorated. The important characters rarely appeared in the street scenes, and in the deep scenes the lower classes strictly kept their place.

The spatial division was ideal to show the gulf between the rulers and the ruled, between the mysterious inner chambers of power politics and the open, public areas of those affected by it. But as I wrote *Tughlaq*, I found it increasingly difficult to maintain the accepted balance between these two regions. Writing in an unprecedented situation where the mass populace was exercising political franchise, in however clumsy a fashion, for the first time in its history, I found the shallow scenes bulging with an energy hard to control. The regions ultimately developed their own logic. The deep scenes became emptier as the play progressed, and in the last scene, the 'comic lead' did the unconventional—he appeared in the deep scene, on a par with the protagonist himself. This violation of traditionally sacred spatial hierarchy, I decided—since there was little I could do about it—was the result of the anarchy which climaxed Tughlaq's times and seemed poised to engulf my own.

(An aside: whatever the fond theories of their creators, plays often develop their own independent existence. In his brilliant production of *Tughlaq*, E. Alkazi ignored my half-hearted tribute to the Parsi theatre and placed the action on the ramparts of the Old Fort at Delhi; and it worked very well.)

Another school of drama had arisen in the 1930s, at the height of the struggle for national independence. When social reform was acknowledged as a goal next only to independence in importance, a group of 'realistic' playwrights had challenged the emptiness and vapidity of Parsi drama. The contemporary concerns of these playwrights gave their work an immediacy and a sharp edge lacking in the earlier theatre, and a few plays of great power were written. While trying to awaken their audience to the humiliation of political enslavement, many of these new playwrights made a coruscating analysis of the ills that had eaten into Indian society. This was essentially the playwright's theatre; the plays were presented by amateur or semiprofessional groups and were mostly directed by the playwrights themselves. Unlike in the Parsi theatre, where a hard-headed financial logic was the guide, here the writers, the actors, and the audience were all united by a genuine idealism. They created a movement, if not a theatre, for the times.

Although its form aimed at being realistic, it must be pointed out at once that this drama concentrated on only a small corner of the vast canvas explored by Western realistic theatre.

The door banged by Nora in *The Doll's House* did not merely announce feminist rebellion against social slavery. It summed up what was to be the main theme of Western realistic drama over the next hundred years: a person's need to be seen as an individual, as an entity valuable in itself, independent of family and social circumstance. Indian realism, however, could not progress beyond analyses of social problems, for in India, despite the large urban population, there really has never been a bourgeoisie with its faith in individualism as the ultimate value. 'Westernization' notwithstanding, Indians define themselves in terms of their relationships to the other members of their family, caste, or class. They are defined by the role they have to play. In Sudhir Kakar's words, they see themselves in 'relational' terms in their social context, and they naturally extend the same references to theatre as well.

Let me give an example. A few years ago Arthur Miller's *A View from the Bridge* was presented in Madras. Eddie Carbone, the play's protagonist, is an Italian dock worker. He is a good man, but tragedy is brought about by his incestuous passion for his orphaned niece. He harbours two young, illegal Italian immigrants in his house, one of whom falls in love with the niece. Consumed by jealousy, Eddie breaks his code of honour, betrays the immigrants to the authorities, and is killed by one of them.

The audience watching the play in Madras was English educated, familiar with Western literature. Many of them frequently were abroad and had a living contact with the Western way of life. The production was a success. But most of the audience entirely missed the element of incest in the play; rather, they chose to ignore it as an unnecessary adjunct to an otherwise perfectly rational tale. After all, Eddie was his niece's guardian, a surrogate father. It was only right that he should be interested in her welfare. You certainly could not blame him for trying to safeguard her future. On the contrary, the illegal immigrants emerged as unsympathetic, for they had betrayed their host's confidence by seducing the niece's affections.

Even apart from consideration of social roles that led the Madras audience to write its own *A View from the Bridge*, Eddie Carbone perfectly fits an Indian archetype: the father figure aggressing toward its offspring. Our mythology is replete with parental figures demanding sacrifices from their children—as in my own *Yayati*; Eddie's position was not one in which the Indian audience was likely to find any tragic flaw.

To get back to realistic theatre, its great improvement over the Parsi theatre was that it took itself seriously both as art and as an instrument of social change. Yet it remained saddled with the European model. Bernard Shaw was its presiding deity. The proscenium continued, only now the grand spectacles gave way to the *interior set* with the invisible fourth wall. And that three-walled living room succinctly defined the basic limitation of this school of writing.

From Ibsen to Albee, the living room has symbolized all that is valuable to the Western bourgeoisie. It is one's refuge from the sociopolitical forces raging in the world outside, as well as the battleground where values essential to one's individuality are fought out and defended. But nothing of consequence ever happens or is supposed to happen in an Indian living room! It is the no-man's-land, the empty, almost defensive front the family presents to the world outside.

Space in a traditional home is ordered according to the caste hierarchy as well as the hierarchies within the family. Whether a person is permitted inside the compound, allowed as far as the outer verandah, or admitted into the living room depends on his or her caste and social status. And it is in the interior of the house, in the kitchen, in the room where the gods are kept, or in the backyard, where family problems are tackled, or allowed to fester, and where the women can have a say. Thus the living room as the location of dramatic action made nonsense of the very social problems the playwright set out to analyze, by distorting the caste dimensions as well as the position of women in the family.

How could these playwrights have so misunderstood the geography of their own homes? The three-walled living room was a symptom of a much more serious malaise: the conceptual tools they were using to analyze India's problems were as secondhand and unrealistic as the European parlour. The writers were young, angry, and in a hurry. The concepts defined for them by their English educators were new and refreshing and seemed rational. If the tools didn't quite fit the shifting ambiguities of social life, reality could be adjusted to fit these attractive imports. It may also be said that the refusal to go beyond the living room exactly mirrored the reluctance of these Westernized, upper-caste writers to go to the heart of the issues they were presenting.

To my generation, a hundred crowded years of urban theatre seemed to have left almost nothing to hang on to, to take off from. And where was one to begin again? Perhaps by looking at our audience again, by trying to understand what experience this audience expected to receive from theatre? This at least partly meant looking again at the traditional forms that had been sidelined by the Parsi theatre. The attempt, let me hasten to add, was not to find and reuse forms that had worked successfully in some other cultural context. The hope, rather, was to discover whether there was a structure of expectations—and conventions—about entertainment underlying these forms from which one could learn.

The most obvious starting point should have been the Sanskrit theatre. *Sakuntala* and *Mrcchakatika*, two Sanskrit masterpieces, had been presented successfully on the Marathi stage in the early part of this century. Recently, Ratan Thiyam, K.N.Panicker, and Vijaya Mehta have brought Sanskrit plays alive again for today's audience. But no modern playwright has claimed, or shown in his work, any allegiance to Sanskrit sensibility. Sanskrit drama assumed a specific social setting, a steady, well-ordered universe in which everyone from the gods to the meanest mortals was in his or her allotted slot. Even in its heyday it was an elitist phenomenon, confined to a restricted group of wealthy and educated courtiers, remote from the general populace.

Along with this court theatre there had existed other, more popular forms—more flexible, varying in their emphasis on formal purity. The exact relationship between Sanskrit theatre and these popular forms is of course difficult to determine. Sanskrit was not a language spoken in the homes; it was the language of courtly, literary, and philosophical discourse. The popular forms, on the other hand, used the natural languages of the people. Further, most of these languages came into their own as vehicles for artistic expression only about A.D. 1000, by which time Sanskrit literature—particularly drama—was already moribund. Even the aesthetics of these two theatre traditions differed. Sanskrit drama underplayed action and emphasized mood. It avoided scenes that unduly excited the audience. The popular forms wallowed in battles and hard-won marriages, blood and thunder. The biggest hurdle from our perspective is that unlike in Sanskrit, in which plays were written as independent works of art, this class of performing arts eschewed written texts and depended on improvisation within limits prescribed by their separate conventions, making it difficult to trace their historical growth. But in India, as has often been pointed out, the past is never totally lost; it coexists with the present as a parallel flow. A rich variety of regional theatre forms still exists, with a continuous history stretching over centuries, though through these centuries they have undoubtedly undergone changes and even mutilations.

For the first two decades after independence, how traditional forms could be utilized to revitalize our own work in the urban context was a ceaseless topic of argument among theatre people. The poet Vallathol had given a new identity to *Kathakali*, Shivaram Karanth a new lease on life to *Yakshagana*. Habib Tanvir has gone to areas in which the traditional troupes operate, taking with him his urban discipline. He has taught, lived, worked, and toured with the local troupes and evolved through them a work that is rich, vital, and meaningful.

But what were we, basically city-dwellers, to do with this stream? What did the entire paraphernalia of theatrical devices, half-curtains, masks, improvisation, music, and mime mean?

I remember that the idea of my play *Hayavadana* started crystallizing in my head right in the middle of an argument with B.V. Karanth (who ultimately produced the play) about the meaning of masks in Indian theatre and theatre's relationship to music. The play is based on a story from a collection of tales called the *Kathasaritsagara* and the further development of this story by Thomas Mann in 'The Transposed Heads.'

A young woman is travelling with her insecure and jealous husband and his rather attractive friend. The husband, suspecting his wife's loyalties, goes to a temple of Goddess Kali and beheads himself. The friend finds the body and, terrified that he will be accused of having murdered the man for the sake of his wife, in turn beheads himself. When the woman, afraid of the scandal that is bound to follow, prepares to kill herself too, the goddess takes pity and comes to her aid. The woman has only to rejoin the heads to the bodies and the goddess will bring them back to life. The woman follows the instructions, the men come back to life—except that in her confusion she has mixed up the heads. The story ends with the question: who is now the real husband, the one with the husband's head or the one with his body?

The answer given in the *Kathasaritsagara* is: since the head represents the man, the person with the husband's head is the husband.

Mann brings his relentless logic to bear upon this solution. If the head is the determining limb, then the body should change to fit the head. At the end of Mann's version, the bodies have changed again and adjusted themselves to the heads so perfectly that the men are physically exactly as they were at the beginning. We are back to square one; the problem remains unsolved.

As I said, the story initially interested me for the scope it gave for the use of masks and music. Western theatre has developed a contrast between the *face* and the *mask*—the real inner person and the exterior one presents, or wishes to present, to the world outside. But in traditional Indian theatre, the mask is only the face 'writ large'; since a character represents not a complex psychological entity but an ethical archetype, the mask merely presents in enlarged detail its essential moral nature. (This is why characters in *Hayavadana* have no real names. The heroine is called Padmini after one of the six types into which Vatsyayana classified all women. Her husband is Devadatta, a formal mode of addressing a stranger. His friend is Kapila, simply 'the dark one.') Music—usually percussion—then further distances the action, placing it in the realm of the mythical and the elemental.

The decision to use masks led me to question the theme itself in greater depth. All theatrical performances in India begin with worship of Ganesha, the god who ensures successful completion of any endeavour. According to mythology, Ganesha was beheaded by Shiva, his father, who had failed to recognize his own son (another aggressive father!). The damage was repaired by substituting an elephant's head, since the original head could not be found. Ganesha is often represented onstage by a young boy wearing the elephant mask, who then is worshipped as the incarnation of the god himself.

Ganesha's mask then says nothing about his nature. It is a mask, pure and simple. Right at the start of the play, my theory about masks was getting subverted. But the elephant head also questioned the basic assumption behind the original riddle: that the head represents the thinking part of the person, the intellect.

It seemed unfair, however, to challenge the thesis of the riddle by using a god. God, after all, is beyond human logic, indeed beyond human comprehension itself. The dialectic had to grow out of grosser ground, and I sensed a third being hovering in the spaces between the divine and the human, a horse-headed man. The play *Hayavadana*, meaning 'the one with a horse's head', is named after this character. The story of this horse-headed man, who wants to shed the horse's head and become human, provides the outer panel—as in a mural—within which the tale of the two friends is framed. Hayavadana, too, goes to the same Goddess Kali and wins a boon from her that he should become complete. Logic takes over. The head is the person: Hayavadana becomes a complete horse. The central logic of the tale remains intact, while its basic premise is denied.

The energy of folk theatre comes from the fact that although it seems to uphold traditional values, it also has the means of questioning these values, of making them literally stand on their head. The various conventions—the chorus, the masks, the seemingly unrelated comic episodes, the mixing of human and nonhuman worlds—permit the simultaneous presentation of alternative points of view, of alternative attitudes to the central problem. To use a phrase from Bertolt Brecht, these conventions then allow for 'complex seeing'. And it must be admitted that Brecht's influence, received mainly through his writings and without the benefit of his theatrical productions, went some way in making us realize what could be done with the design of traditional theatre. The theatrical conventions Brecht was reacting against—character as a psychological construct providing a focus for emotional identification, the willing-suspension-of-disbelief syndrome, the notion of a unified spectacle—were never a part of the traditional Indian theatre. There was therefore no question of arriving at an 'alienation' effect by using

Brechtian artifice. What he did was to sensitize us to the potentialities of nonnaturalistic techniques available in our own theatre.

How invigorating this legacy of traditional theatre has proved for Indian theatre can be illustrated by two other plays, which appeared soon after *Hayavadana*. In his *Ghashiram Kotwal*, Tendulkar uses *Dashavatara*, a traditional semiclassical form, to investigate a contemporary political problem, the emergence of 'demons' in public. These demons are initially created by political leaders for the purposes of their own power games, but ultimately go out of control and threaten to destroy their own creators. It is a theme recurrent in Indian mythology: the demon made indestructible by the boon of gods and then turning on the gods themselves. (A decade after the play was written, in Punjab, Sant Bhindranwale and Mrs Indira Gandhi seemed to be re-enacting the theme in real life in horrifying detail.)

The central theatrical device in the play is the use of about a dozen singers who start conventionally enough as a chorus. But as the play progresses, they become the human curtain alternately hiding the action and revealing bits of it as in a peep show. From neutral commentators, they slide into the roles of voyeurs who enjoy the degeneration they condemn, of courtiers who perpetrate atrocities, and of the populace that suffers the harassment. In the final scene the demon is ritually destroyed, torn limb from limb; the city is exorcised, and the now-purified stage is filled with revellers led by the politician who initially created the demon.

In Jabbar Patel's production, music and dance become the instruments of comment and analysis. Ritualistic movements turn imperceptibly into an orgy or a political procession; the music by Bhaskar Chandavarkar, based on traditional devotional tunes, continually turns upon itself, sometimes indulgently, sometimes critically. Unexpected breaks jangle the nerves of the audience. There is no explicit political analysis, but the matrix of the myth and the ironic use of *Dashavatara* drive the point home.

Unlike most Indian playwrights writing today, Chandrasekhar Kambar does not come from an urban background. As he was born and brought up in the country, there is no self-consciousness in his use of *Bayalata*, a secular folk form of his region. He draws upon the rich resources of popular speech and folklore with an effortlessness that conceals a rare sophistication of sensibility and technique.

He is a poet at ease with the ballad, and his approach to poetry on stage is through the ballad rather than the lyric; the imagery is the action, the metaphors serve to resonate the narrative at different levels of meaning.

*Jokumaraswamy* starts with a fertility rite in honor of the phallic deity Jokumara, who is worshipped in the form of a snake gourd. and then consumed by those desirous of bearing children. The basic situations as well as the music are all traditional, in the sense that they are set pieces, familiar in *Bayalata* drama. The impotent chieftain's virgin wife feeds the snake gourd by mistake to the village rake and has a child by him. The rake's death at the hands of the chieftain's men is a kind of gang rape-cum-fertility offering. The chieftain himself is literally left holding a baby he cannot disown.

Through this semicomic tale, Kambar makes a very Brechtian statement about the right of the peasants to the land on which they work virtually as serfs for an absentee landlord. But the analysis goes beyond this rather obvious political manifesto to a complex exploration in action of political power as a compensation for sexual inadequacy, of philandering as a psychosexual equivalent of anarchism, which can be controlled by love and responsibility. By working out the psychological, social, and political implications of the concept of virility, the play brings out the ambiguous nature of the very fertility rite it had set out to celebrate.

It must be admitted that the popularity of traditional forms on the urban stage has much to do with the technical freedom they offer the director. Music, mime, and exotic imagery open up vast opportunities for colorful improvisation, which nevertheless can—and alas! all too often does—degenerate into self-indulgence. While there are productions today which combine traditional theatre techniques with modern choreography and visual design to an effect unimaginable in the '60s, most such efforts tend to be imitative and soul-less. It is as though now that the problem has found a technical solution, the spirit of the quest has been lost.

*Naga-Mandala* is based on two oral tales I heard from A.K. Ramanujan. These tales are narrated by women—normally the older women in the family—while children are being fed in the evenings in the kitchen or being put to bed. The other adults present on these occasions are also women. Therefore these tales, though directed at the children, often serve as a parallel system of communication among the women in the family.

They also express a distinctly woman's understanding of the reality around her, a lived counterpoint to the  patriarchal structures of classical texts and institutions. The position of Rani in the story of *Naga-Mandala*, for instance, can be seen as a metaphor for the situation of a young girl in the bosom of a joint family where she sees her husband only in two unconnected roles—as a stranger during the day and as lover at night. Inevitably, the pattern of relationships she is forced to weave from these disjointed encounters must be something of a fiction. The empty house Rani is locked in could be the family she is married into.

Many of these tales also talk about the nature of tales. The story of the flames comments on the paradoxical nature of oral tales in general: they have an existence of their own, independent of the teller and yet live only when they are passed on from the possessor of the tale to the listener. Seen thus, the status of a tale becomes akin to that of a daughter, for traditionally a daughter too is not meant to be kept at home too long but has to be passed on. This identity adds poignant and ironic undertones to the relationship of the teller to the tales.

It needs to be stressed here that these tales are not left-overs from the past. In the words of Ramanujan, 'Even in a large modern city like Madras, Bombay or Calcutta, even in western-style nuclear families with their well-planned 2.2 children, folklore . . . is only a suburb away, a cousin or a grandmother away'.[*]

The basic concern of the Indian theatre in the post-independence period has been to try to define its 'Indianness'. The distressing fact is that most of these experiments have been carried out by enthusiastic amateurs or part-timers, who have been unable to devote themselves entirely to theatre. I see myself as a playwright but make a living in film and television. There is a high elasticity of substitution

---

[*] A.K. Ramanujan, 'Introduction', *Folktales from India* (New Delhi: Viking, 1993), p. xiii.

A.K. Ramanujan, 'Two Realms of Kannada Folklore', Stuart H. Blackburn and A.K. Ramanujan, ed., *Another Harmony* (Berkeley: University of California Press, 1987).

A.K. Ramanujan, 'Telling Tales', *Daedalus*, Fall, 1989.

between the different performing media in India; the participants—as well as the audiences—get tossed about.

The question therefore of what lies in store for the Indian theatre should be rephrased to include other media as well—radio, cinema, audio cassettes, television and video. Their futures are inextricably intertwined and in this shifting landscape, the next electronic gadget could easily turn a mass medium into a traditional art from.

Perhaps quite unrealistically, I dream of the day when a similar ripple will reestablish theatre—flesh-and-blood actors enacting a well-written text to a gathering of people who have come to witness the performance—where it belongs, at the centre of the daily life of the people.

# Nāga-Mandala

## Play with a Cobra

# Note to Nāga-Mandala

Nāga-Mandala is based on two oral tales from Karnataka which I first heard several years ago from Professor A.K. Ramanujan. But that is only the least of the reasons for dedicating this play to him.

I wrote Nāga-Mandala during the year I spent at the University of Chicago as Visiting Professor and Fulbright Scholar-in-Residence. I am most grateful to Professor Stuart M. Tave, Dean, Division of Humanities, and Professor C.M. Naim, Chairman, Department of South Asian Languages and Civilizations as well as to the Council for International Exchange of Scholars for having made that visit possible. I am further indebted to Professor Naim for persuading me to put the play into English.

I write in Kannada. English is the language of my adulthood. This translation must therefore be seen only as an approximation to the original. My deepest thanks are due to the colleagues and students who helped with the production of the play at the University Theater at Chicago, for their many valuable suggestions and textual corrections, as well as to Shri Shankar Nag who first presented the play in Kannada with his group, Sanket.

I am conscious that Naga's long speech on p. 45 owes much to Jean Anouilh, although I have been unable to identify the play.

Bombay                                                                 G.K.
28 November 1988

# *Characters*

### *(In the order of their appearance)*

THE MAN

THE FLAMES

THE STORY


RANI (*which means* QUEEN)

APPANNA (*which means* ANY MAN)

KURUDAVVA (*which means* THE BLIND ONE)

KAPPANNA (*which means* THE DARK ONE)

NAGA (*which means* THE COBRA)


THREE VILLAGE ELDERS

CROWDS

*Appanna and Naga are played by the same actor.*

# Prologue

(*The inner sanctum of a ruined temple. The idol is broken, so the presiding deity of the temple cannot be identified.*

*It is night. Moonlight seeps in through the cracks in the roof and the walls.*

*A man is sitting in the temple. Long silence. Suddenly, he opens his eyes wide. Closes them. Then uses his fingers to pry open his eyelids. Then he goes back to his original morose stance.*

*He yawns involuntarily. Then reacts to the yawn by shaking his head violently, and turns to the audience.*)

MAN:   I may be dead within the next few hours.

(*Long pause.*)

I am not talking of 'acting' dead. Actually dead. I might die right in front of your eyes.

(*Pause.*)

A mendicant told me: 'You must keep awake at least one whole night this month. If you can do that, you'll live. If not, you will die on the last night of the month.' I laughed out loud when I heard him. I thought nothing would be easier than spending a night awake.

(*Pause.*)

I was wrong. Perhaps death makes one sleepy. Every night this month I have been dozing off before even being aware of it. I am convinced I am seeing something with these eyes of mine, only to wake up and find I was dreaming. Tonight is my last chance.

(*Pause.*)

For tonight is the last night of the month. Even of my life, perhaps? For how do I know sleep won't creep in on me again as it has every night so far? I may doze off right in front of you. And that will be the end of me.

(*Pause.*)

I asked the mendicant what I had done to deserve this fate. And he said: 'You have written plays. You have staged them. You have caused so many good people, who came trusting you, to fall asleep twisted in miserable chairs, that all that abused mass of sleep has turned against you and become the Curse of Death.'

(*Pause.*)

I hadn't realized my plays had had that much impact.

(*Pause.*)

Tonight may be my last night. So I have fled from home and come to this temple, nameless and empty. For years I've been lording it over my family as a writer. I couldn't bring myself to die a writer's death in front of them.

(*Pause.*)

I swear by this absent God, if I survive this night I shall have nothing more to do with themes, plots or stories. I abjure all story-telling, all play-acting.

(*Female voices are heard outside the temple. He looks.*)

Voices! Here? At this time of night? Lights! Who could be coming here now?

(*He hides behind a pillar. Several Flames enter the temple, giggling, talking to each other in female voices.*)

MAN: I don't believe it! They are naked lamp flames! No wicks, no lamps. No one holding them. Just lamp flames on their own—floating in the air! Is that even possible?

(*Another three or four Flames enter, talking among themselves.*)

FLAME 3: (*Addressing Flame I, which is already in the temple.*)

Hello! What a pleasant surprise! You are here before us tonight.

FLAME 1: That master of our house, you know what a skinflint he is! He is convinced his wife has a hole in her palm, so he buys all the groceries himself. This evening, before the dark was even an hour old, they ran out of *kusbi* oil. The tin of peanut oil didn't go far. The bowl of castor oil was empty anyway. So they had to retire to bed early and I was permitted to come here.

(*Laughter.*)

FLAME 2: (*Sneering.*) *Kusbi* oil! Peanut oil! How disgusting! My family comes from the coast. We won't touch anything but coconut oil.

FLAME 1: . . . But at least I come here every night. What about your friend, the kerosene flame? She hasn't been seen here for months. She is one of the first tonight.

FLAME 4:   Actually, from today on I don't think I'll have any difficulty getting out . . . and early.
        (*They all laugh.*)
FLAME 1:   Why? What's happened?
        (*The other Flames giggle.*)
FLAMES:   Tell her! Tell her!
FLAME 4:   My master had an old, ailing mother. Her stomach was bloated, her back covered with bed sores. The house stank of cough and phlegm, pus and urine. No one got a wink of sleep at night. Naturally, I stayed back too. The old lady died this morning, leaving behind my master and his young wife, young and juicy as a tender cucumber. I was chased out fast.
        (*Giggles.*)
FLAME 3:   You are lucky. My master's eyes have to feast on his wife limb by limb if the rest of him is to react. So we lamps have to bear witness to what is better left to the dark.
        (*They all talk animatedly. New Flames come and join them. They group and regroup, chattering.*)
MAN:   (*To the audience.*) I had heard that when lamps are put out in the village, the flames gather in some remote place and spend the night together, gossiping. So this is where they gather!
        (*A new Flame enters and is enthusiastically greeted.*)
FLAME 1:   You are late. It is well past midnight.
NEW FLAME:   Ah! There was such a to-do in our house tonight.
FLAMES:   What happened? Tell us!
NEW FLAME:   You know I have only an old couple in my house. Tonight the old woman finished eating, swept and cleaned the floor, put away the pots and pans, and went to the room in which her husband was sleeping. And what should she see, but a young woman dressed in a rich, new sari step out of the room! The moment the young woman saw my mistress, she ran out of the house and disappeared into the night. The old woman woke her husband up and questioned him. But he said he knew nothing. Which started the rumpus.
FLAMES:   But who was the young woman? How did she get into your house?
NEW FLAME:   Let me explain: My mistress, the old woman, knows a story and a song. But all these years she has kept them to herself, never told the story, nor sung the song. So the story

and the song were being choked, imprisoned inside her. This afternoon the old woman took her usual nap after lunch and started snoring. The moment her mouth opened, the story and the song jumped out and hid in the attic. At night, when the old man had gone to sleep, the story took the form of a young woman and the song became a sari. The young woman wrapped herself in the sari and stepped out, just as the old lady was coming in. Thus, the story and song created a feud in the family and were revenged on the old woman.

FLAME 1:    So if you try to gag one story, another happens.

FLAMES:    (*All together.*) But where are they now, the poor things? . . . How long will they run around in the dark? What will happen to them?

NEW FLAME:    I saw them on my way here and told them to follow me. They should be here any moment . . . There they are! The story with the song!

(*The Story, in the form of a woman dressed in a new, colourful sari, enters, acknowledges the enthusiastic welcome from the Flames with a languid wave of the hand and goes and sits in a corner, looking most despondent. The Flames gather around her.*)

NEW FLAME:    Come on. Why are you so despondent? We are here and are free the whole night. We'll listen to you.

STORY:    Thank you, my dears. It is kind of you. But what is the point of your listening to a story? You can't pass it on.

FLAMES:    That's true . . . What can we do? Wish we could help.

(*While the Flames make sympathetic noises, the Man jumps out from behind the pillar and grabs the Story by her wrist.*)

MAN:    I'll listen to you!

(*The Flames flee helter-skelter in terror. The Story struggles to free herself.*)

STORY:    Who are you? Let me go!

MAN:    What does it matter who I am, I'll listen to you. Isn't that enough? I promise you, I'll listen all night!

(*The Story stops struggling. There is a new interest in her voice.*)

STORY:    You will?

MAN:    Yes.

STORY:    Good. Then let me go.

(*He does not.*) I need my hands to act out the parts.

(*He lets her go.*)

There is a condition, however—

MAN: What?

STORY: You can't just listen to the story and leave it at that. You must tell it again to someone else.

MAN: That I certainly shall, if I live. But first I must be alive to . . . That reminds me. I have a condition, too.

STORY: Yes?

MAN: I must not doze off during the tale. If I do, I die. All your telling will be wasted.

STORY: As a self-respecting story, that is the least I can promise.

MAN: All right then. Start. (*Suddenly.*) But no! No! It's not possible. I take back my word. I can't repeat the story.

STORY: And why not?

MAN: I have just now taken a vow not to have anything to do with themes, plots or acting. If I live, I don't want to risk any more curses from the audience.

STORY: (*Gets up.*) Good-bye then. We must be going.

MAN: Wait! Don't go. Please.

(*Thinks.*)

I suppose I have no choice.

(*To the audience.*)

So now you know why this play is being done. I have no choice. Bear with me, please. As you can see, it is a matter of life and death for me.

(*Calls out.*)

Musicians, please!

(*Musicians enter and occupy their mat.*)

The Story and the Song!

(*Throughout the rest of the play, the Man and the Story remain on stage. The Flames too listen attentively though from a distance.*)

(*To the Story.*) Go on.

# Act One

*(The locked front door of a house with a yard in front of the house, and on the right, an enormous ant-hill. The interior of the house—the kitchen, the bathroom as well as Rani's room—is clearly seen.)*

STORY:  A young girl. Her name . . . it doesn't matter. But she was an only daughter, so her parents called her Rani. Queen. Queen of the whole wide world. Queen of the long tresses. For when her hair was tied up in a knot, it was as though a black King Cobra lay curled on the nape of her neck, coil upon glistening coil. When it hung loose, the tresses flowed, a torrent of black, along her young limbs, and got entangled in her silver anklets. Her fond father found her a suitable husband. The young man was rich and his parents were both dead. Rani continued to live with her parents until she reached womanhood. Soon, her husband came and took her with him to his village. His name was—well, any common name will do—

MAN:  Appanna?

STORY:  Appanna.

*(Appanna enters, followed by Rani. They carry bundles in their arms, indicating that they have been travelling. Appanna opens the lock on the front door of the house. They go in.)*

APPANNA:  Have we brought in all the bundles?

RANI:  Yes.

APPANNA:  Well, then, I'll be back tomorrow at noon. Keep my lunch ready. I shall eat and go.

*(Rani looks at him nonplussed. He pays no attention to her, goes out, shuts the door, locks it from outside and goes away. She runs to the door, pushes it, finds it locked, peers out of the barred window. He is gone.)*

RANI:  Listen—please—

*(She does not know what is happening, stands perplexed. She cannot even weep. She goes and sits in a corner of her room. Talks to herself indistinctly. Her words become distinct as the lights dim. It is night.)*

. . . So Rani asks him: 'Where are you taking me?' And the

Eagle answers: 'Beyond the seven seas and the seven isles. On the seventh island is a magic garden. And in that garden stands the tree of emeralds. Under that tree, your parents wait for you.' So Rani says: 'Do they? Then please, please take me to them—immediately. Here I come.' So the Eagle carries her clear across the seven seas . . .

(*She falls asleep. Moans 'Oh, Mother!' 'Father' in her sleep. It gets light. She wakes up with a fright, looks around, then runs to the bathroom, mimes splashing water on her face, goes into the kitchen, starts cooking. Appanna comes. Opens the lock on the front door and comes in. Goes to the bathroom. Mimes bathing, then comes to the kitchen and sits down to eat. She serves him food.*)

RANI:   Listen—(*Fumbling for words*) Listen—I feel—frightened—alone at night—

APPANNA:   What is there to be scared of? Just keep to yourself. No one will bother you. Rice!

(*Pause.*)

RANI:   Please, you could—

APPANNA:   Look, I don't like idle chatter. Do as you are told, you understand?

(*Finishes his meal, gets up.*)

I'll be back tomorrow, for lunch.

(*Appanna washes his hands, locks her in and goes away. Rani watches him blankly through the window.*)

STORY:   And so the days rolled by.

(*Mechanically, Rani goes into the kitchen, starts cooking. Talks to herself.*)

RANI:   Then Rani's parents embrace her and cry. They kiss her and caress her. At night she sleeps between them. So she is not frightened any more. 'Don't worry,' they promise her. 'We won't let you go away again ever!' In the morning, the stag with the golden antlers comes to the door. He calls out to Rani. She refuses to go. 'I am not a stag,' he explains, 'I am a prince' . . .

(*Rani sits staring blankly into the oven. Then begins to sob. Outside, in the street, Kappanna enters, carrying Kurudavva on his shoulders. She is blind. He is in his early twenties.*)

KAPPANNA:   Mother, you can't do this! You can't start meddling in other people's affairs the first thing in the morning. That

Appanna should have been born a wild beast or a reptile. By some mistake, he got human birth. He can't stand other people. Why do you want to tangle with him?

KURUDAVVA:  Whatever he is, he is the son of my best friend. His mother and I were like sisters. Poor thing, she died bringing him into this world. Now a new daughter-in-law comes to her house. How can I go on as though nothing has happened? Besides, I haven't slept a wink since you told me you saw Appanna in his concubine's courtyard. He has got himself a bride—and he still goes after that harlot?

KAPPANNA:  I knew I shouldn't have told you. Now you have insomnia—and I have a backache.

KURUDAVVA:  Who's asked you to carry me around like this? I haven't, have I? I was born and brought up here. I can find my way around.

KAPPANNA:  Do you know what I ask for when I pray to Lord Hanuman of the Gymnasium every morning? For more strength. Not to wrestle. Not to fight. Only so I can carry you around.

KURUDAVVA:  (*Pleased.*) I know, I know.
    (*Suddenly Kappanna freezes.*)
What is it? Why have you stopped?
    (*He doesn't answer. Merely stands immobile and stares. A touch of panic in Kurudavva's voice.*)
What is it, Kappanna? Kappanna!

KAPPANNA:  Nothing, Mother. It's just that I can see Appanna's front door from here.

KURUDAVVA:  (*Relieved.*) Oh! For a moment I was worried it was that—who-is-that-again? That witch or fairy, whatever she is—who you say follows you around.

KAPPANNA:  Mother, she is not a witch or a fairy. When I try to explain, you won't even listen. And then, when I'm not even thinking of her, you start suspecting all kinds of—

KURUDAVVA:  Hush! Enough of her now. Tell me why we have stopped.

KAPPANNA:  There doesn't seem to be anyone in Appanna's house. There is a lock on the front door.

KURUDAVVA:  How is that possible? Even if he is lying in his concubine's house, his bride should be home.

KAPPANNA:  Who can tell about Appanna? He's a lunatic . . .

KURUDAVVA: You don't think he could have sent his wife back to her parents already, do you? Come, let us look in through the window and check.

KAPPANNA: Of course not, Mother! If someone sees us—

KURUDAVVA: Listen to me. Go up to the house and peep in. Tell me what you see.

KAPPANNA: I refuse.

KURUDAVVA: (*Tearful.*) I wouldn't have asked you if I had eyes. I don't know why God has been cruel to me, why he gave me no sight . . .

KAPPANNA: (*Yielding.*) All right, Mother.

(*They go near the house. Kappanna peers through the window.*)

KAPPANNA: The house is empty.

KURUDAVVA: Of course it is, silly! How can anyone be inside when there is a lock outside on the door? Tell me, can you see clothes drying inside? What kind of clothes? Any saris? Skirts? Or is it only men's clothes?

KAPPANNA: I can't see a thing!

RANI: Who is it? What is that outside?

KAPPANNA: Oh my God!

(*Lifts Kurudavva and starts running.*)

KURUDAVVA: Stop! Stop, I tell you! Why are you running as though you've seen a ghost?

KAPPANNA: There is someone inside the house—a woman!

KURUDAVVA: You don't have to tell me that! So what if there is a woman inside the house? We have come here precisely because a woman is supposed to be in the house.

KAPPANNA: Mother, what does it mean when a man locks his wife in?

KURUDAVVA: You tell me.

KAPPANNA: It means he does not want anyone to talk to his wife.

RANI: (*Comes to the window.*) Who is it?

KAPPANNA: Let's go.

(*Starts running again. Kurudavva hits him on the back.*)

KURUDAVVA: Stop! Stop! (*To Rani*) I am coming, child! Right now! Don't go away! (*To Kappanna*) He keeps his wife locked up like a caged bird? I must talk to her. Let me down—instantly!

(*He lets her down.*)

You go home if you like.

KAPPANNA: I'll wait for you here under the tree. Come back soon. Don't just sit there gossiping . . .

KURUDAVVA: (*Approaching Rani.*) Dear girl . . .

RANI: Who are you?

KURUDAVVA: Don't be afraid. I am called Kurudavva, because I am blind. Your mother-in-law and I were like sisters. I helped when your husband was born. Don't be frightened. Appanna is like a son to me. Is he not in?

RANI: No.

KURUDAVVA: What is your name?

RANI: They call me Rani.

KURUDAVVA: And where is Appanna?

RANI: I don't know.

KURUDAVVA: When did he go out?

RANI: After lunch yesterday.

KURUDAVVA: When will he come back?

RANI: He will be back for lunch later in the day.

KURUDAVVA: You don't mean, he is home only once a day, and that too . . . only for lunch?

(*No reply.*)

And you are alone in the house all day?

(*Rani begins to sob.*)

Don't cry child, don't cry. I haven't come here to make you cry. Does he lock you up every day like this?

RANI: Yes, since the day I came here . . .

KURUDAVVA: Does he beat you or ill-treat you?

RANI: No.

KURUDAVVA: (*Pause.*) Does he . . . 'talk' to you?

RANI: Oh, that he does. But not a syllable more than required. 'Do this', 'Do that', 'Serve the food.'

KURUDAVVA: You mean—? That means—you are—still—hmm! Has he . . . ?

RANI: Apart from him, you are the first person I have seen since coming here. I'm bored to death. There is no one to talk to!

KURUDAVVA: That's not what I meant by 'talk'. Has your husband touched you? How can I put it? (*Exasperated.*) Didn't anyone explain to you before your wedding? Your mother? Or an aunt?

RANI: Mother started shedding tears the day I matured and was still crying when I left with my husband. Poor her! She is probably crying even now.

(*Starts sobbing.*)

KURUDAVVA: Dear girl, it's no use crying. Don't cry! Don't! Come here. Come, come to the window. Let me touch you. My eyes are all in my fingers.

(*She feels Rani's face, shoulder, neck through the bars of the window.*)

Ayyo! How beautiful you are. Ears like hibiscus. Skin like young mango leaves. Lips like rolls of silk. How can that Appanna gallivant around leaving such loveliness wasting away at home?

RANI: I am so frightened at night, I can't sleep a wink. At home, I sleep between Father and Mother. But here, alone—Kurudavva, can you help me, please? Will you please send word to my parents that I am, like this, here? Will you ask them to free me and take me home? I would jump into a well—if only I could—

KURUDAVVA: Chih! Chih! You shouldn't say such things. I'll take care of everything.

(*Calls out.*)

Son! Son!

KAPPANNA: (*From behind the tree.*) Yes?

KURUDAVVA: Come here.

KAPPANNA: No, I won't.

KURUDAVVA: Come here, you idiot.

KAPPANNA: I absolutely refuse, Mother. I told you right at the start that I won't.

KURUDAVVA: Honestly!

(*Comes to him.*)

Listen, Son. Run home now. Go into the cattle shed—the left corner—

KAPPANNA: The left corner—

KURUDAVVA: Just above where you keep the plough, behind the pillar, on the shelf—

KAPPANNA: Behind the pillar—on the shelf—

KURUDAVVA: There is an old tin trunk. Take it down. It's full of odds and ends, but take out the bundle of cloth. Untie it. Inside there is a wooden box.

KAPPANNA: A wooden box. All right—

KURUDAVVA:   In the right hand side of the wooden box is a coconut shell wrapped in a piece of paper. Inside are two pieces of a root. Bring them.

KAPPANNA:   Now?

KURUDAVVA:   Now. At once. Before Appanna returns home.

KAPPANNA:   Mother, listen to me. If he finds you here—

KURUDAVVA:   Don't waste time now. Do as I say. Run.

(*Gets up and comes back to the house. Kappanna leaves.*)
Are you still there?

RANI:   Yes. Who is that?

KURUDAVVA:   My son, Kappanna. Oh, don't let his name mislead you. He isn't really dark. In fact, when he was born, my husband said: 'Such a fair child! Let's call him the Fair One!' I said: 'I don't know what Fair means. My blind eyes know only the dark. So let's call this little parrot of my eyes the Dark One!' And he became Kappanna.

RANI:   And where have you sent him?

KURUDAVVA:   I'll tell you. I was born blind. No one would marry me. My father wore himself out going from village to village looking for a husband. But to no avail. One day a mendicant came to our house. No one was home. I was alone. I looked after him in every way. Cooked hot food specially for him and served him to his heart's content. He was pleased with me and gave me three pieces of a root. 'Any man who eats one of these will marry you', he said.

RANI:   And then?

KURUDAVVA:   'Feed him the smallest piece first', he said. 'If that gives no results, then try the middle-sized one. Only if both fail, feed him the largest piece.'

RANI:   (*Entranced.*) And then?

KURUDAVVA:   One day a boy distantly related to me came to our village and stayed with us. That day I ground one of the pieces into paste, mixed it in with the food, and served him. Can you guess which piece I chose?

RANI:   (*Working it out.*) Which one now? The smallest one, as the mendicant said? No, no, surely the biggest piece.

KURUDAVVA:   No, I was in such a hurry I barely noticed the small one. The biggest scared me. So I used the middle-sized root.

RANI:   And then?

KURUDAVVA:   He finished his meal, gave me one look and fell in
love. Married me within the next two days. Never went back
to his village. It took the plague to detach him from me.
(*Rani laughs.*)
KAPPANNA:   (*Entering.*) Mother—
KURUDAVVA:   Ha! There he is! Wait!
(*Goes to him.*)
Have you brought them?
(*Kappanna gives her the two pieces of root. Kurudavva hurries back
to Rani.*)
Are you still there?
RANI:   Yes, I am.
KURUDAVVA:   Here.
RANI:   What is that?
KURUDAVVA:   The root I was telling you about.
(*Rani starts.*) Here. Take this smaller piece. That should do for
a pretty jasmine like you. Take it! Grind it into a nice paste and
feed it to your husband. And watch the results. Once he smells
you he won't go sniffing after that bitch. He will make you a
wife instantly.
RANI:   But I am his wife already.
KURUDAVVA:   Just do as I say.
(*Rani takes the piece. Kurudavva tucks the other one in the knot
of her sari. Kappanna whistles. She turns.*)
That must be Appanna coming.
RANI:   (*Running in.*) Go now, Kurudavva. But come again.
KURUDAVVA:   I shall too. But don't forget what I told you.
(*Kurudavva starts to go. Appanna crosses her.*)
APPANNA:   (*Suspicious.*) Who is that? Kurudavva?
KURUDAVVA:   How are you, Appanna? It's been a long time—
APPANNA:   What are you doing here?
KURUDAVVA:   I heard you had brought a new bride. Thought I
would talk to her. But she refuses to come out.
APPANNA:   She won't talk to any one. And no one need talk to
her.
KURUDAVVA:   If you say so.
(*Exits.*)
APPANNA:   (*So she can hear.*) I put a lock on the door so those with

sight could see. Now what does one do about blind meddlers?
I think I'll keep a watch dog.

(*Opens the door and goes in. To Rani.*)

I am lunching out today. I'll have my bath and go. Just heat up
a glass of milk for me.

(*Goes into the bathroom. Mimes bathing. Rani boils the milk.
Pours it in a glass and starts to take it out. Notices the piece of
root. Stops. Thinks. Runs out. Sees that he is still bathing. Runs
back into the kitchen, makes a paste of the root.*)

APPANNA:   (*Dressing.*) Milk!

(*Rani jumps with fright. Hurriedly mixes the paste into the milk.
Comes out and gives Appanna the glass of milk. He drinks it in
a single gulp. Hands the glass back to her. Goes to the door, ready
to put the lock on. She watches him intently. He tries to shut the
door. Suddenly clutches his head. Slides down to the floor. Stretches
out and goes to sleep on the door-step, half inside and half outside
the house. Rani is distraught. Runs to him. Shakes him. He doesn't
wake up. He is in a deep sleep. She tries to drag him into the
house, but he is too heavy for her. She sits down and starts crying.*)

APPANNA:   (*Groggily.*) Water! Water!

(*She brings a pot of water. Splashes it on his face. He wakes up
slowly, staggers up. Washes his face. Pushes her in. Locks the door
from outside. Goes away. Rani watches, stunned. Slowly goes back
to her bedroom. Starts talking to herself. It becomes night.*)

RANI:   . . . So the demon locks her up in his castle. Then it rains
for seven days and seven nights. It pours. The sea floods the
city. The waters break down the door of the castle. Then a big
whale comes to Rani and says: 'Come, Rani, let us go . . .'

(*She falls asleep. Midnight. Kappanna enters carrying Kurudavva.
Stumbles on a stone. They fall.*)

KURUDAVVA:   Thoo! That's the problem with having eyes: one
can't see in the dark. That's why I have been telling you to let
me go on my own at least at night—

KAPPANNA:   Go! Go! From this point on you can certainly go on
alone. I refuse to come any closer to that house. And what are
you doing, Mother? Suppose he is in the house. And he hears
you. What will you say? That you have come to gossip with
his wife in the dead of night?

KURUDAVVA:   Shut up! We are here only to find out if the lock is gone yet. If it's gone, he is inside now. That means success is ours. We'll leave right away.

(*Goes and touches the door. It is closed. Tip-toes to feel the latch. The lock is still there. Recoils in surprise.*)

I can't believe it. The lock is still there! (*Thinks.*)

Perhaps he has taken her out to the fields or the garden!

(*Laughs.*)

RANI:     (*Wakes up.*) Who is that?

KURUDAVVA:     Me.

RANI:     (*Comes running.*) Who? Kurudavva? This time of the night?

KURUDAVVA:     What happened, child? Why is the lock still there? (*No reply.*)

Did you feed him the root?

RANI:     Yes.

KURUDAVVA:     And what happened?

RANI:     Nothing. He felt giddy. Fainted. Then got up and left.

KURUDAVVA:     That's bad. This is no ordinary infatuation then. That concubine of his is obviously—

RANI:     Who?

KURUDAVVA:     Didn't want to tell you. There is a woman, a bazaar woman. She has your husband in her clutches. Squeezes him dry. Maybe she's cast a spell. There is only one solution to this—

RANI:     What?

KURUDAVVA:     (*Giving her the bigger piece.*) Feed him this larger piece of root.

RANI:     No!

KURUDAVVA:     Yes!

RANI:     That little piece made him sick. This one—

KURUDAVVA:     It will do good, believe me. This is not hearsay. I am telling you from my own experience. Go in. Start grinding it. Make a tasty curry. Mix the paste in it. Let him taste a spoonful and he will be your slave. And then? Just say the word and he will carry you to my house himself.

(*Rani blushes.*)

Son! Son!

(*To Rani.*) Remember. Don't let anything frighten you.

(*Rani goes into the kitchen. Kurudavva wakes up Kappanna. They exit. It gets brighter. Appanna comes. He has a vicious-looking dog on a chain with him. He brings it to the front yard and ties it*

*to a tree stump there. Then comes to the front door and unlocks it.*
*The dog begins to bark. Surprised at the bark, Rani peers out of*
*the window.*)

RANI:   Oh! A dog—

APPANNA:   That blind woman and her son! Let them step here again
and they'll know—! I'll bathe and come to eat. Serve my food.
(*Goes to the bathroom and starts bathing. Rani takes down her pot*
*of curry. Removes the lid. Takes out the paste of the root.*)

RANI:   (*To the Story.*) Shall I pour it in?
(*Appanna calmly continues his bath. It is evident he has heard*
*nothing.*)

RANI:   Oh my god! What horrible mess is this? Blood. Perhaps
poison. Shall I serve him this? That woman is blind, but he
isn't. How could he possibly not see this boiling blood, this
poisonous red? And then—even if he doesn't see it—how do I
know it is not dangerous? Suppose something happens to my
husband? What will my fate be? That little piece made him ill.
Who knows . . . ?
(*Slaps herself on her cheeks.*)
No, no. Forgive me, God. This is evil. I was about to commit
a crime. Father, Mother, how could I, your daughter, agree to
such a heinous act? No, I must get rid of this before he notices
anything.
(*She brings the pot out. Avoids the husband in the bathroom. Steps*
*out of the house. Starts pouring out the curry. Stops.*)

RANI:   No! How awful! It's leaving a red stain. He is bound to
notice it, right here on the door-step! What shall I do? Where
can I pour it, so he won't see?

STORY:   Rani, put it in that ant-hill.

RANI:   Ah, the ant-hill!
(*Runs to the tall ant-hill. Starts pouring the liquid into it. The dog*
*starts howling in the front yard.*)

APPANNA:   Rani! See what is bothering the dog!
(*Surprised at receiving no reply.*) Rani! Rani!
(*Goes to the kitchen, drying himself. She is not there. Comes to*
*the front door looking for her. By this time Rani has poured the*
*curry into the ant-hill and is running back to the house. The moment*
*she turns her back to the ant-hill, a King Cobra lifts its hood,*
*hissing, out of the ant-hill. Looks around. It sees Rani and follows*

*her at a distance. By the time she has reached the front door of her house, it is behind a nearby tree, watching her.*

*Rani comes to the front door and freezes. Appanna is waiting for her.)*

APPANNA:  Rani, where have you been?

*(No answer.)*

I said, where have you been? Rani, answer me!

*(Moves aside so she can go in. But the moment she steps in, Appanna slaps her hard. Rani collapses to the floor. He does not look at her again. Just pulls the door shut, locks it from outside and goes away. There is not a trace of anger in anything he does. Just cold contempt. The dog barks loudly at the King Cobra which watches from behind the tree, hissing, excited, restless. Appanna goes away. Rani goes to her bedroom. Throws herself down in her usual corner, crying.*

*It gets dark.*

*The King Cobra is still watching from under the tree. The dog continues to bark.*

*When it is totally dark, the Cobra moves toward the house. The barking becomes louder, more continuous. Rani wakes up, goes to the window, curses and shouts. Goes back to bed. The Cobra enters the house through the drain in the bathroom.)*

STORY:  As you know, a cobra can assume any form it likes. That night, it entered the house through the bathroom drain and took the shape of—

*(The Cobra takes the shape of Appanna. To distinguish this Appanna from the real one, we shall call him Naga, meaning a 'Cobra'.*

*Naga searches for Rani in the house. Finds her sleeping in the bedroom. Watches her.)*

# Act Two

(*Rani is sleeping and Naga is watching her from a distance, exactly as at the end of* ACT ONE. *He moves nearer her and then gently caresses her. She wakes up with a start.*)

RANI: You—you—
NAGA: Don't get up.
RANI: But, when did you come? Shall I serve the food?
NAGA: (*Laughs.*) Food? At midnight?
RANI: Then something else. Perhaps—
(*Doesn't know what to say. Stands dazed, leaning against the wall.*)
NAGA: Why don't you sit? Are you so afraid of me?
(*She shakes her head.*)
Then sit down.
RANI: No.
NAGA: I will go and sit there. Away from you. Will you at least sit then?
(*Moves away, sits on the floor at a distance from her.*)
Now?
(*Rani sits on the edge of the bed. Long silence. She is dozing but struggles to keep her eyes open.*)
NAGA: You are very beautiful.
RANI: (*Startled.*) Hm? What? Do you—want something?
NAGA: No. I said you are very beautiful. Poor thing!
RANI: Poor thing—?
NAGA: That a tender bud like you should get such a rotten husband.
RANI: I didn't say anything!
NAGA: You didn't. I am saying it. Did it hurt . . . the beating this morning?
RANI: No.
NAGA: Locked up in the house all day . . . You must be missing your parents.
RANI: (*Struggles to hold back a sob.*) No.
NAGA: They doted on you, didn't they?
(*She suddenly bursts out into a fit of weeping.*)

NAGA: (*Startled.*) What is it?
(*Rani continues to howl.*)
I know, you want to see your parents, don't you? All right.
I'll arrange that.
(*She looks at him dumbfounded.*)
Truly. Now, smile. Just a bit. Look, I'll send you to them only
if you smile now.
(*Rani tries to smile. A new outburst of barking from the dog.*)
Oh! Does this dog carry on like that all night? How long is it
since you had a good night's sleep?

RANI: But—

NAGA: (*Happy to see her react.*) But what?

RANI: Nothing.

NAGA: (*In order to provoke her.*) Listen to that racket! Have you had
even one good night's sleep since coming here?

RANI: But—

NAGA: What are you 'but'ting about? But what?

RANI: But you brought the dog here only this morning! There
was no problem all these days.

NAGA: (*Trying to cover up.*) Yes, of course.

RANI: Till this morning, once the housework was over . . . what
was there to do? I used to sleep through the day and lie awake
at night. Today this wretched dog has been barking away since
it was brought here. That's why I was dozing when you came
in. I'm sorry—

NAGA: (*Teasing.*) Quite right! That won't do any more. From
tomorrow I want you to be fresh and bright when I come home
at night—

RANI: (*Uncertain.*) At night?

NAGA: Yes. I shall come home every night from now on. May I?
(*Rani laughs shyly. Pause. She is sleepy.*)
May I sit by you now? Or will that make you jump out of your
skin again?
(*Rani shakes her head. Naga comes and sits very close to her. When
she tries to move away, he suddenly grabs her, with frightening
speed.*)

NAGA: Don't be afraid. Put your head against my shoulder.
(*She slowly puts her head on his shoulder. He gently puts his arm
around her.*)

NAGA:  Now, don't be silly. I am not a mongoose or a hawk that
you should be so afraid of me. Good. Relax. Tell me about
your parents. What did all of you talk about? Did they pamper
you? Tell me everything—
(*She has fallen asleep against his chest. He slowly unties her hair.
It is long and thick and covers them both. He picks up her hair in
his hand, smells it.*)

NAGA:  What beautiful, long hair! Like dark, black, snake princesses!
(*He lays her down gently. Gets up. Goes to the bathroom, turns
into his original self and slithers away. Morning. Rani wakes up,
and looks around. No husband. Comes to the front door. Pushes
it. It is still locked. Baffled, she washes her face, goes to the kitchen
and starts cooking.*
The dog starts barking. Appanna comes. Pats the dog.*)

APPANNA:  Hello, friend! No intruders tonight, eh?
(*He unlocks the door and steps in. At the noise of the door, Rani
comes out running. She is laughing.*)

RANI:  But when did you go away? I'm . . .
(*Freezes when she sees the expression of distaste on his face.*)

APPANNA:  Yes?

RANI:  Oh! Nothing.

APPANNA:  Good.
(*Goes to the bathroom. Rani stares after him, then returns to the
kitchen.*)

RANI;  I must have been dreaming again—
(*Appanna bathes, then eats silently as usual and leaves. It grows
dark. Night. Rani lies in bed, wide awake. A long silence. The
Cobra comes out of the ant-hill and enters the darkened front yard
of her house. The dog suddenly begins to bark. Then, sounds of
the dog growling and fighting, mixed with the hiss of a snake. The
racket ends when the dog gives a long, painful howl and goes silent.
Rani rushes to the window to see what is happening. It is dark.
She cannot see anything. When silence is restored, she returns to
her bed.*
The Cobra enters the house through the drain and becomes
Naga. In the bathroom, he washes blood off his cheeks and shoulder
and goes to Rani's room. When she hears his step on the stairs,
she covers her head with the sheet. Naga comes, sees her, smiles,*

*sits on the edge of her bed. Waits. She peeps out, sees him, closes her eyes tight.*)

NAGA:   What nonsense is this?

(*Without opening her eyes, Rani bites her forefinger. Gives a cry of pain.*)

What is going on, Rani?

RANI:   (*Rubbing her finger.*) I must be going mad.

NAGA:   Why?

RANI:   (*To herself.*) His visit last night—I assumed I must have dreamt that. I am certainly not dreaming now. Which means I am going mad. Spending the whole day by myself is rotting my brain.

NAGA:   It is not a dream. I am not a figment of your imagination either. I am here. I am sitting in front of you. Touch me. Come on! You won't? Well, then. Talk to me. No? All right. Then I had better go.

RANI:   Don't. Please.

NAGA:   What is the point of sitting silent like a stone image?

RANI:   What do you—want me to say?

NAGA:   Anything. Tell me about yourself. About your parents. Whatever comes into your head. If you want me to stay, tell me why. If you want me to go, say why.

RANI:   (*Pouting.*) What can I say if you behave like this?

NAGA:   Like what?

RANI:   You talk so nicely at night. But during the day I only have to open my mouth and you hiss like a . . . stupid snake.

(*Naga laughs.*)

It's all very well for you to laugh. I feel like crying.

NAGA:   What should I do then—stop coming at night? Or during the day?

RANI:   Who am I to tell you that? It's your house. Your pleasure.

NAGA:   No, let's say, the husband decides on the day visits. And the wife decides on the night visits. So I won't come at night if you don't want me to.

RANI:   (*Eyes filling up.*) Why do you tease me like this? I am sick of being alone. And then tonight, I was terrified you might not come—that what I remembered from last night may be just a dream. I was desperate that you should come again tonight. But, what am I to say if you spin riddles like this?

NAGA: (*Seriously.*) I am afraid that is how it is going to be. Like *that* during the day. Like *this* at night. Don't ask me why.

RANI: I won't.

NAGA: Come. You slept like a child in my arms last night. You must be sleepy now. Come. Go to sleep.

RANI: (*Moves into his arms, suddenly stops.*) But, what is this? (*Touches his cheek.*)

Blood on your cheeks! And your shoulders! That looks like tooth-marks. Did you run into a thorn bush or a barbed-wire fence on your way here?

NAGA: Don't worry about it.

RANI: Wait. Let me apply that ointment Mother gave me. Where is it? I took it out the other day when I cut my thumb slicing onions. Where did I put it? Oh, yes! The mirror-box!

(*She rushes to the mirror-box and opens it. Before Naga can move away so Rani won't see his reflection, she looks at him in the mirror. Screams in fright. He moves with lightening speed, pulls her away from the mirror and holds her in his arms. She is trembling.*)

NAGA: What is it? What is it, Rani?

(*He gently shuts the mirror-box and pushes it away. Rani turns and looks at where he had been sitting.*)

RANI: When I looked in the mirror, I saw there—where you were sitting—instead of you, I saw a—

(*Mimes a cobra hood with her fingers.*)

—sitting there.

NAGA: What? A cobra?

RANI: (*Silencing him.*) Shh! Don't mention it. They say that if you mention it by name at night, it comes into the house.

NAGA: All right. Suppose a cobra does come into this house . . .

RANI: Don't! Why are you tempting fate by calling that unmentionable thing by its name?

NAGA: . . . why shouldn't it come with love?

RANI: May God bless our house and spare us that calamity. The very thought makes me shudder.

NAGA: I am here now. Nothing more to fear.

(*They sit on the bed together.*)

RANI: Oh no! What am I to do with myself? In all this, I forgot to put the ointment on your wounds.

(*She tries to get up. He forces her down. She gently touches his wounds. Shivers.*)
Your blood is so cold. It's the way you wander about day and night heedless of wind and rain—
    (*Stares into his eyes. Suddenly shuts her eyes and clasps him.*)

NAGA:    What is it now?

RANI:    (*Looking up.*) Since I looked into the mirror I seem to be incapable of thinking of anything else. Father says: 'If a bird so much as looks at a cobra—'

NAGA:    There! Now you said 'cobra'. Now he is bound to come—
    (*He mimes a cobra's hood with his hand.*)

RANI:    Let it. I don't feel afraid anymore, with you beside me. Father says: 'The cobra simply hooks the bird's eyes with its own sight. The bird stares—and stares—unable to move its eyes. It doesn't feel any fear either. It stands fascinated, watching the changing colours in the eyes of the cobra. It just stares, its wings half-opened as though it was sculpted in the sunlight.'

NAGA:    Then the snake strikes and swallows the bird.
    (*He kisses her. They freeze. The Flames surround them and sing the Song of the Flames (See p. 49). Rani gets up and goes and sits in a corner hiding her face behind her knees, her arms wrapped around her legs.*)

NAGA:    What is it now?

RANI:    Go away! Don't talk to me.

NAGA:    But why are you crying?

RANI:    I said be quiet.
    (*Pause.*)
I didn't know you were such a bad man. I should have known the moment you started using honeyed words.
    (*Pause.*)
Had I known, I would never have agreed to marry you. What will Father and Mother say if they come to know?

NAGA:    They will say: 'Good! Our daughter is following nicely in our footsteps—'

RANI:    (*Exploding.*) Quiet! I warn you, I am your wife and you don't have to answer anyone about me. But I will not have you say such things about my parents. They are not like—like—like dogs!

NAGA:    (*Laughs.*) What have dogs done to deserve sole credit for it, you silly goose? Frogs croaking in pelting rain, tortoises singing soundlessly in the dark, foxes, crabs, ants, rattlers, sharks, swallows—even the geese! The female begins to smell like the wet earth. And stung by her smell, the King Cobra starts searching for his Queen. The tiger bellows for his mate. When the flame of the forest blossoms into a fountain of red and the earth cracks open at the touch of the aerial roots of the banyan, it moves in the hollow of the cottonwood, in the flow of the estuary, the dark limestone caves from the womb of the heavens to the dark netherworlds, within everything that sprouts, grows, stretches, creaks and blooms—everywhere, those who come together, cling, fall apart lazily! It is there and there and there, everywhere.

RANI:     Goodness! Goats have to be sacrificed and buffaloes slaughtered to get a word out of you in the mornings. But at night—how you talk! Snakes and lizards may do what they like, but human beings should have some sense of shame.

NAGA:     (*Suddenly looks out.*) It is almost dawn. I must go.

RANI:     No! No!

NAGA:     The birds. Listen!

RANI:     Why don't those birds choke on their own songs? Who has given them the right to mess about with other creatures' nights?

NAGA:     I'll be back again at night.

RANI:     Only at night? Not for lunch?

NAGA:     Of course. There's always that. (*Pause.*) Listen, Rani. I shall come home every day twice. At night and of course again at mid-day. At night, wait for me here in this room. When I come and go at night, don't go out of this room, don't look out of the window—whatever the reason. And don't ask me why.

RANI:     No, I won't. The pig, the whale, the eagle—none of them asks why. So I won't either. But they ask for it again. So I can too, can't I?

          (*Runs to him and embraces him.*)
          (*While the above scene is in progress, Kurudavva and Kappanna have arrived outside. As usual, he lowers her to the ground and sits under the tree. She goes to the door. Stumbles over the dog. Surprised, she feels it, makes sure it is dead. Feels the lock on the door. Calls out in a whisper.*)

KURUDAVVA:  Kappanna!

KAPPANNA:  Yes.

KURUDAVVA:  Come here.

KAPPANNA:  No, I won't.

KURUDAVVA:  I said come here. This fool doesn't understand a thing. Quick. Something funny is happening here.

(*Reluctantly, Kappanna comes to the door.*)

Look here.

KAPPANNA:  A dog. And it is dead!

KURUDAVVA:  It wasn't here the night before. And the lock is still there. I wonder what the silly girl has gone and done. Look inside the house. Can you see anything?

KAPPANNA:  (*Looking*) No!

KURUDAVVA:  Listen.

(*They listen. Naga walks toward the bathroom.*)

KAPPANNA:  Footsteps.

KURUDAVVA:  It's a man.

KAPPANNA:  Appanna! He is inside. He will be out any minute!

KURUDAVVA:  He can't! What about the lock? (*Thinks.*) And if Appanna locked the door from the outside, who is in there now? Look, look. See who it is.

KAPPANNA:  I can't see anything from here.

KURUDAVVA:  Try the window at the back.

(*Reluctantly he goes to the backyard. Naga goes to the bathroom, turns into a King Cobra and goes out of the drain, just as Kappanna arrives at the spot and sees the Cobra emerge.*)

KAPPANNA:  (*Screams.*) Snake! Snake! A cobra!

(*Rushes to the front door, picks up Kurudavva and starts to run.*)

KURUDAVVA:  Where?

KAPPANNA:  In the backyard! Out of the bathroom drain!

KURUDAVVA:  Then why are you running? It isn't following us, is it? It should be gone by now. Let me down! Let me down!

(*Rani hears the commotion, comes running to the front door.*)

RANI:  Who is it? Kurudavva?

KURUDAVVA:  Let me down! Yes, it's me, child.

(*Comes back to the door.*)

KAPPANNA:  Don't go too near, Mother. It may still be there—

RANI:  What is it, Kurudavva? Who was that shouting?

KURUDAVVA:  I won't come any closer. I'll speak from here. Kappanna says he saw a cobra there.

RANI:  Where?

KURUDAVVA: Coming out of your bathroom drain.

RANI: Oh my God! I hope he didn't go to the bathroom—
(*Rushes to the bathroom.*)

KURUDAVVA: We have been here the last half hour. No one has come out.

RANI: He certainly isn't in the house!
(*Pushes the door.*)
There! The door is locked from the outside. It wouldn't be if he was in here, would it? Perhaps you didn't see him come out?

KURUDAVVA: Maybe so. Well, my child, have you started your married life?

RANI: (*Blushing*) Yes, Kurudavva.
(*Yawns.*)

KURUDAVVA: (*Laughs.*) Tired? Poor thing! So you see the power of my root? Didn't I tell you your husband will cling to you once he tastes it?
(*Rani embarrassed, tries to laugh.*)

KURUDAVVA: Well, my work is done. I'll be off now. Bless you. Burn incense in a ladle and stick it into the drain. Keeps the reptiles out.

RANI: Please come again.
(*Kappanna lifts up Kurudavva: They talk in whispers.*)

KAPPANNA: If the steps we heard were Appanna's, well, he certainly hasn't come out of the house.

KURUDAVVA: Of course, he is in there. Once couples start playing games, they begin to invent some pretty strange ones. Come on. Let's go.
(*They move. Rani thinks for a while, goes into the bedroom. Kappanna, carrying Kurudavva, suddenly stiffens. Stands frozen, staring at something in the distance.*)

KURUDAVVA: Kappanna—Kappanna—
(*He does not respond. She hits him on his back in an effort to wake him up. But he is immobile.*)

KURUDAVVA: (*Panicky.*) Kappanna! What is it? Why do you act like this? Kappanna—
(*He suddenly wakes up.*)

KAPPANNA: Eh? Nothing.

KURUDAVVA: What do you mean nothing? Giving me a scare like that—

KAPPANNA: You won't believe me if I tell you. It was her again—

KURUDAVVA: Why shouldn't I believe you if you talked sense? Just admit it's one of the girls from a nearby village, instead of making up fancy stories about some—

KAPPANNA: She is not a village girl. Which village girl will dare step out at this hour? And I am not making up stories. That day she floated out from the haunted well. Just now she stepped out of the cemetery. Looked at me. Smiled and waved.

KURUDAVVA: Perhaps she is an ogress. Of demon birth. Or some-one from the netherworld, perhaps. A spirit. Why don't you just say who it is—

KAPPANNA: You won't let me—

KURUDAVVA: When you talk like this I feel we are falling apart. It's a fear I have never felt before.

KAPPANNA: Mother, just listen—

KURUDAVVA: Shut up now!

*(They exit, arguing: It gets brighter. It is mid-day. Appanna enters. Sees the dead dog.)*

APPANNA: What's wrong with this dog? Why is it asleep in the hot sun?

*(Whistles. Then comes nearer and inspects.)*

It is dead! Dead! I paid fifty rupees for it!

*(Rani comes to the front window and looks out.)*

APPANNA: Something has bitten it. Perhaps that cobra—from that ant-hill . . .

*(To Rani)* This was no ordinary hound. It cornered a cheetah once. It must have sensed the cobra. It must have given a fight. Didn't you hear anything at night?

*(She shakes her head. He gets up.)*

APPANNA: I'd better go and find an Untouchable to bury the carcass.

*(Appanna exits. Rani stares after him nonplussed. Touches herself on her cheek.)*

RANI: But last night . . . he had blood on his cheeks . . . and shoulders. Now . . .

*(Goes to the kitchen. Starts cooking. Appanna comes, bathes, sits down to eat. She serves him food. He gets up. Locks the door and goes away.*

*While all this is going on, the story narrates the following.)*

STORY:   The death of the dog infuriated Appanna. He next brought a mongoose. The mongoose lasted only one day. But it had evidently given a tougher fight: its mouth was full of blood. There were bits of flesh under its claws. Bits of snakeskin were found in its teeth.

Rani fainted when she saw the dead mongoose. That night he did not visit her. There was no sign of him the next fifteen days. Rani spent her nights crying, wailing, pining for him. When he started coming again, his body was covered with wounds which had only partly healed. She applied her ointment to the wounds, tended him. But she never questioned him about them. It was enough that he had returned. Needless to say, when her husband came during the day, there were no scars on him.

(*It gets dark on stage. Rani hurriedly lights the lamps in the house. As she does so, some of the Flames get into position.*)

RANI:   (*to the Flames*) Wait now. Don't be impatient. It won't be long . . . It will open out. Reach out with its fragrance.

(*Rushes into her bedroom. Waits tensely. Suddenly jumps up, breathes in deeply.*)

RANI:   There it is . . . The smell of the blossoming nightqueen! How it fills the house before he comes! How it welcomes him! God, how it takes me, sets each fibre in me on fire!

(*Naga comes, they embrace. The Flames surround them and sing. Naga and Rani dance.*)

### SONG OF THE FLAMES

*Come let us dance*
      *through the weaver-bird's nest*
      *and light the hanging lamps*
      *of glow-worms*
      *through the caverns in the ant-hill*
      *and set the diamond*
      *in the cobra's crown ablaze*
      *through the blind woman's dream*
      *through the deaf-mute's song*
*Come let us flow*
      *down the tresses of time*
      *all light and song.*

*(It is night. Rani and Naga are in bed together. Naga plays with her loose hair. She suddenly laughs.)*

NAGA: What is it?

RANI: Thank God.

NAGA: Why?

RANI: All these days I was never sure I didn't just dream up these nightly visits of yours. You don't know how I have suffered. When I saw your scowling face in the mornings, I would be certain everything was a fantasy and almost want to cry. But my real anxiety began as the evening approached. I would merely lie here, my eyes shut tight. What is there to see after all? The same walls. The same roof. As the afternoon passed my whole being got focused in my ears. The bells of cattle returning home—that means it is late afternoon. The cacophony of birds in a far-away tree—it is sunset. The chorus of crickets spreading from one grove to another—it is night. Now he will come. Suppose he doesn't tonight? Suppose the nightqueen bush does not blossom? Suppose it's all a dream? Every night the same anxiety. The same cold feeling deep within me! Thank God. That's all past now.

NAGA: Why?

RANI: I have definite evidence to prove I was not fantasizing.

NAGA: What evidence?

RANI: I am pregnant.

*(He stares at her, dumbfounded.)*

Why are you looking at me like that? There is a baby in my womb.

*(He stares blankly.)*

We are going to have a baby.

*(Pause.)*

It doesn't make you happy?

*(Anguished.)* What am I going to do with you? Laugh? Cry? Bang my head against the wall? I can never guess how you'll react. I thought you would dance with joy on hearing the news. That you would whirl me around and fondle me. Feel my stomach gently and kiss me. All that—

*(Pause.)*

Actually, I was also afraid you might not do anything of that sort. That's why I hid the news from you all these months. I can't make any sense of you even when it is just the two of us. Now a third life joins us! I didn't know if that would be too much for you. So I was silent.

(*Her eyes fill up.*)

What I feared has come true. What kept me silent has happened. You are not happy about the baby. You are not proud that I am going to be a mother. Sometimes you are so cold-blooded— you cannot be human.

(*Forcibly puts his hand on her belly.*)

Just feel! Feel! Our baby is crouching in there, in the darkness, listening to the sounds from the world outside—as I do all day long.

NAGA: (*Dully.*) I am glad you hid the news from me all this time. Even now, try to keep from speaking about it as long as possible. Keep it a secret.

RANI: From whom?

NAGA: From me.

RANI: What are you talking about? I have already told you. How can it be a secret again? And how long can it remain a secret? Another fifteen days? Three weeks?

NAGA: (*Sadly.*) I realize it cannot remain a secret for long. That is why I said, as long as possible. Please, do as I tell you.

RANI: (*Blankly.*) Yes, I shall. Don't ask questions. Do as I tell you. Don't ask questions. Do as I tell you. No. I won't ask questions. I shall do what you tell me. Scowls in the day. Embraces at night. The face in the morning unrelated to the touch at night. But day or night, one motto does not change: Don't ask questions. Do as I tell you.

(*He is silent.*)

I was a stupid, ignorant girl when you brought me here. But now I am a woman, a wife, and I am going to be a mother. I am not a parrot. Not a cat or a sparrow. Why don't you take it on trust that I have a mind and explain this charade to me? Why do you play these games? Why do you change like a chameleon from day to night? Even if I understood a little, a tiny bit—I could bear it. But now—sometimes I feel my head is going to burst!

(*Naga opens his mouth to say something.*)

RANI: I know. Don't ask questions. Do as I say.

NAGA: (*Laughs.*) That is not what I was going to say.

RANI: You don't want the child, do you? If I had remained barren, I could have spent my whole life happily trying to work out whether all of this was real or a dream. But this is no dream now. Dreams remain in heads. This one has sent roots deep down into my womb.

(*Suddenly.*)

What shall I do? Shall I have an abortion?

(*Naga stares, blankly.*)

I may find a sharp instrument in the kitchen—a ladle, a knife. Or I can ask Kurudavva's help. No, it's too late. It's five months old. Too big to be kept a secret. Forgive me. I know it's *my* fault. But the secret will be out whatever I do.

NAGA: It's almost morning. I must go.

RANI: (*Waking up.*) What?

NAGA: I have to go.

RANI: (*Gently.*) Go.

(*She turns away. Naga takes a step to go. They both freeze. The lights change sharply from night to mid-day. In a flash, Naga becomes Appanna: Pushes her to the floor and kicks her.*)

APPANNA: Aren't you ashamed to admit it, you harlot? I locked you in, and yet you managed to find a lover! Tell me who it is. Who did you go to with your sari off?

RANI: I swear to you I haven't done anything wrong!

APPANNA: You haven't? And yet you have a bloated tummy. Just pumped air into it, did you? And you think I'll let you get away with that? You shame me in front of the whole village, you darken my face, you slut—!

(*He beats her. The Cobra watches this through a window and moves about, frantic. Neither notices it.*)

APPANNA: I swear to you I am not my father's son, if I don't abort that bastard! Smash it into dust! Right now—

(*Drags her into the street. Picks up a huge stone to throw on her. The Cobra moves forward, hissing loudly, drawing attention to itself. Rani screams.*)

RANI: Oh my God! A snake! A cobra!

(*Appanna throws the stone at the Cobra which instantly withdraws. Rani uses this moment to run into the house and lock herself in. Appanna runs behind her and bangs on the door.*)

APPANNA:　Open the door! Open the door, you whore! All right then, I'll show you. I'll go to the Village Elders. If they don't throw that child into boiling oil and you along with it, my name is not Appanna.

(*He exits. She rushes to her bedroom. Lights change to night. She is crying on the floor. Naga comes and sits glumly nearby.*)

RANI:　Why are you humiliating me like this? Why are you stripping me naked in front of the whole village? Why don't you kill me instead? I would have killed myself. But there's not even a rope in this house for me to use.

NAGA:　Rani, the Village Elders will sit in judgement. You will be summoned. That cannot be avoided.

RANI:　Look at the way you talk—as if you were referring to someone else. After all, you complained to the Elders about me. Now you can go and withdraw the complaint. Say my wife isn't a whore.

NAGA:　I'm sorry, but it can't be done. Rani, listen. You do trust me, don't you?

RANI:　You ask me that? Isn't all this a result of trusting you? (*Suddenly helpless.*) Who else is there for me?

NAGA:　Then listen to me carefully. When you face the Elders, tell them you will prove your innocence. Say you will undertake the snake ordeal.

RANI:　Snake ordeal? What is that?

NAGA:　There is an enormous ant-hill under the banyan tree. Almost like a mountain. A King Cobra lives in it. Say you will put your hand into the ant-hill—

RANI:　(*Screams.*) What?

NAGA:　Yes. And pull out the King Cobra. And take your oath by that cobra.

RANI:　I can't! I can't!

NAGA:　There is no other way.

RANI:　Yes, there is. Give me poison instead. Kill me right here. At least I'll be spared the humiliation. Won't the cobra bite me the moment I touch it? I'll die like your dog and your mongoose.

NAGA:　No, it won't bite. Only, you must tell the truth.

RANI:　What truth?

NAGA:　The truth. Tell the truth while you are holding the cobra.

RANI: What truth? Shall I say my husband forgets his nights by next morning? Shall I say my husband brought a dog and a mongoose to kill this cobra, and yet suddenly he seems to know all about what the cobra will do or not do?

NAGA: Say anything. But you must speak the truth.

RANI: And if I lie?

NAGA: It will bite you.

RANI: God!

(*And then gently, almost menacingly.*)

And suppose what I think is the truth turns out to be false?

NAGA: I'm afraid it will have to bite you. What you think is not of any consequence. It must be the truth.

(*Anguished.*)

I can't help it, Rani. That's how it has always been. That's how it will always be.

RANI: Oh, God!

NAGA: (*Gets up.*) All will be well, Rani. Don't worry. Your husband will become your slave tomorrow. You will get all you have ever wanted.

(*He turns to go.*)

RANI: Wait!

(*She suddenly runs to him and embraces him.*)

Please hold me tight. I'm afraid. Not of the cobra. Nor of death! Of you. For you. You say you'll become my slave tomorrow. That we will be together again. Why then does your heart hammer so frantically? I had not even noticed it until now. And now, why is it fluttering like a bird ambushed in a net? Why this welcome to my child?

(*He slowly moves her away. Unable to look at him, unable to keep quiet, she leans her forehead against the wall.*)

The night is almost over. You must go. But I know this is not a morning like any before. Tomorrow won't be a day like any other day. I don't want any tomorrows. Or days after. I want this night to last forever. Remain unchanged. I mustn't let you go. I must listen to my heart and hold you back. Take you like a baby in my arms and keep you safe.

(*As she talks, Naga moves down the steps, turns into a snake and goes away. She suddenly turns to him. He is not there.*)

Listen. Please. Wait.

(*She rushes out. Runs to the front door. Lifts her hand to open the latch. And freezes.*)

But the door . . . I had locked it from inside. And it is still locked.

(*A new thought occurs to her. Almost unconsciously she runs to the bathroom. Looks inside, it is empty.*)

Where are you? Where are you?

(*Sudden commotion. Crowds of villagers fill the stage from all sides. The three Elders come and take their positions near the ant-hill. The stage becomes the village square.*)

ELDER I:  Dear child, we have done our best. But you refuse to listen to us. We have no alternative now but to give in to your demands.

ELDER II:  It brings no credit to the village to have a husband publicly question his wife's chastity. But Appanna here says: Since the day of our wedding, I have not once touched my wife or slept by her side. And yet she is pregnant. He has registered the complaint, so we must judge its merits.

ELDER III:  The traditional test in our Village Court has been to take the oath while holding a red-hot iron in the hand. Occasionally, the accused has chosen to plunge the hand in boiling oil. But you insist on swearing by the King Cobra. The news has spread and, as you can see, attracted large crowds.

ELDER I:  This Village Court has turned into a Country Fair. Such curiosity is not healthy for the village, nor conducive to justice.

ELDER III:  Listen to us even now. If something goes wrong and the Cobra bites you, not just your life but the life of the child you carry will be in jeopardy. We risk the sin of killing your unborn child.

ELDER II:  To risk visiting such a sin on the whole village and the Village Elders purely for a personal whim of yours is not right. Think again. Listen to us. Desist from this stupidity.

ELDER I:  We shall be content if you go through the ordeal of the red-hot iron.

RANI:  I am young and immature. I know nothing. But I ask pardon of the Elders. I must swear by the King Cobra.

(*The Elders discuss animatedly among themselves.*)

ELDER I:  All right. If you insist. Come now child. Truth shall prevail. Come.

(*Rani steps up to the ant-hill. The crowds surge forward. The Cobra rears its head out of the ant-hill. The crowd steps back in terror. Even Rani is scared and runs back. The Cobra waits, swaying its hood. Rani steps farther and farther back. The Cobra goes back into the ant-hill.*)

ELDER II:   Go on, child. Don't delay now.

RANI:   I am scared. Please—if the Cobra bites me, what shall I do? I am afraid—
(*Runs to Appanna.*)
Please, please, help me—

APPANNA:   You whore—!

ELDER III:   Appanna, there is no need to be vituperative. She may have erred. But she is a child yet. Even we feel shaken by the sight of the King Cobra. So her fright is quite understandable.

ELDER I:   If you are afraid, there is no need to go through with the ordeal. Accept your guilt. We shall then go on to consider the punishment.

RANI:   But I have not done anything wrong. I am not guilty of anything. What shall I plead guilty to?

ELDER II:   (*Angry*) Listen to me. We have been patient until now because of your youth. We have given in to your whims. But you have tested us enough. Either confess or accept the ordeal.

ELDER III:   Remember, child, you have a choice of ordeals even now.

RANI:   (*Looking at the ant-hill.*) Yes, I shall take my oath . . . holding the red-hot iron.
(*A roar of disappointment from the crowds. But the Elders are delighted.*)

APPANNA:   This is ridiculous! You can't allow this harlot . . .

ELDER I:   Heaven be praised. It's a load off our conscience.

ELDER II:   We have been saved.

ELDER III:   Hurry up now . . . Heat the iron rod. Quick!
(*In all this confusion, Kurudavva enters calling her son.*)

KURUDAVVA:   Kappanna, my son—Where are you? Can you hear me?

RANI:   Kurudavva—

KURUDAVVA:   Has my son come here? Why is he teasing me like this? Kappanna—

RANI:   Kurudavva—

(*Tries to rush after her but is stopped by Appanna.*)

APPANNA:   Where do you think you are going?

ELDER I:   Do you know that old woman? Don't you know she has gone mad?

ELDER II:   Her son disappeared a week ago.

ELDER III:   We have all told her he is not in the village. But she won't listen. Wanders around day and night calling him—

KURUDAVVA:   Kappanna, Son—

RANI:   (*Snarling at Appanna.*) If you don't let go, I'll—
(*Taken aback by her fury, Appanna lets her go.*)

ELDER III:   Let her. The rod isn't hot yet.

RANI:   (*Runs to Kurudavva.*) Help me, Kurudavva. Help me, please—

KURUDAVVA:   Do you know where he is? He—

RANI:   It's me. Rani. What shall I do? I don't know . . .

KURUDAVVA:   My Kappanna is gone. Melted away.

RANI:   I am innocent, Kurudavva. I haven't done anything, what shall I do?

KURUDAVVA:   I woke up. It was midnight. I heard him panting. He was not in his bed. He was standing up . . . stiff . . . like a wooden pillar. Suddenly I knew. There was someone else in the house. A third person . . .

RANI:   (*Mesmerized.*) Who was it?

KURUDAVVA:   If only I had my eyes! I would have seen her. I would have recognized. But what can one do with these pebbles? When he tried to tell me I didn't listen. I was deaf. A temptress from beyond? A *yaksha* woman—Perhaps a snake woman? But not a human being. No. What woman would come inside our house at that hour? And how? She wasn't even breathing. I shouted: 'Who are you? What do you want from us? Go away!' Suddenly the door burst open. The rushing wind shook the rafters. He slipped from my hands and was gone. Never came back.

ELDER I:   Rani—

KURUDAVVA:   Now I wander about calling him. They tell me he is not in the village. They think I am mad. I know he is not here. I know he won't come back. But what can I do? How can I sit in the house doing nothing? I must do something for him.

ELDER II:   Rani—

KURUDAVVA:   (*Getting up.*) I must go. Look for my son. Can't waste time like this—Kappanna, Son, it's your Mother. Don't torment me now, child . . .

> (*Goes out. Rani stands staring in her direction. Then turns to the Story.*)

RANI:   Why should she suffer like this? Would sight have helped? Do desires really reach out from some world beyond right into our beds?

> (*The crowd has become restive. So Rani's remaining questions get lost in the increasing hubub. We only see her addressing the Story, who does not answer.*)

ELDER I:   Silence! Silence!

> (*The crowd falls silent. Only the last part of Rani's dialogue is heard.*)

RANI:   (*To the Story.*) Why should I let you push me around? Isn't it better to accept the kiss of the Cobra and the dark silence of the ant-hill?

ELDER II:   Come, child. The iron rod is hot and ready.

RANI:   No. I want the ordeal by the Cobra.

> (*Goes to the ant-hill, plunges her hand into it and pulls the Cobra out.*)

ELDER III:   Be quick, now.

RANI:   Since coming to this village, I have held by this hand, only two . . .

APPANNA:   (*Triumphant.*) There. She admits it. Two, she says. Two! Who are they?

RANI:   My husband and . . .

APPANNA:   And—say it, who else?

RANI:   And this Cobra.

> (*Suddenly words pour out.*)

Yes, my husband and this King Cobra. Except for these two, I have not touched any one of the male sex. Nor have I allowed any other male to touch me. If I lie, let the Cobra bite me.

> (*The Cobra slides up her shoulder and spreads its hood like an umbrella over her head. The crowd gasps. The Cobra sways its hood gently for a while, then becomes docile and moves over her shoulder like a garland. Music fills the skies. The light changes into a soft, luminous glow. Rani stares uncomprehending as the Cobra*

*slips back into the ant-hill. There are hosannas and cheers from the crowd.*)

ELDER I:   A miracle! A miracle!

ELDER II:   She is not a woman. She is a Divine Being!

ELDER III:   Indeed, a Goddess—!

(*They fall at her feet. The crowd surges forward to prostrate itself before her. Appanna stands, uncomprehending. The Elders shout, 'Palanquin! Music!' They lift her into the palanquin. Then, as an afterthought, Appanna is seated next to her. The couple is taken in procession to their house.*)

ELDER I:   Appanna, your wife is not an ordinary woman. She is a goddess incarnate. Don't grieve that you judged her wrongly and treated her badly. That is how goddesses reveal themselves to the world. You were the chosen instrument for revealing her divinity.

ELDER II:   Spend the rest of your life in her service. You need merit in ten past lives to be chosen for such holy duty.

ELDER III:   Bless us, Mother. Bless our children.

(*All disperse, except Rani and Appanna. Appanna opens the lock on the door, throws it away. He goes in and sits, mortified, baffled. She comes and stands next to him. Long pause. Suddenly he falls at her feet.*)

APPANNA:   Forgive me. I am a sinner. I was blind . . .

RANI:   Hush, now!

(*She gently takes him in her arms. Music starts in the background and the words they speak to each other cannot be heard.*)

STORY:   So Rani got everything she wished for, a devoted husband, a happy life. She even got a life-long servant to draw water for her house. For Appanna's concubine was present at the trial. When she saw Rani's glory, she felt ashamed of her sinful life and volunteered to do menial work in Rani's house. In due course, Rani gave birth to a beautiful child. A son. Rani lived happily ever after with her husband, child and servant.

(*Her last sentence is drowned in the hubub created by the Flames as they prepare to leave. 'That was a nice story!', 'Has it dawned yet?', 'I don't want to be late', 'Poor girl!'*)

MAN:   (*Exasperated.*) These Flames are worse than my audience. Can't they wait till the story is over?

FLAME 1:   But isn't it?

MAN: It can't be. No one will accept this ending.

STORY: But why not?

MAN: Too many loose ends. Take Kappanna's disappearance, for instance . . .

STORY: Oh, that is Kurudavva's story. If you are interested in that one, you may find her yet, meet her unexpectedly as you met me here, in some remote place. Even in the market place perhaps. Or someone in the audience may know. Or you can invent the missing details. That would be quite in order. I am only Rani's story.

MAN: Even then, the present ending just doesn't work.

STORY: And why not?

MAN: It's all right to say Rani lived happily ever after. But what about Appanna, her husband? As I see him, he will spend the rest of his days in misery.

(*Appanna suddenly moves out of Rani's embrace. Speaks to himself.*)

APPANNA: What am I to do? Is the whole world against me? Have I sinned so much that even Nature should laugh at me? I know I haven't slept with my wife. Let the world say what it likes. Let any miracle declare her a goddess. But *I* know! What sense am I to make of my life if that's worth nothing?

STORY: Well then, what about her?

(*Rani does not speak but responds restlessly to the Story's following dialogue.*)

STORY: No two men make love alike. And that night of the Village Court, when her true husband climbed into bed with her, how could she fail to realize it was someone new? Even if she hadn't known earlier? When did the split take place? Every night this conundrum must have spread its hood out at her. Don't you think she must have cried out in anguish to know the answer?

MAN: So? The story is not over then?

STORY: When one says, 'And they lived happily ever after', all that is taken for granted. You sweep such headaches under the pillow and then press your head firmly down on them. It is something one has to live with, like a husband who snores, or a wife who is going bald.

(*As the Story speaks, Rani and Appanna come together, smile, embrace and are plunged into darkness.*)

MAN: But that ending lacks something. (*Remembering.*) Of course, the Cobra!

STORY: Yes, the Cobra. One day the Cobra was sitting in its ant-hill and it thought of Rani and said: 'Why should I not go and take a look?'

(*During the above dialogue, the Cobra enters the house, takes on his human form.*)

NAGA: Why should I not take a look? I have given her everything. Her husband. Her child. Her home. Even her maid. She must be happy. But I haven't seen her . . . It is night. She will be asleep. This is the right time to visit her. The familiar road. At the familiar hour. (*Laughs.*) Hard to believe now I was so besotted with her.

(*Goes into Rani's bedroom. Rani is sleeping next to her husband, her head on his shoulders, her long loose tresses hanging down from the edge of the cot. Her child is by her side. There is a quiet smile of contentment on her face. Naga looks at the group and recoils in sudden anguish. Covers his face as though he cannot bear to see the scene.*)

NAGA: Rani! My queen! The fragrance of my nights! The blossom of my dreams! In another man's arms? In another man's bed? Does she curl around him as passionately every night now? And dig her nails into his back? Bite his lips? And here I am—a sloughed-off skin on the tip of a thorn. An empty sac of snake-skin. No. I can't bear this. Someone must die. Someone has to die. Why shouldn't I kill her? If I bury my teeth into her breast now, she will be mine—mine forever.

(*Moves to her swiftly. But stops.*)

No, I can't. My love has stitched up my lips. Pulled out my fangs. Torn out my sac of poison. Withdraw your veils of light, Flames. Let my shame float away in the darkness. Don't mock, gecko. Yes, this King Cobra is now no better than a grass snake. Yes, that is it. A grass snake. A common reptile. That's what I am and I had forgotten that. I thought I could become human. Turn into my own creation. No! Her thighs, her bosom, her lips are for one who is forever a man. I shed my own skin every season. How could I even hope to retain the human form? For me—yes, only her long locks. Dark, jet-black snake princesses.

(*Smells them.*)

They are like me. Reptilian. Cold. Long. They are right for
me. I shall summon my magical powers for the last time—to
become the size of her tresses. To become so thin, so small,
that I can hide in them, play with them, swim away in their
dark flow.

(*Presses her hair to his body.*)

Become their size now! Enter her tresses! Make love to them.
They have no sensation. They will not disturb her dreams. But
for you, that will suffice.

(*A beam of light on him. The rest is plunged into darkness. Long
dark hair appear to descend and cover him. He covers himself and
dances.*

    *Finally, Naga ties a tress into a noose and places it around his
neck. The stage slowly becomes dark.*

    *Long silence.*

    *Then Kurudavva's voice is heard in the distance.*)

KURUDAVVA'S VOICE:   Son! Where are you?

(*Lights come on. Rani, Appanna and child are sleeping.*)

KURUDAVVA'S VOICE:   Kappanna—

(*Appanna sits up.*)

APPANNA:   Yes?

RANI:   (*Waking up.*) What is it?

APPANNA:   I thought I heard someone calling me.

KURUDAVVA'S VOICE:   Kappanna! Where are you?

RANI:   That poor soul: Kurudavva.

APPANNA:   In my sleep, it sounded like—my Mother calling me—

RANI:   Poor you!

(*Tries to sit up. Groans and clutches her hair.*)

APPANNA:   What is it?

RANI:   My head. It feels so heavy. Ahh! Please. Can you give me
a comb? My head weighs a ton. Let me comb my hair.

(*He gives her a comb. She tries to comb her hair, but cannot. There
is something caught up in her tresses.*)

(*To Appanna.*) Could you please?

APPANNA:   Certainly.

(*He combs her hair. He has to struggle to get the comb through. A
dead cobra falls to the ground.*)

A cobra! Stay away!

(*They look at it from afar.*)

RANI: Oh! Poor thing, it is dead!

APPANNA: (*Examining the dead snake.*) You know—it seems to have got caught in your hair and strangled itself. Your long hair saved us, Rani. The Elders were right. You are no common person. You are a goddess.

RANI: We are not important. But our son is the blossom of our family. He has been saved. He has been given the gift of life by the Cobra, as by a father.

APPANNA: So?

RANI: (*Almost to herself.*) A cobra. It has to be ritually cremated. Can you grant me a favour?

APPANNA: Certainly.

RANI: When we cremate this snake, the fire should be lit by our son.

APPANNA: As you say.

RANI: And every year on this day, our son should perform the rituals to commemorate its death.

APPANNA: But aren't you going too far? I mean—that's done only for one's own father. And I am still alive.

RANI: Please don't say no.

APPANNA: Of course, there is no question of saying no. You are the goddess herself incarnate. Any wish of yours will be carried out.

(*He exits. She sits staring at the snake. Her eyes fill with tears. Music. She bows down to the dead snake, then picks it up and presses it to her cheeks. Freezes. It gets brighter, the Flames disappear, one by one. The Story of course is gone.*)

FLAMES: Is it really over? . . . Oh! What a lovely tale! etc.

MAN: (*Looks out.*) No sign of any light yet!

FLAME 3: Pity it has to end like that.

FLAME 2: These unhappy endings . . .

FLAME 4: Why can't things end happily for a change?

MAN: But death! It's the only inescapable truth, you know.

FLAME 5: Don't be so pompous!

FLAME 1: (*Sharply.*) Then why are you running away from it?

FLAME 2: If darkness were the only option, we might as well have embraced it at home!

MAN: But—that's how the story is. That's how it ends. I'm not to blame.

FLAMES: Stop making excuses! . . . The story may be over. But
    you are still here and still alive! . . . Listen, we don't have much
    time left. . . . Get on with it, for goodness' sake, etc.

MAN: All right! All right! Let me try.
    (*The Flames rush back to their corners and wait expectantly.*
    *Rani and Appanna are sleeping, with the child next to them.*
    *Rani suddenly moans and sits up, holding her hair. Appanna wakes*
    *up.*)

APPANNA: What is it?

RANI: My head! It hurts—as though someone were pulling out
    my hair! Ahh! Please. Can you give me a comb? I can't bear
    the pain . . .
    (*He gives her a comb. She tries to comb her hair, but cannot. She*
    *gives the comb to Appanna.*)
    Would you, please?
    (*He takes the comb. Combs her hair. A live snake falls out of her*
    *hair and lies writhing on the floor.*)

APPANNA: A snake! Stay away! It's tiny, but it's a cobra, all right.
    And alive. How did it get into your hair? Thank god for your
    thick tresses. They saved you. Wait. We must kill it—
    (*Backs away from the snake, then runs out shutting the bedroom*
    *door behind him. Searches for a stick in the kitchen.*
    *Rani watches the snake transfixed.*)

APPANNA: Isn't there a stick anywhere here?

RANI: (*Softly, to the Cobra.*) You? What are you doing here? He'll
    kill you. Go. Go away. No! Not that way. He's there. What
    shall we do? What shall we do? Why did you ever come in
    here, stupid? (*Suddenly.*) My hair! Of course. Come, quick.
    Climb into it.
    (*She lets her hair down to the floor.*)
    Quick now. Get in. Are you safely in there? Good. Now stay
    there. And lie still. You don't know how heavy you are. Let
    me get used to you, will you?
    (*Appanna comes in with a stick.*)
    It went that way—toward the bathroom.
    (*Appanna rushes out of the bedroom, toward the bathroom, looking*
    *for the snake. Rani pats her hair.*)
    This hair is the symbol of my wedded bliss. Live in there happily,
    for ever.

*(Lifts the baby up. Starts feeding it. She and Appanna freeze. It gets brighter. The flames disappear, one by one.*

*We are back in the inner sanctum of the temple. The Man is sitting alone. He looks up. Sunlight pours in through the cracks in the temple roof. It is morning. The man vigorously stretches himself, bows to the audience and goes out.)*

# Hayavadana

# Note to Hayavadana

*Hayavadana* was originally written in Kannada and I must express my thanks to the Homi Bhabha Fellowships Council for the fellowship which enabled me to write the play.

The central episode in the play—the story of Devadatta and Kapila—is based on a tale from the *Kathasaritsagara*, but I have drawn heavily on Thomas Mann's reworking of the tale in *The Transposed Heads* and am grateful to Mrs Mann for permission to do so.

My special thanks are also due to Mr Rajinder Paul who persuaded me to translate the play into English and first published this translation in his journal, *Enact*, and to Mrs Lakshmi Krishnamurty and Mrs Yamuna Prabhu who jointly produced it for the Madras Players in 1972.

In translating this play, I have not tried to be consistent while rendering the songs into English. Some have been put in a loose verse form while, for others, only a straightforward prose version has been given.

This play is dedicated to S——.

G.R.K.

# Introduction to Hayavadana

Until very recently playwriting in Kannada was a mere literary exercise, with no contact whatever with the living stage. The professional theatre was, as it continues to be, so naive and rudimentary that both Kailasam and Adya Rangacharya, the two major playwrights in Kannada, rejected it out of hand. But they could not create an enduring substitute for it and were forced to work in isolation.

Fortunately the situation has changed now and a group of young directors and actors have been able to create a theatre which, though entirely dependent on non-professionals, has proved congenial to the growth of new drama. With this new theatre growing around them, new playwrights like Girish Karnad have been able to bring to drama a first-hand knowledge of the practical demands of the stage and a better understanding of dramatic style and technique.

In his works, Karnad has moved away from the regionalist tradition that had given Kannada literature its identity in the early years of the century. None of his three plays has a specifically Kannada theme. *Yayati*, his first play, reinterprets an ancient myth. *Tughlaq*, his second play, is based on history. And both the plays are thoroughly modern in outlook and spirit.

The plot of *Hayavadana* comes from *Kathasaritsagara*, an ancient collection of stories in Sanskrit. But Karnad has borrowed it through Thomas Mann's retelling of the story in *The Transposed Heads*. The Sanskrit tale, told by a ghost to an adventurous king, gains a further mock-heroic dimension in Mann's version. The original poses a moral problem while Mann uses it to ridicule the mechanical conception of life which differentiates between body and soul. He ridicules the philosophy which holds the head superior to the body. The human body, Mann argues, is a fit instrument for the fulfilment of human destiny. Even the transposition of heads will not liberate the protagonists from the psychological limits imposed by nature.

Karnad's play poses a different problem, that of human identity in a world of tangled relationships. When the play opens, Devadatta and Kapila are the closest of friends—'one mind, one heart', as the Bhagavata describes them. Devadatta is a man of intellect, Kapila a 'man of the body'. Their relations get complicated when Devadatta marries Padmini. Kapila falls in love with Padmini and she too starts drifting towards him. The friends kill themselves and in a scene, hilariously comic but at the same time full of profound dramatic implications, Padmini transposes their heads, giving Devadatta Kapila's body and Kapila Devadatta's.

The result is a confusion of identities which reveals the ambiguous nature of human personality.

Initially Devadatta—actually the head of Devadatta on Kapila's body—behaves differently from what he was before. But ever so gradually he changes to his former self. So does Kapila. But there is a difference. Devadatta stops writing poetry while Kapila is haunted by the memories in Devadatta's body. Padmini who, after the exchange of heads, had felt that she had the best of both the men, gets slowly disillusioned. Of the three, only she has the capacity for complete experience. She understands but cannot control the situation in which she is placed. Her situation is beautifully summed up by the images of the river and the scarecrow in the choric songs.

A duel that leaves both the friends dead brings the puzzling story to an end. Neither the death of the lovers nor the subsequent *sati* of Padmini is presented as tragic; the deaths serve only to emphasize the logic behind the absurdity of the situation.

The sub-plot of 'Hayavadana', the horse-man, deepens the significance of the main theme of incompleteness by treating it on a different plane. The horse-man's search for completeness ends comically, with his becoming a complete horse. The animal body triumphs over what is considered the best in man, the *Uttamanga*, the human head!

Karnad uses the conventions and motifs of folk tales and folk theatre—masks, curtains, dolls, the story-within-a-story—to create a bizarre world. It is a world of incomplete individuals, indifferent gods, dolls that speak and children who cannot, a world indifferent to the desires and frustrations, joys and sorrows of human beings. What is real is only the tremendous, irrational energy of the horse and its rider who move round the stage symbolizing the powerful but monotonous rhythm of life.

Karnad has published only three plays so far and it is too early to judge his dramatic achievement. But his work has the tone and expression of great drama. He has the genius and the power to transform any situation into an aesthetic experience, the quality of which, to use Joyce's vocabulary, would be 'static' rather than 'kinetic'. One looks forward to works of greater and more enduring worth.

Vallabh Vidyanagar                                   KIRTINATH KURTKOTI
25 June 1973

# Characters

*(In the order of their appearance)*

BHAGAVATA

ACTOR I

HAYAVADANA

DEVADATTA

KAPILA

PADMINI

DOLL I

DOLL II

KALI

CHILD

ACTOR II

*Actors I and II may also play Kapila and Devadatta.*

# Act One

(*The stage is empty except for a chair, kept centre-stage, and a table on stage right—or at the back—on which the Bhagavata and the musicians sit.*

*At the beginning of the performance, a mask of Ganesha is brought on stage and kept on the chair. Pooja is done. The Bhagavata sings verses in praise of Ganesha, accompanied by his musicians.*)

*Then the mask is taken away.*

> O Elephant-headed Herambha
> whose flag is victory
> and who shines like a thousand suns,
> O husband of Riddhi and Siddhi,
> seated on a mouse and decorated with a snake,
>  O single-tusked destroyer of incompleteness,
> we pay homage to you and start our play.

BHAGAVATA:  May Vighneshwara, the destroyer of obstacles, who removes all hurdles and crowns all endeavours with success, bless our performance now. How indeed can one hope to describe his glory in our poor, disabled words? An elephant's head on a human body, a broken tusk and a cracked belly—whichever way you look at him he seems the embodiment of imperfection, of incompleteness. How indeed can one fathom the mystery that this very Vakratunda-Mahakaya, with his crooked face and distorted body, is the Lord and Master of Success and Perfection? Could it be that this Image of Purity and Holiness, this Mangalamoorty, intends to signify by his very appearance that the completeness of God is something no poor mortal can comprehend? Be that as it may. It is not for us to understand this Mystery or try to unravel it. Nor is it within our powers to do so. Our duty is merely to pay homage to the Elephant-headed god and get on with our play.

This is the city of Dharmapura, ruled by King Dharmasheela whose fame and empire have already reached the ends of the eight directions. Two youths who dwell in this city are our heroes. One is Devadatta. Comely in appearance, fair in colour, unrivalled in intelligence, Devadatta is the only son of the Revered Brahmin, Vidyasagara. Having felled the mightiest pundits of the kingdom in debates on logic and love, having blinded the greatest poets of the world with his poetry and wit, Devadatta is as it were the apple of every eye in Dharmapura.

The other youth is Kapila. He is the only son of the iron-smith, Lohita, who is to the King's armoury as an axle to the chariotwheel. He is dark and plain to look at, yet in deeds which require drive and daring, in dancing, in strength and in physical skills, he has no equal.

(*A scream of terror is heard off-stage. The Bhagavata frowns, quickly looks in the direction of the scream, then carries on.*)

The world wonders at their friendship. The world sees these two young men wandering down the streets of Dharmapura, hand in hand, and remembers Lava and Kusha, Rama and Lakshmana, Krishna and Balarama.

(*Sings.*) Two friends there were
　　　—one mind, one heart—

(*The scream is heard again. The Bhagavata cannot ignore it any more.*)

Who could that be—creating a disturbance at the very outset of our performance? (*Looks.*) Oh! It's Nata, our Actor. And he is running. What could have happened, I wonder?

(*The Actor comes running in, trembling with fear. He rushes on to the stage, runs round the stage once, then sees the Bhagavata and grabs him.*)

ACTOR: Sir, Bhagavata Sir—

BHAGAVATA: (*Trying to free himself.*) Tut! Tut! What's this? What's this?

ACTOR: Sir . . . oh my God!—God!—

BHAGAVATA: Let me go! I tell you, let go of me!
(*Freeing himself.*) Now what's this? What . . .

ACTOR: I—I—I—Oh God! (*Grabs him again.*)

BHAGAVATA: Let me go!
(*The Actor moves back.*)

What nonsense is this? What do you mean by all this shouting and screaming? In front of our audience too! How dare you disturb . . .

ACTOR: Please, please, I'm—sorry . . . But—but . . .

BHAGAVATA: (*More calmly.*) Now, now, calm down! There's nothing to be afraid of here. I am here. The musicians are here. And there is our large-hearted audience. It may be that they fall asleep during a play sometimes. But they are ever alert when someone is in trouble. Now, tell us, what's the matter?

ACTOR: (*Panting.*) Oh—Oh—My heart . . . It' going to burst . . .

BHAGAVATA: Sit down! Sit. Right! Now tell me everything quietly, slowly.

ACTOR: I was on my way here . . . I was already late . . . didn't want to annoy you . . . So I was hurrying down when . . . Ohh!

(*Covers his face with his hands.*)

BHAGAVATA: Yes, yes. You were hurrying down. Then?

ACTOR: I'm shivering! On the way . . . you see . . . I had drunk a lot of water this morning . . . my stomach was full . . . so to relieve myself . . .

BHAGAVATA: Watch what you are saying! Remember you are on stage . . .

ACTOR: I didn't do anything! I only wanted to . . . so I sat by the side of the road—and was about to pull up my dhoti when . . .

BHAGAVATA: Yes?

ACTOR: A voice—a deep, thick voice . . . it said: 'Hey, you there —don't you know you are not supposed to commit nuisance on the main road?'

BHAGAVATA: Quite right too. You should have known that much.

ACTOR: I half got up and looked around. Not a man in sight—no one! So I was about to sit down again when the same voice said . . .

BHAGAVATA: Yes?

ACTOR: 'You irresponsible fellow, can't you understand you are not to commit nuisance on the main road?' I looked up. And there—right in front of me—across the fence . . .

BHAGAVATA: Who was there?

ACTOR: A horse!

BHAGAVATA: What?

ACTOR: A horse! And it was talking.

BHAGAVATA: What did you have to drink this morning?

ACTOR: Nothing, I swear. Bhagavata Sir, I haven't been near a toddy-shop for a whole week. I didn't even have milk today.

BHAGAVATA:　Perhaps your liver is sensitive to water.

ACTOR:　(*Desperate.*) Please believe me. I saw it clearly—it was a horse—and it was talking.

BHAGAVATA:　(*Resigned.*) It's no use continuing this nonsense. So you saw a talking horse? Good. Now go and get made up . . .

ACTOR:　Made up? I fall to your feet, Sir, I can't . . .

BHAGAVATA:　Now look here . . .

ACTOR:　Please, Sir . . .

> (*He holds up his hand. It's trembling.*)

You see, Sir? How can I hold up a sword with this? How can I fight?

BHAGAVATA:　(*Thinks.*) Well then. There's only one solution left. You go back . . .

ACTOR:　Back?

BHAGAVATA. . . . back to that fence, have another look and make sure for yourself that whoever was talking, it couldn't have been that horse.

ACTOR:　No!

BHAGAVATA:　Nata . . .

ACTOR:　I can't!

BHAGAVATA:　It's an order.

ACTOR:　(*Pleading.*) Must I?

BHAGAVATA:　Yes, you must.

ACTOR:　Sir . . .

> (*The Bhagavata turns to the audience and starts singing.*)

BHAGAVATA:　Two friends there were
　　　　　　—one mind, one heart—

Are you still here?

> (*The Actor goes out looking at the Bhagavata, hoping for a last minute reprieve. It doesn't come.*)

Poor boy! God alone knows what he saw—and what he took it to be! There's Truth for you . . . Pure Illusion.

> (*Sings.*) Two friends there were
　　　　　　—one mind, one heart—

> (*A scream in the wings. The Actor comes rushing in.*)

Now look here . . .

ACTOR:　It's coming. Coming . . .

BHAGAVATA:　What's coming?

ACTOR:　Him! He's coming . . . (*Rushes out.*)

BHAGAVATA:   Him? It? What's coming? Whatever or whoever it
is, the Actor has obviously been frightened by its sight. If even
a hardened actor like him gets frightened, it's more than likely
that our gentle audience may get frightened too. It's not proper
to let such a sight walk on stage unchallenged. (*To the wings.*)
Hold up the entry-curtain!

    (*Two stage- hands enter and hold up a half-curtain, about six feet
in height—the sort of curtain used in* Yakshagana *or* Kathakali.
*The curtain masks the entry of Hayavadana, who comes and stands
behind it.*)

Who's that?

    (*No reply. Only the sound of someone sobbing behind the curtain.*)

How strange! Someone's sobbing behind the curtain. It looks
as though the Terror which frightened our Actor is itself now
crying!

    (*To the stage-hand.*) Lower the curtain!

    (*The curtain is lowered by about a foot. One sees Hayavadana's
head, which is covered by a veil. At a sign from the Bhagavata,
one of the stage-hands removes the veil, revealing a horse's head.
For a while the horse-head doesn't realize that it is exposed to the
gaze of the audience. The moment the realization dawns, the head
ducks behind the curtain.*)

BHAGAVATA:   A horse! No, it can't be!

    (*He makes a sign. The curtain is lowered a little more—just enough
to show the head again. Again it ducks. Again the curtain is lowered.
This goes on till the curtain is lowered right down to the floor.
Hayavadana, who has a man's body but a horse's head, is sitting
on the floor hiding his head between his knees.*)

Incredible! Unbelievable!

    (*At a sign from the Bhagavata, the stage-hands withdraw. The
Bhagavata goes and stands near Hayavadana. Then he grunts to
himself as though he has seen through the trick.*)

Who are you?

    (*Hayavadana lifts his head, and wipes the tears away. The
Bhagavata beckons to him to come centre-stage.*)

Come here!

    (*Hayavadana hesitates, then comes forward.*)

First you go around scaring people with this stupid mask. And
then you have the cheek to disturb our show with your

clowning? Have you no sense of proportion? . . . Enough of this nonsense now. Take it off—I say, take off that stupid mask!

(*Hayavadana doesn't move.*)

You won't?—Then I'll have to do it myself!

(*Holds Hayavadana's head with both his hands and tries to pull it off. Hayavadana doesn't resist.*)

It is tight. Nata—My dear Actor . . .

(*The Actor comes in, warily, and stands open-mouthed at the sight he sees.*)

Why are you standing there? Don't you see you were taken in by a silly mask? Come and help me take it off now.

(*The Actor comes and holds Hayavadana by his waist while the Bhagavata pulls at the head. Hayavadana offers no resistance, but can't help moaning when the pain becomes unbearable. The tug-of-war continues for a while. Slowly, the truth dawns on the Bhagavata.*)

Nata, this isn't a mask! It's his real head!

(*The Actor drops Hayavadana with a thud. Hayavadana gets up and sits as before, head between knees.*)

Truly, surprises will never cease! If someone had told me only five minutes ago that there was a man with a horse's head, I would have laughed out in his face.

(*To Hayavadana.*) Who are you?

(*Hayavadana gets up and starts to go out. The Actor hurriedly moves out of his way.*)

Wait! Wait! That's our green room there. It's bad enough that you scared this actor. We have a play to perform today, you know.

(*Hayavadana stands, dejected.*)

(*Softly.*) Who are you?

(*No reply.*)

What brought you to this? Was it a curse of some *rishi*? Or was it some holy place of pilgrimage, a *punyasthana*, which you desecrated? Or could it be that you insulted a *pativrata*, dedicated to the service of her husband? Or did you . . .

HAYAVADANA:  Hey . . .

BHAGAVATA:  (*Taken aback.*) Eh?

HAYAVADANA:  What do you mean, Sir? Do you think just because you know the *puranas* you can go about showering your Sanskrit

on everyone in sight? What temple did I desecrate? What
woman did I insult? What . . .

BHAGAVATA:   Don't get annoyed . . .

HAYAVADANA:   What else? What *rishi*? What sage? What? Who have
I wronged? What have I done to anyone? Let anyone come
forward and say that I've done him any wrong. I haven't—I
know I haven't yet . . .

(*He is on the point of beginning to sob again.*)

BHAGAVATA:   Don't take it to heart so much. What happened?
What's your grief? You are not alone here. I am here. The
musicians are here. And there is our large-hearted audience. It
may be that they fall asleep during a play sometimes . . .

HAYAVADANA:   What can anyone do? It's my fate.

BHAGAVATA:   What's your name?

HAYAVADANA:   Hayavadana.

BHAGAVATA:   How did you get this horse's head?

HAYAVADANA:   I was born with it.

BHAGAVATA:   Then why didn't you stop us when we tried to take
it off? Why did you put up with our torture?

HAYAVADANA:   All my life I've been trying to get rid of this head.
I thought—you with all your goodness and *punya* . . . if at least
you managed to pull it off . . .

BHAGAVATA:   Oho! Poor man! But, Hayavadana, what can anyone
do about a head one's born with? Who knows what error
committed in the last birth is responsi . . .

HAYAVADANA:   (*Annoyed.*) It has nothing to do with my last birth.
It's this birth which I can't shake off.

BHAGAVATA:   Tell us what happened. Don't feel ashamed.

HAYAVADANA:   (*Enraged.*) Ashamed? Me? Why should I . . .

BHAGAVATA:   Sorry. I beg your pardon. I should have said 'shy'.

HAYAVADANA:   (*Gloomy.*) It's a long story.

BHAGAVATA:   Carry on.

HAYAVADANA:   My mother was the Princess of Karnataka. She was
a very beautiful girl. When she came of age, her father decided
that she should choose her own husband. So princes of every
kingdom in the world were invited—and they all came. From
China, from Persia, from Africa. But she didn't like any of them.
The last one to come was the Prince of Araby. My mother took

one look at that handsome prince sitting on his great white
stallion—and she fainted.

ACTOR:  Ah!

HAYAVADANA:  Her father at once decided that this was the man.
All arrangements for the wedding were made. My mother woke
up—and do you know what she said?

ACTOR, BHAGAVATA:  What?

HAYAVADANA:  She said she would only marry that horse!

ACTOR:  What!

HAYAVADANA:  Yes. She wouldn't listen to anyone. The Prince of
Araby burst a blood-vessel.

ACTOR:  Naturally.

HAYAVADANA:  No one could dissuade her. So ultimately she was
married off to the white stallion. She lived with him for fifteen
years. One morning she wakes up—and no horse! In its place
stood a beautiful Celestial Being, a *gandharva*. Apparently this
Celestial Being had been cursed by the god Kuvera to be born
a horse for some act of misbehaviour. After fifteen years of
human love he had become his original self again.

BHAGAVATA:  I must admit several such cases are on record.

HAYAVADANA:  Released from his curse, he asked my mother to
accompany him to his Heavenly Abode. But she wouldn't. She
said she would come only if he became a horse again. So he
cursed her . . .

ACTOR:  No!

HAYAVADANA:  He cursed her to become a horse herself. So my
mother became a horse and ran away happily. My father went
back to his Heavenly Abode. Only I—the child of their marriage
—was left behind.

BHAGAVATA:  It's a sad story.

ACTOR:  Very sad.

HAYAVADANA:  What should I do now, Bhagavata Sir? What can I
do to get rid of this head?

BHAGAVATA:  Hayavadana, what's written on our foreheads cannot
be altered.

HAYAVADANA:  (*Slapping himself on the forehead.*)
But what a forehead! What a forehead! If it was a forehead like
yours, I would have accepted anything. But this! . . . . I have
tried to accept my fate. My personal life has naturally been

blameless. So I took interest in the social life of the Nation—
Civics, Politics, Patriotism, Nationalism, Indianization, the
Socialist Pattern of Society . . . I have tried everything. But
where's my society? Where? You must help me to become a
complete man, Bhagavata Sir. But how? What can I do?

(*Long silence. They think.*)

BHAGAVATA:  Banaras?

HAYAVADANA:  What?

BHAGAVATA:  If you go to Banaras and make a vow in front of the
god there . . .

HAYAVADANA:  I've tried that. Didn't work.

ACTOR:  Rameshwar.

HAYAVADANA:  Banaras, Rameshwar, Gokarn, Haridwar, Gaya,
Kedarnath—not only those but the *Dargah* of Khwaja Yusuf
Baba, the Grotto of Our Virgin Mary—I've tried them all.
Magicians, mendicants, maharshis, fakirs, saints and sadhus—
sadhus with short hair, sadhus with beards—sadhus in saffron,
sadhus in the altogether—hanging, singing, rotating, gyrating
—on the spikes, in the air, under water, under the ground
. . . I've covered them all. And what did I get out of all this?
Everywhere I went I had to cover my head with a veil—and I
started going bald. (*Pause. Shyly.*) You know, I hate this head—
but I just can't help being fond of this lovely, long mane. (*Pause.*)
So—I had to give the miss to Tirupati.

(*Long silence.*)

BHAGAVATA:  Come to think of it, Hayavadana, why don't you try
the Kali of Mount Chitrakoot?

HAYAVADANA:  Anything you say.

BHAGAVATA:  It's a temple at the top of Mount Chitrakoot. The
goddess there is famous for being ever-awake to the call of
devotees. Thousands used to flock to her temple once. No one
goes now, though.

HAYAVADANA:  Why not?

BHAGAVATA:  She used to give anything anyone asked for. As the
people became aware of this they stopped going.

HAYAVADANA:  Fools!

BHAGAVATA:  Why don't you try her?

HAYAVADANA:  (*Jumps up.*) Why not? I'll start at once . . .

BHAGAVATA:  Good. But I don't think you should go alone. It's a wild road . . . You'll have to ask a lot of people, which won't be easy for you. So . . .

(*To the Actor.*) You'd better go with him.

ACTOR:   Me?

BHAGAVATA:   Yes, that way you can make up for having insulted him.

HAYAVADANA:   But, Bhagavata Sir, may I point out that his roadside manners . . .

ACTOR:   There! He's insulting me now! Let him find his own way. What do I care?

BHAGAVATA:   Come, come, don't let's start fighting now. (*To Hayavadana.*) Don't worry. There's no highway there. Only a cart-track at best.

(*To the Actor.*) You've no reason to feel insulted—Actually you should admire him. Even in his dire need, he doesn't lose his civic sense. Be off now.

HAYAVADANA:   (*To the Actor.*) Please, don't get upset. I won't bother you, I promise.

(*To the Bhagavata.*) I am most grateful . . .

BHAGAVATA:   (*Blessing him.*) May you become successful in your search for completeness.

(*The two go.*)

Each one to his own fate. Each one to his own desire. Each one to his own luck. Let's now turn to our story.

(*He starts singing. The following is a prose rendering of the song.*)

BHAGAVATA:   (*Sings.*) Two friends there were—one mind, one heart. They saw a girl and forgot themselves. But they could not understand the song she sang.

FEMALE CHORUS:   (*Sings.*) Why should love stick to the sap of a single body? When the stem is drunk with the thick yearning of the many-petalled, many-flowered lantana, why should it be tied down to the relation of a single flower?

BHAGAVATA:   (*Sings.*) They forgot themselves and took off their bodies. And she took the laughing heads, and held them high so the pouring blood bathed her, coloured her red. Then she danced around and sang.

FEMALE CHORUS:   (*Sings.*) A head for each breast. A pupil for each eye. A side for each arm. I have neither regret nor shame. The blood pours into the earth and a song branches out in the sky.

(*Devadatta enters and sits on the chair. He is a slender, delicate-looking person and is wearing a pale-coloured mask. He is lost in thought. Kapila enters. He is powerfully built and wears a dark mask.*)

KAPILA: (*Even as he is entering.*) Devadatta, why didn't you come to the gymnasium last evening? I'd asked you to. It was such fun . . .

DEVADATTA: (*Preoccupied.*) Some work . . .

KAPILA: Really, you should have come. The wrestler from Gandhara—he's one of India's greatest, you know—he came. Nanda and I were wrestling when he arrived. He watched us. When I caught Nanda in a crocodile-hold, he first burst into applause and said . . .

(*Notices that Devadatta isn't listening and stops. Pause.*)

DEVADATTA: (*Walking up.*) Then?

KAPILA: Then what?

DEVADATTA: (*Flustered.*) I mean . . . what did Nanda do?

KAPILA: He played the flute.

DEVADATTA: (*More confused.*) No . . . I mean . . . you were saying something about the wrestler from Gandhara, weren't you?

KAPILA: He wrestled with me for a few minutes, patted me on the back and said, 'You'll go far'.

DEVADATTA: That's nice.

KAPILA: Yes, it is . . . Who's it this time?

DEVADATTA: What do you mean?

KAPILA: I mean—who—is—it—this—time?

DEVADATTA: What do you mean who?

KAPILA: I mean—who is the girl?

DEVADATTA: No one. (*Pause.*) How did you guess?

KAPILA: My dear friend, I have seen you fall in love fifteen times in the last two years. How could I not guess?

DEVADATTA: Kapila, if you've come to make fun of me . . .

KAPILA: I am not making fun of you. Every time, you have been the first to tell me about it. Why so shy this time?

DEVADATTA: How can you even talk of them in the same breath as her? Before her, they're as . . .

KAPILA: . . . . as stars before the moon, as the glow-worms before a torch. Yes, yes, that's been so fifteen times too.

DEVADATTA: (*Exploding.*) Why don't you go home? You are becoming a bore.

KAPILA:   Don't get annoyed.

DEVADATTA:   You call yourself my friend. But you haven't understood me at all.

KAPILA:   And have you understood me? No, you haven't. Or you wouldn't get angry like this. Don't you know I would do anything for you? Jump into a well—or walk into fire? Even my parents aren't as close to me as you are. I would leave them this minute if you asked me to.

DEVADATTA:   (*Irritated.*) Don't start on that now. You've said it fifty times already.

KAPILA:   . . . . And I'll say it again. If it wasn't for you I would have been no better than the ox in our yard. You showed me that there were such things as poetry and literature. You taught me . . .

DEVADATTA:   Why don't you go home? All I wanted was to be by myself for a day. Alone. And you had to come and start your chatter. What do you know of poetry and literature? Go back to your smithy—that's where you belong.

KAPILA:   (*Hurt.*) Do you really want me to go?

DEVADATTA:   Yes.

KAPILA:   All right. If that's what you want.
   (*He starts to go.*)

DEVADATTA:   Sit down.
   (*This is of course exactly what Kapila wants. He sits down on the floor.*)
   And don't speak . . .
   (*Devadatta gets down on the floor to sit beside Kapila. Kapila at once leaps up and gestures to Devadatta to sit on the chair. Devadatta shakes his head but Kapila insists, pulls him up by his arm. Devadatta gets up.*)
   You are a pest.
   (*Sits on the chair. Kapila sits down on the ground happily. A long pause.*)

DEVADATTA:   (*Slowly.*) How can I describe her, Kapila? Her forelocks rival the bees, her face is . . .
   (*All this is familiar to Kapila and he joins in, with great enjoyment.*)

BOTH:   . . . . is a white lotus. Her beauty is as the magic lake. Her arms the lotus creepers. Her breasts are golden urns and her waist . . .

DEVADATTA:  No. No!

KAPILA:  Eh?

DEVADATTA:  I was blind all these days. I deceived myself that I understood poetry. I didn't. I understood nothing.

*Tanvee shyama* —

BOTH:    . . . *shikharidashana pakvabimbadharoshthi* — *Madhye kshama chakitaharineeprekshana nimnanabhih.*

DEVADATTA:  The Shyama Nayika — born of Kalidasa's magic description — as Vatsyayana had dreamt her. Kapila, in one appearance, she became my guru in the poetry of love. Do you think she would ever assent to becoming my disciple in love itself?

KAPILA:  (*Aside.*) This is new!

DEVADATTA:  (*His eyes shining.*) If only she would consent to be my Muse, I could outshine Kalidasa. I'd always wanted to do that — but I thought it was impossible . . . But now I see it is within my reach.

KAPILA:  Then go ahead. Write . . .

DEVADATTA:  But how can I without her in front of me? How can I concentrate when my whole being is only thinking of her, craving for her?

KAPILA:  What's her name? Will you at least tell me that?

DEVADATTA:  Her name? She has no name.

KAPILA:  But what do her parents call her?

DEVADATTA:  (*Anguished.*) What's the use? She isn't meant for the likes of me . . .

KAPILA:  You don't really believe that, do you? With all your qualities — achievements — looks — family — grace . . .

DEVADATTA:  Don't try to console me with praise.

KAPILA:  I'm not praising you. You know very well that every parent of every girl in the city is only waiting to catch you . . .

DEVADATTA:  Don't! Please. I know this girl is beyond my wildest dreams. But still — I can't help wanting her — I can't help it. I swear, Kapila, with you as my witness I swear, if I ever get her as my wife, I'll sacrifice my two arms to the goddess Kali, I'll sacrifice my head to Lord Rudra . . .

KAPILA:  Ts! Ts! (*Aside.*) This is a serious situation. It does look as though this sixteenth girl has really caught our Devadatta in her net. Otherwise, he isn't the type to talk with such violence.

DEVADATTA: I mean it! What's the use of these hands and this head if I'm not to have her? My poetry won't live without her. The *Shakuntalam* will never be excelled. But how can I explain this to her? I have no cloud for a messenger. No bee to show the way. Now the only future I have is to stand and do penance in Pavana Veethi . . .

KAPILA: Pavana Veethi? Why there?

DEVADATTA: She lives in that street.

KAPILA: How do you know?

DEVADATTA: I saw her in the market yesterday evening. I couldn't remove my eyes from her and followed her home.

KAPILA: Tut! Tut! What must people have thought . . . ?

DEVADATTA: She went into a house in Pavana Veethi. I waited outside all evening. She didn't come out.

KAPILA: Now tell me. What sort of a house was it?

DEVADATTA: I can't remember.

KAPILA: What colour?

DEVADATTA: Don't know.

KAPILA: How many storeys?

DEVADATTA: I didn't notice.

KAPILA: You mean you didn't notice anything about the house?

DEVADATTA: The door-frame of the house had an engraving of a two-headed bird at the top. I only saw that. She lifted her hand to knock and it touched the bird. For a minute, the bird came alive.

KAPILA: (*Jumps up.*) Then why didn't you tell me before? You've been wasting all this precious time . . .

DEVADATTA: I don't understand . . .

KAPILA: My dear Devadatta, your cloud-messenger, your bee, your pigeon is sitting right in front of you and you don't even know it? You wait here. I'll go, find out her house, her name . . .

DEVADATTA: (*Incredulous.*) Kapila—Kapila . . .

KAPILA: I'll be back in a few minutes . . .

DEVADATTA: I won't ever forget this, Kapila . . .

KAPILA: Shut up! . . . And forget all about your arms and head. This job doesn't need either Rudra or Kali. I'm quite enough. (*Goes out.*)

DEVADATTA: Kapila—Kapila . . . He's gone. How fortunate I am to have a friend like him. Pure gold. (*Pause.*) But should I have trusted this to him? He means well—and he is a wizard in his smithy, in his farm, in his field. But here? No. He is too rough, too indelicate. He was the wrong man to send. He's bound to ruin the whole thing. (*Anguished.*) Lord Rudra, I meant what I said. If I get her my head will be a gift to you. Mother Kali, I'll sacrifice my arms to you. I swear . . .

(*Goes out. The Bhagavata removes the chair. Kapila enters.*)

KAPILA: This is Pavana Veethi—the street of merchants. Well, well, well. What enormous houses! Each one a palace in itself. It's a wonder people don't get lost in these houses.

(*Examines the doors one by one.*)

Now. This is not a double-headed bird. It's an eagle—This? A lotus. This is—er—a lion. Tiger. A wheel. And this? God alone knows what this is. And the next? (*In disgust.*) A horse!—a rhinoceros—another lion. Another lotus!—Where the hell is that stupid two-headed bird? (*Stops.*) What was the design? I couldn't make out? (*Goes back and stares at it. Shouts in triumph.*) That's it! Almost gave me the slip! A proper two-headed bird. But it's so tiny you can't see it at all unless you are willing to tear your eyes staring at it. Well now. Whose house could this be? (*Looks around.*) No one in sight. Naturally. Why should anyone come here in this hot sun? Better ask the people in the house.

(*Mimes knocking. Listens. Padmini enters humming a tune.*)

PADMINI: . . . Here comes the rider—from which land does he come? . . .

KAPILA: (*Gapes at her. Aside.*) I give up, Devadatta. I surrender to your judgment. I hadn't thought anyone could be more beautiful than the wench Ragini who acts Rambha in our village troupe. But this one! You're right—she is Yakshini, Shakuntala, Urvashi, Indumati—all rolled into one.

PADMINI: You knocked, didn't you?

KAPILA: Er—yes . . .

PADMINI: Then why are you gaping at me? What do you want?

KAPILA: I—I just wanted to know whose house this was.

PADMINI: Whose house do you want?

KAPILA: This one.

PADMINI:   I see. Then who do you want here?

KAPILA:   The master . . .

PADMINI:   Do you know his name?

KAPILA:   No.

PADMINI:   Have you met him?

KAPILA:   No.

PADMINI:   Have you seen him?

KAPILA:   No.

PADMINI:   So. You haven't met him, seen him or known him. What do you want with him?

KAPILA:   (*Aside.*) She is quite right. What have I to do with him? I only want to find out his name . . .

PADMINI:   Are you sure you want this house? Or were you . . .

KAPILA:   No. I'm sure this is the one.

PADMINI:   (*Pointing to her head.*) Are you all right here?

KAPILA:   (*Taken aback.*) Yes—I think so.

PADMINI:   How about your eyes? Do they work properly?

KAPILA:   Yes.

PADMINI:   (*Showing him four fingers.*) How many?

KAPILA:   Four.

PADMINI:   Correct. So there's nothing wrong with your eyes. As for the other thing, I'll have to take you on trust. Well then. If you are sure you wanted this house why were you peering at all those doors? And what were you mumbling under your breath?

KAPILA:   (*Startled.*) How did you know?

PADMINI:   I am quite sane . . . and I've got good eyes.

KAPILA:   (*Looks up and chuckles.*) Oh, I suppose you were watching from the terrace . . .

PADMINI:   (*In a low voice, mysteriously.*) Listen, you'd better be careful. We have any number of thefts in this street and people are suspicious. Last night there was a man standing out there for nearly two hours without moving. And today you have turned up. It's just as well I saw you. Anyone else would have taken you to the police—Beware! (*Aloud.*) Now tell me. What are you doing here?

KAPILA:   I—I can't tell you.

PADMINI:   Really! Who will you tell it to?

KAPILA:   Your father . . .

PADMINI: Do you want my father or do you want the master of this house?

KAPILA: Aren't they the same?

PADMINI: (*As though explaining to a child.*) Listen, my father could be a servant in this house. Or the master of this house could be my father's servant. My father could be the master's father, brother, son-in-law, cousin, grandfather or uncle. Do you agree?

KAPILA: Er—Yes.

PADMINI: Right. Then we'll start again. Whom should I call?

KAPILA: Your father.

PADMINI: And if he's not in?

KAPILA: (*Lost.*) Anyone else.

PADMINI: Which anyone?

KAPILA: Perhaps—your brother.

PADMINI: Do you know him?

KAPILA: No.

PADMINI: Have you met him?

KAPILA: No.

PADMINI: Do you know his name?

KAPILA: (*Desperate.*) Please, please—call your father or the master or both, or if they are the same, anyone . . . please call someone!

PADMINI: No. No. That won't do.

KAPILA: (*Looking around; aside.*) No one here. Still I have to find out her name. Devadatta must be in pain and . . . He will never forgive me if I go back now. (*Aloud.*) Madam, please. I have some very important work. I'll touch your feet . . .

PADMINI: (*Eager.*) You will? Really? Do you know, I've touched everyone's feet in this house some time or the other, but no one's ever touched mine? You will?

KAPILA: (*Slapping his forehead as he sinks to the ground.*) I'm finished— decimated—powdered to dust—powdered into tiny specks of flour. (*To Padmini.*) My mother, can I at least talk to a servant?

PADMINI: I knew it. I knew you wouldn't touch my feet. One can't even trust strangers any more. All right, my dear son! I opened the door. So consider me the door-keeper. What do you want?

KAPILA: (*Determined.*) All right! (*Gets up.*) You have no doubt heard of the Revered Brahmin Vidyasagara.

PADMINI: It's possible.

KAPILA: In which case you'll also know of Devadatta, his only son. A poet. A pundit. Knows the Vedas backwards. Writes the grandest poetry ever. Long, dark hair. Delicate, fair face. Age twenty. Height five feet seven inches. Weight . . .

PADMINI: Wait a minute! What's he to you?

KAPILA: Friend. Greatest in the world! But the main question now: What's he going to be to you?

(*Sudden silence.*)

PADMINI: (*Blushing as the import of the remark dawns on her.*) Mother! (*Runs in. Kapila stands, staring after her.*)

KAPILA: Devadatta, my friend, I confess to you I'm feeling uneasy. You are a gentle soul. You can't bear a bitter word or an evil thought. But this one is fast as lightning—and as sharp. She is not for the likes of you. What she needs is a man of steel. But what can one do? You'll never listen to me. And I can't withdraw now. I'll have to talk to her family . . .

(*Follows her in.*)

BHAGAVATA: Need one explain to our wise and knowing audience what followed next? Padmini is the daughter of the leading merchant in Dharmapura. In her house, the very floor is swept by the Goddess of Wealth. In Devadatta's house, they've the Goddess of Learning for a maid. What could then possibly stand in the way of bringing the families together? (*Marriage music.*) Padmini became the better half of Devadatta and settled in his house. Nor did Devadatta forget his debt to Kapila. The old friendship flourished as before. Devadatta—Padmini—Kapila! To the admiring citizens of Dharmapura, Rama—Sita—Lakshmana.

(*Enter Devadatta and Padmini.*)

PADMINI: Why is he so late? He should have been here more than an hour ago . . .

(*Looks out of a window.*)

DEVADATTA: Have you packed your clothes properly?

PADMINI: The first thing in the morning.

DEVADATTA: And the mattresses? We may have to sleep out in the open. It's quite chilly . . . we'll need at least two rugs.

PADMINI: Don't worry. The servant's done all that.

DEVADATTA: And your shawl? Also some warm clothes . . .

PADMINI: What's happened to you today? At other times you are so full of your books, you even forget to wash your hands after a meal. But today you've been going on and on and on all morning.

DEVADATTA:   Padmini, I've told you ten times already . . . I don't like the idea of this trip. You should rest—not face such hazards. The cart will probably shake like an earthquake. It's dangerous in your condition. But you won't listen . . .

PADMINI:   My condition! What's happened to me? To listen to you, one would think I was the first woman in this world to become pregnant. I only have to stumble and you act as though it's all finished and gone . . .

DEVADATTA:   For God's sake . . . will you stop it?

PADMINI:   (*Laughs.*) Sorry! (*Bites her tongue in repentance.*) I won't say such things again.

DEVADATTA:   You've no sense of what not to say. So long as you can chatter and run around like a child . . .

PADMINI:   (*Back at the window.*) Where is Kapila?

DEVADATTA   . . . and drool over Kapila all day.

PADMINI:   (*Taken aback.*) What do you mean?

DEVADATTA:   What else should I say? The other day I wanted to read out a play of Bhasa's to you and sure enough Kapila drops in.

PADMINI:   Oh! That's biting you still, is it? . . . But why are you blaming me? He was your friend even before you married me, wasn't he? He used to drop in every day even then . . .

DEVADATTA:   But shouldn't he realize I'm married now? He just can't go on as before . . .

PADMINI:   Don't blame him. It's my fault. He learnt a bit about poetry from you and I thought he might enjoy Bhasa. So I asked him to come . . . He didn't want to—but I insisted.

DEVADATTA:   I know that.

PADMINI:   Had I realized you would get so upset, I wouldn't have.

DEVADATTA:   I'm not upset, Padmini. Kapila isn't merely a friend— he's like my brother. One has to collect merit in seven lives to get a friend like him. But is it wrong for me to want to read to you alone—or to spend a couple of days with you without anyone else around? (*Pause.*) Of course, once he came, there wasn't the slightest chance of my reading any poetry. You had to hop around him twittering 'Kapila! Kapila!' every minute.

PADMINI:   You aren't jealous of him, are you?

DEVADATTA:   Me? Jealous of Kapila? Why do you have to twist everything I say . . .

PADMINI:   (*Laughs. Affectionately.*) Don't sulk now. I was just trying to be funny. Really you have no sense of humour.

DEVADATTA:   It's humour for you. But it burns my insides . . .

PADMINI:   Aw, shut up. Don't I know how liberal and largehearted you are? You aren't the sort to get jealous. If I fall into a well tomorrow, you won't even miss me until my bloated corpse floats up . . .

DEVADATTA:   (*Irritated.*) Padmini!

PADMINI:   Sorry, I forgot. I apologize —I slap myself on the cheeks. (*Slaps herself on both cheeks with her right hand several times in punishment.*) Is that all right? The trouble is I grew up saying these awful things and it's become a habit now. But you are so fragile! I don't know how you're going to go through life wrapped in silk like this! You are still a baby . . .

DEVADATTA:   I see.

PADMINI:   Look now. You got annoyed about Kapila. But why? You are my saffron, my marriage-thread, my deity. Why should you feel upset? I like making fun of Kapila—he is such an innocent. Looks a proper devil, but the way he blushes and giggles and turns red, he might have been a bride.

DEVADATTA:   (*Smiles.*) Well, this bride didn't blush.

PADMINI:   No one taught this bride to blush. But now I'm learning from that yokel.

(*They both laugh. She casually goes back to the window and looks out.*)

DEVADATTA:   (*Aside.*) Does she really not see? Or is she deliberately playing this game with him? Kapila was never the sort to blush. But now, he only has to see her and he begins to wag his tail. Sits up on his hind legs as though he were afraid to let her words fall to the ground. And that pleading in his eyes—can't she really see that? (*Aloud.*) Padmini, Kapila isn't used to women. The only woman he has known in his life is his mother . . .

PADMINI:   You mean it's dangerous to be with him? The way you talk one would never imagine he was your best friend.

DEVADATTA:   (*Incensed.*) Why do you have to paint everything I say . . .

PADMINI:   (*Conciliatory.*) What did I say? Listen, if you really don't want to go to Ujjain today, let's not. When Kapila comes, tell him I'm ill.

DEVADATTA:   But . . . you will be disappointed.

PADMINI:   Me? Of course not. We'll do as you feel. You remember what the priest said—I'm your 'half' now. The better half! We can go to Ujjain some other time . . . In another couple of months, there's the big Ujjain fair. We'll go then—just the two of us. All right? We'll cancel today's trip.

DEVADATTA:   (*Trying to control his excitement.*) Now—if you aren't going to be disappointed—then—truly—that's what I would like most. Not because I'm jealous of Kapila—No, I'm not, I know that. He has a heart of gold. But this is your first baby . . .

PADMINI:   What do you mean first? How many babies can one have in six months?

DEVADATTA:   You aren't going to start again . . .

PADMINI:   No, no, no, I won't say a word.

DEVADATTA:   (*Pinching her cheek.*) Bad upbringing—that's what it is. I don't like the idea of your going so far in a cart in your present condition, that's all.

PADMINI:   Ordinarily I would have replied I had a womb of steel, but I won't—in the present condition.

     (*Both laugh.*)

All right. If you are happy, so am I.

DEVADATTA:   (*Happy.*) Yes, we'll spend the whole day by ourselves. The servants are going home anyway. They can come back tomorrow. But for today—only you and me. It's been such a long time since we've been on our own.

KAPILA:   (*Off-stage.*) Devadatta . . .

PADMINI:   There's Kapila now. You tell him.

     (*She pretends to go in, but goes and stands in a corner of the stage, listening. Kapila enters excited.*)

KAPILA:   I'm late, ain't I? What could I do? That cartman had kept the cart ready but the moment I looked at it, I knew one of the oxen was no good. I asked him to change it. 'We won't reach Ujjain for another fortnight in this one', I said. He started . . .

DEVADATTA:   Kapila . . .

KAPILA:   . . . making a scene, but I stood my ground. So he had to fetch a new one. These cart-hirers are a menace. If ours hadn't gone to Chitrapur that day . . .

DEVADATTA:   Kapila, we have to call off today's trip.

KAPILA:   (*Suddenly silenced.*) Oh!

DEVADATTA:   (*Embarrassed.*) You see, Padmini isn't well . . .

KAPILA:   Well, then of course . . .

(*Silence.*)

I'll return the cart then . . .

DEVADATTA:   Yes.

KAPILA:   Or else he may charge us for the day.

DEVADATTA:   Uhm.

KAPILA:   (*Aside.*) So it's off. What am I to do for the rest of the day? What am I to do for the rest of the week? Why should it feel as though the whole world has been wiped out for a whole week? Why this emptiness . . . Kapila, Kapila, get a tight hold on yourself. You are slipping, boy, control yourself. Don't lose that hold. Go now—don't come here again for a week— Devadatta's bound to get angry with you for not coming. Sister-in-law will be annoyed. But don't come back. Go, Go! (*Aloud.*) Well then—I'll start.

DEVADATTA:   Why don't you sit for a while?

KAPILA:   No, no—we might upset sister-in-law more then with our prattle.

DEVADATTA:   That's true. So—come again.

KAPILA:   Yes, I will.

(*Starts to go. Padmini comes out.*)

PADMINI:   Why are you sitting here? When are we going to start? We are already late . . .

(*They look at her, surprised.*)

KAPILA:   But if you aren't well, we won't . . .

PADMINI:   What's wrong with me? I'm perfect. I had a headache this morning. But a layer of ginger-paste took care of that. Why should we cancel our trip for a little thing like that?

(*Devadatta opens his mouth to say something but stays quiet.*)

(*To Kapila.*) Why are you standing there like a statue?

KAPILA:   No, really, if you have a headache . . .

PADMINI:   I don't have a headache now!

DEVADATTA:   But, Padmini . . .

PADMINI: Kapila, put those bundles out there in the cart. The servant will bring the rest.

(*Kapila stands totally baffled. He looks at Devadatta for guidance. There's none.*)

Be quick. Otherwise I'll put them in myself.

(*Kapila goes out. Padmini goes to Devadatta. Pleading.*)

Please don't get angry. Poor boy, he looked so lost and disappointed, I couldn't bear to see it. He has been running around for us this whole week.

DEVADATTA: (*Turning his head away.*) Where's the box in which I put the books? I'll take it . . .

PADMINI: You are an angel. I knew you wouldn't mind . . . I'll bring it. It's quite light.

(*Goes out.*)

DEVADATTA: (*To himself.*) And my disappointment? Does that mean nothing to you? (*Aloud.*) Don't. I'll take it. You don't lift anything.

(*Goes in after her.*)

BHAGAVATA: Why do you tremble, heart? Why do you cringe like a touch-me-not bush through which a snake has passed? The sun rests his head on the Fortunate Lady's flower.

And the head is bidding good-bye to the heart.

(*Kapila, followed by Padmini and Devadatta, enter, miming a cart-ride. Kapila is driving the cart.*)

PADMINI: How beautifully you drive the cart, Kapila! Your hands don't even move, but the oxen seem to know exactly where to go.

(*Kapila laughs happily.*)

Shall we stop here for a while? We've been in this cart all day and my legs feel like bits of wood.

KAPILA: Right! Ho—Ho . . .

(*Pulls the cart to a halt. They get down. She slips but Devadatta supports her.*)

PADMINI: What a terrible road. Nothing but stones and rocks —but one didn't feel a thing in the cart! You drove it so gently—almost made it float. I remember when Devadatta took me in a cart —that was soon after our marriage—I insisted on being shown the lake outside the city. So we started—only the two of us and Devadatta driving—against my advice, I must say. And we didn't

even cross the city-gates. The oxen took everything except the
road. He only had to pull to the right, and off they would rush
to the left! I've never laughed so much in my life. But of course
he got very angry, so we had to go back home straight!
(*Laughs. But Kapila and Devadatta don't join in.*)
Kapila, what's that glorious tree there? That one—covered with
flowers?

KAPILA:   Oh that! That's called the Fortunate Lady's flower—that
means a married woman . . .

PADMINI:   I know! But why do they call it that?

KAPILA:   Wait. I'll bring a flower. Then you'll see.
(*Goes out.*)

PADMINI:   (*Watching him, to herself.*) How he climbs—like an ape.
Before I could even say 'yes', he had taken off his shirt, pulled
his *dhoti* up and swung up the branch. And what an ethereal
shape! Such a broad back—like an ocean with muscles rippling
across it—and then that small, feminine waist which looks so
helpless.

DEVADATTA:   (*Aside.*) She had so much to talk about all day, she
couldn't wait for breath. Now—not a word.

PADMINI:   (*Aside.*) He is like a Celestial Being reborn as a hunter.
. . . How his body sways, his limbs curve—it's a dance almost.

DEVADATTA:   (*Aside.*) And why should I blame her? It's his strong
body—his manly muscles. And to think I had never *ever* noticed
them all these years . . . I was an innocent—an absolute baby.

PADMINI:   (*Aside.*) No woman could resist him.

DEVADATTA:   (*Aside.*) No woman could resist him—and what does
it matter that she's married? What a fool I've been. All these
days I only saw that pleading in his eyes stretching out its arms,
begging for a favour. But never looked in her eyes. And when
I did—took the whites of her eyes for their real depth. Only
now—I see the depths—now I see these flames leaping up from
those depths. Now! So late! Don't turn away now, Devadatta,
look at her. Look at those yellow, purple flames. Look how
she's pouring her soul in his mould. Look! Let your guts burn
out—let your lungs turn to ash—but don't turn away. Look—
and don't scream. Strangle your agony. But look deep into
these eyes—look until those peacock flames burn out the
blindness in you. Don't be a coward now.

PADMINI: (*Aside.*) How long can one go on like this? How long? How long? If Devadatta notices . . .

> (*Looks at Devadatta. He is looking at her already and their eyes meet. Both look away.*)

PADMINI: (*Aloud.*) There he comes. All I wanted was one flower and he's brought a heap.

> (*Kapila comes in, miming a whole load of flowers in his arms and hands. He pours them out in front of her.*)

KAPILA: Here you are. The Fortunate Lady's flowers.

PADMINI: And why a 'Fortunate Lady', pray?

KAPILA: Because it has all the marks of marriage a woman puts on. The yellow on the petals—then that red round patch at the bottom of the petals—like on your foreheads—then—here—that thin saffron line—like in the parting of your hair—Then—uhm . . . oh yes—here near the stem a row of black dots—like a necklace of black heads—

PADMINI: What imagination! (*To Devadatta.*) You should put it in your poetry. It's good for a simile.

DEVADATTA: Shall we go? It's quite late.

PADMINI: Let's stay. I have been sitting in that cart for I don't know how long. I didn't know the road to Ujjain was so enchanting . . .

KAPILA: The others take a longer route. This is a more wooded area—so very few come this way. But I like this better. Besides, it's fifteen miles shorter.

PADMINI: I wouldn't have minded even if it were fifteen miles longer. It's like a garden . . .

KAPILA: Isn't it? Look there, do you see it? That's the river Bhargavi. The poet Vyasa had a hermitage on its banks. There's a temple of Rudra there now.

DEVADATTA: (*Suddenly awake.*) A temple of Rudra?

KAPILA: Yes, it's beautiful. And—there—beyond that hill is a temple of Kali.

> (*Two stage-hands come and hold up a half-curtain in the corner to which he points. The curtain has a picture of Goddess Kali on it. The Bhagavata puts a sword in front of it.*)

It was very prosperous once. But now it's quite dilapidated.

DEVADATTA: (*As though in a trance.*) The temple of Rudra!

KAPILA:   Yes, that's old too. But not half as ruined as the Kali temple. We can have a look if you like.

PADMINI:   Yes, let's.

DEVADATTA:   Why don't you go and see the Kali temple first?

KAPILA:   No, that's quite terrible . . . I saw it once—bats, snakes, all sorts of poisonous insects—and no proper road. We can go to the Rudra temple, though. It's nearer.

PADMINI:   Come on. Let's go.

DEVADATTA:   You two go. I won't come.

PADMINI:   (*Pause.*) And you?

DEVADATTA:   I'll stay here and watch the cart.

KAPILA:   But there's no fear of thieves here . . . (*Sensing the tension.*) Or else, I'll stay here . . .

DEVADATTA:   No, no. You two go. I'm also a little tired.

PADMINI:   (*Aside.*) He has started it again. Another tantrum. Let him. What do I care? (*Aloud.*) Come, Kapila, we'll go.

KAPILA:   But—perhaps in your condition . . .

PADMINI:   (*Exploding.*) Why are you two hounding me with this condition? If you don't want to come, say so. Don't make excuses . . .

KAPILA:   Devadatta, it's not very far. You come too . . .

DEVADATTA:   I told you to go. Don't force me . . .

PADMINI:   Let's not go. I don't want the two of you to suffer for my sake.

DEVADATTA:   (*To Kapila.*) Go.

KAPILA:   (*He has no choice.*) Come. We'll be back soon.

(*Kapila and Padmini go out.*)

DEVADATTA:   Good-bye, Kapila. Good-bye, Padmini. May Lord Rudra bless you. You are two pieces of my heart—live happily together. I shall find my happiness in that. (*Agonized.*) Give me strength, Lord Rudra. My father, give me courage. I'm already trembling, I'd never thought I would be so afraid. Give me courage, Father, strengthen me.

(*He walks to the temple of Kali. It's a steep and difficult climb. He is exhausted by the time he reaches the temple. He prostrates himself before the goddess.*)

Bhavani, Bhairavi, Kali, Durga, Mahamaya, Mother of all Nature—I had forgotten my promise to you. Forgive me, Mother. You fulfilled the deepest craving of my life—you gave me Padmini—and I forgot my word. Forgive me, for I'm here now to carry out my promise.

(*Picks up the sword.*)

Great indeed is your mercy. Even in this lonely place some devotee of yours—a hunter perhaps or a tribesman—has left this weapon. Who knows how many lives this weapon has sacrificed to you . . . (*Screaming.*) Here, Mother Kali, here's another. My head. Take it, Mother, accept this little offering of my head.

(*Cuts off his head. Not an easy thing to do—he struggles, groans, writhes. Ultimately succeeds in killing himself. The head—that is, the mask—rolls off and blood flows.*

*A long silence. Padmini and Kapila return to the cart.*)

PADMINI: (*Enters talking.*) . . . he should have come. How thrilling it was! Heavenly! But of course he has no enthusiasm for these things. After all . . .

(*Notices Devadatta isn't there.*)

Where's Devadatta?

(*They look around.*)

He said he'd stay here!

KAPILA: (*Calls.*) Devadatta—Devadatta . . .

PADMINI: He's probably somewhere around. Where will he go? He has the tenderest feet on earth. They manage to get blisters, corns, cuts, boils and wounds without any effort. So . . .

KAPILA: (*Calls.*) Devadatta . . .

PADMINI: Why are you shouting? Sit down. He'll come.

(*Kapila inspects the surrounding area. Gives a gasp of surprise.*)

What's it?

KAPILA: His footprints. He has obviously gone in that direction. (*Pause.*) But—that's where the Kali temple is!

PADMINI: You don't mean he's gone there! How absurd!

KAPILA: You stay here. I'll bring him back.

PADMINI: But why do you have to go? There's nothing to fear in this broad daylight!

KAPILA: (*Hurrying off.*) It's very thick wood there. If he gets lost, he'll have to spend the whole night in the jungle. You stay here. I'll come back soon.

(*Runs out.*)

PADMINI: (*Exasperated.*) He's gone! Really, he seems more worried about Devadatta than me.

(*She sits down. Kapila goes to the Kali temple—but naturally faster than Devadatta did. He sees the body and his mouth half opens in a scream. He runs to Devadatta and kneels beside him. Lifts his truncated head and moans.*)

KAPILA:   You've cut off your head! You've cut off your head! Oh my dear friend, my brother, what have you done? Were you so angry with me? Did you feel such contempt for me—such abhorrence? And in your anger you forgot that I was ready to die for you? If you had asked me to jump into fire, I would have done it. If you had asked me to leave the country, I would have done it. If you had asked me to go and drown in a river, I would have accepted. Did you despise me so much that you couldn't even ask me that? I did wrong. But you know I don't have the intelligence to know what else I should have done. I couldn't think—and so you've pushed me away? No, Devadatta, I can't live without you. I can't breathe without you. Devadatta, my brother, my father, my friend . . .

(*Picks up the sword.*)

You spurned me in this world. Accept me as your brother at least in the next. Here, friend, here I come. As always, I follow in your path.

(*Cuts off his head. It's an easier death this time. Padmini, who has been still till now, moves.*)

PADMINI:   Where are they? Now this Kapila's disappeared too. He couldn't still be searching for him. That's not possible. Devadatta's too weak to have gone far. They must have met. Perhaps they're sitting now, chatting as in the old days. For once no bother of a wife around . . . No, more likely Devadatta's sulking. He's probably tearing poor Kapila to shreds by just being silent and grumpy. Yes, that would be more like him.

(*Pause.*)

It's almost dark. And they aren't back. Shameless men—to leave me alone like this here!

No, it's no use sitting here any longer. I had better go and look for them. If I die of a snake-bite on the way, so much the better for them.

(*Walks to the temple, slowly. Rubs her eyes when she reaches there.*)

How dark it is! Can't see a thing. (*Calls.*) Kapila—Kapila— Devadatta isn't here either. What shall I do here? At this time

of night! Alone! (*Listens.*) What's that? Some wild beast. A wolf!
It's right outside—what shall I do if it comes in? . . . Ah! It's
gone. Mother Kali, only you can protect me now.

(*Stumbles over the bodies.*)

What's this? What's this?

(*Stares at the bodies and then lets out a terrified scream.*)

Oh God! What's this? Both! Both gone! And didn't even think
of me before they went? What shall I do? What shall I do? Oh,
Devadatta, what did I do that you left me alone in this state?
Was that how much you loved me? And you, Kapila, who
looked at me with dog's eyes—you too? How selfish you
are—how unkind! What shall I do now—where shall I go?
How can I go home?

(*Pause.*)

Home? And what shall I say when I get there? What shall I say
happened? And who'll believe me? They'll all say the two fought
and died for this whore. They're bound to say it. Then what'll
happen to me? No, Mother Kali, no,—it's too horrible to think
of. No! Kapila's gone—Devadatta's gone. Let me go with them.

(*Picks up the sword.*)

I don't have the strength to hack off my head. But what does
it matter how I die, Mother? You don't care. It's the same to
you—another offering! All right. Have it then—here's another
offering for you.

(*Lifts the sword and puts its point on her breast when, from behind
the curtain, the goddess's voice is heard.*)

VOICE:    Hey . . .

(*Padmini freezes.*)

Put it down! Put down that sword!

(*Padmini jumps up in fright and, throwing the sword aside, tries
to run out of the temple. Then stops.*)

PADMINI:  Who's that?

(*No reply.*)

Who's that?

(*A tremendous noise of drums. Padmini shuts her eyes in terror.
Behind the curtain one sees the uplifted blood-red palms of the
goddess. The curtain is lowered and taken away and one sees a
terrifying figure, her arms stretched out, her mouth wide open with
the tongue lolling out. The drums stop and as the goddess drops*

*her arms and shuts her mouth, it becomes clear she has been
yawning.*)

KALI: (*Completes the yawn.*) All right. Open your eyes and be quick.
Don't waste time.

(*Padmini opens her eyes and sees the goddess. She runs and falls
at her feet.*)

PADMINI: Mother—Kali . . .

KALI: (*Sleepy.*) Yes, it's me. There was a time—many many years
ago—when at this hour they would have the *mangalarati*. The
devotees used to make a deafening racket with drums and
conch-shells and cymbals. So I used to be wide awake around
now. I've lost the habit. (*Yawns.*) Right. What do you want?
Tell me. I'm pleased with you.

PADMINI: Save me, Mother . . .

KALI: I know. I've done that already.

PADMINI: Do you call this saving, Mother of all Nature? I can't
show my face to anyone in the world. I can't . . .

KALI: (*A little testily.*) Yes, yes, you've said that once. No need to
repeat yourself. Now do as I tell you. Put these heads back
properly. Attach them to their bodies and then press that sword
on their necks. They'll come up alive. Is that enough?

PADMINI: Mother, you are our breath, you are our bread—and—
water . . .

KALI: Skip it! Do as I told you. And quickly. I'm collapsing with
sleep.

PADMINI: (*Hesitating*) May I ask a question?

KALI: If it's not too long.

PADMINI: Can there ever be anything you already don't know,
Mother? The past and the future are mere specks in your palm.
Then why didn't you stop Devadatta when he came here? Why
didn't you stop Kapila? If you'd saved either of them, I would
have been spared all this terror, this agony. Why did you wait
so long?

KALI: (*Surprised.*) Is that all you can think of now?

PADMINI: Mother . . .

KALI: I've never seen anyone like you.

PADMINI: How could one possibly hide anything from you,
Mother?

KALI: That's true enough.

PADMINI:   Then why didn't you stop them?

KALI:   Actually if it hadn't been that I was so sleepy, I would have thrown them out by the scruff of their necks . . .

PADMINI:   But why?

KALI:   The rascals! They were lying to their last breaths. That fellow Devadatta—he had once promised his head to Rudra and his arms to me! Think of it—head to him and arms to me! Then because you insisted on going to the Rudra temple, he comes here and offers his head. Nobly too—wants to keep his word, he says—no other reason!

Then this Kapila, died right in front of me—but 'for his friend'. Mind you! Didn't even have the courtesy to refer to me. And what lies! Says he is dying for friendship. He must have known perfectly well he would be accused of killing Devadatta for you. Do you think he wouldn't have grabbed you if it hadn't been for that fear? But till his last breath—'Oh my friend! My dear brother!'

Only you spoke the truth.

PADMINI:   It's all your grace, Mother . . .

KALI:   Don't drag me into it. I had nothing to do with it. You spoke the truth because you're selfish—that's all. Now don't go on talking. Do what I told you and shut your eyes.

PADMINI:   Yes, Mother . . .

(*Eagerly, Padmini puts the heads—that is, the masks—back. But in her excitement she mixes them up so that Devadatta's mask goes to Kapila's body and vice versa. Then presses the sword on their necks, does* namaskara *to the goddess, walks downstage and stands with her back to the goddess, her eyes shut tight.*)

PADMINI:   I'm ready, Mother.

KALI:   (*In a resigned tone.*) My dear daughter, there should be a limit even to honesty. Anyway—So be it!

(*Again the drums. The curtain is held up again and the goddess disappears behind it. During the following scene the stage-hands, the curtain as well as the goddess leave the stage.*

*Padmini stands immobile with her eyes shut. The drums stop. A long silence follows. The dead bodies move. Their breathing becomes loud and laboured. They sit up, slowly, stiffly. Their movement is mechanical, as though blood-circulation has not started properly yet. They feel their own arms, heads and bodies, and look around, bewildered.*

*Henceforth the person wearing the mask of Devadatta will be called Devadatta. Similarly with Kapila.*

*They stand up. It's not easy and they reel around a bit. Padmini is still.)*

DEVADATTA: What—happened?

KAPILA:  . . . . what happened?

(*Padmini opens her eyes, but she still doesn't dare to look at them.*)

PADMINI:   Devadatta's voice! Kapila's voice!

(*Screaming with joy.*) Kapila! Devadatta!

(*Turns and runs to them. Then suddenly stops and stands paralysed.*)

KAPILA:   Who . . .?

DEVADATTA:   Padmini?

KAPILA:   What—happened? My head—Ooh! It feels so heavy!

DEVADATTA:   My body—seems to weigh—a ton.

PADMINI:   (*Running around in confusion.*) What have I done? What have I done? What have I done? Mother Kali, only you can save me now—only you can help me—What have I done? What have I done? What should I do? Mother—Mother . . .

DEVADATTA:   (*A little more alive.*) Why are you—crying?

KAPILA:   What's—wrong?

PADMINI:   What shall I tell you, Devadatta? How can I explain it, Kapila? You cut off your heads—but the goddess gave you life—but—I—I—in the dark . . . Mother, only you can protect me now—Mother! I—mixed up your heads—I mixed them up! Forgive me—I don't deserve to live—forgive me . . .

KAPILA:   (*Looking at Devadatta.*) You mixed up . . .

DEVADATTA:   . . . . the heads?

(*The stare at each other. Then burst into laughter. She doesn't know how to react. Watches them. Then starts laughing.*)

DEVADATTA:   Mixed-up heads!

KAPILA:   Heads mixed-up!

DEVADATTA:   Exchanged heads!

KAPILA:   Heads exchanged!

DEVADATTA:   How fantastic! All these years we were only friends . . .

KAPILA: Now we are blood-relations! Body-relations! (*Laughing.*)
What a gift!

DEVADATTA: Forgive you? We must thank you . . .

KAPILA: We'll never be able to thank you—enough . . .

DEVADATTA: Exchanged heads!

(*They roar with laughter. Then all three hold hands and run round in a circle, singing.*)

ALL THREE: (*Together.*)
What a good mix!
No more tricks!
Is this one that
Or that one this?
Ho! Ho!

(*They sing this over and over again until they collapse on the floor.*)

KAPILA: Oooh—I'm finished!

PADMINI: . . . . dead!

DEVADATTA: Nothing like this could have ever happened before.

PADMINI: You know, seeing you two with your heads off was bad enough. But when you got up it was terrible! I almost died of fright . . .

(*They laugh.*)

KAPILA: No one will believe us if we tell them.

PADMINI: (*Suddenly.*) We won't tell anyone.

DEVADATTA: We'll keep our secrets inside us.

PADMINI: 'Inside us' is right.

(*Laughter.*)

KAPILA: But how can we not tell? They'll know soon . . .

DEVADATTA: No one'll know.

KAPILA: I'm sure they'll . . .

DEVADATTA: I'll take any bet.

KAPILA: But how's that possible?

DEVADATTA: You'll see. Why worry now?

PADMINI: Come. Let's go . . .

KAPILA: It's late.

DEVADATTA: No Ujjain now. We go back home!

KAPILA: Absolutely.

PADMINI: This Ujjain will last us a lifetime. Come.

(*They get up. Every now and then someone laughs and then all burst out together.*)

PADMINI:   Devadatta, I really don't know how we're going to keep this from your parents. They'll guess as soon as they see you bare-bodied.

DEVADATTA:   They won't, I tell you. They take us too much for granted . . .

KAPILA:   What do you mean?

DEVADATTA:   Who ever looks hard at a person he sees every day?

KAPILA:   I don't mean that . . .

PADMINI:   I'm not so sure. I'm afraid I'll get the blame for it ultimately . . .

DEVADATTA:   Stop worrying! I tell you it . . .

KAPILA:   But what has she got to do with you now?

DEVADATTA:   (*Stops.*) What do you mean?

KAPILA:   I mean Padmini must come home with me, shouldn't she? She's my wife, so she must . . .

       (*Exclamations from Devadatta and Padmini.*)

PADMINI:   What are you talking of, Kapila?

KAPILA:   (*Explaining.*) I mean, you are Devadatta's wife. I have Devadatta's body now. So you have to be my wife . . .

PADMINI:   Shut up . . .

DEVADATTA:   Don't blather like an idiot! I am Devadatta . . .

PADMINI:   Aren't you ashamed of yourself?

KAPILA:   But why, Padmini? I have Devadatta's body now . . .

DEVADATTA:   We know that. You don't have to repeat yourself like a parrot. According to the *Shastras*, the head is the sign of a man . . .

KAPILA:   (*Angry now.*) That may be. But the question now is simply this: Whose wife is she? (*Raising his right hand.*) This is the hand that accepted her at the wedding. This the body she's lived with all these months. And the child she's carrying is the seed of this body.

PADMINI:   (*Frightened by the logic.*) No, no, no. It's not possible. It's not. (*Running to Devadatta.*) It's not, Devadatta.

DEVADATTA:   Of course, it isn't, my dear. He is ignorant . . . (*To Kapila.*) When one accepts a partner in marriage, with the holy fire as one's witness, one accepts a person, not a body. She didn't marry Devadatta's body, she married Devadatta—the person.

KAPILA:   If that's your argument, I have Devadatta's body, so I am Devadatta—the person.

DEVADATTA:  Listen to me. Of all the human limbs the topmost—in position as well as in importance—is the head. I have Devadatta's head and it follows that I am Devadatta. According to the Sacred Texts . . .

KAPILA:  Don't tell me about your Sacred Texts. You can always twist them to suit your needs. She married Devadatta's body with the holy fire as her witness and that's enough for me.

DEVADATTA:  (*Laughs.*) Did you hear that, Padmini? He claims to be Devadatta and yet he condemns the Texts. You think Devadatta would ever do that?

KAPILA:  You can quote as many Texts as you like, I don't give a nail. Come on, Padmini . . .

(*Takes a step towards her. But Devadatta steps in between.*)

DEVADATTA:  Take care!

PADMINI:  Come, Devadatta. It's no use arguing with this rascal. Let's go.

DEVADATTA:  Come on . . .

KAPILA:  (*Stepping between them.*) Where are you taking my wife, friend?

DEVADATTA:  Will you get out of our way or should . . .

KAPILA:  It was you who got in my way.

DEVADATTA:  (*Pushing Kapila aside.*) Get away, you pig.

KAPILA:  (*Triumphant.*) He's using force! And what language! Padmini, think! Would Devadatta ever have acted like this? This is Kapila's violence . . .

DEVADATTA:  Come. Padmini.

KAPILA:  Go. But do you think I'll stay put while you run away with my wife? Where will you go? How far can you go? Only to the city, after all. I'll follow you there. I'll kick up a row in the streets. Let's see what happens then.

(*Devadatta stops.*)

PADMINI:  Let him scream away. Don't pay him any attention.

DEVADATTA:  No. He's right. This has to be solved here. It'll create a scandal in the city . . .

PADMINI:  But who'll listen to him? Everyone will take you for Devadatta by your face.

KAPILA:  Ha! You think the people in Dharmapura don't know my body, do you? They've seen me a thousand times in the wrestling pit. I've got I don't know how many awards for body-building. Let's see whom they believe.

PADMINI: (*Pleading.*) Why are you torturing us like this? For so many years you have been our friend, accepted our hospitality . . .

KAPILA: I know what you want, Padmini. Devadatta's clever head and Kapila's strong body . . .

PADMINI: Shut up, you brute.

DEVADATTA: Suppose she did. There's nothing wrong in it. It's natural for a woman to feel attracted to a fine figure of a man . . .

KAPILA: I know it is. But that doesn't mean she can just go and live with a man who's not her husband. That's not right.

PADMINI: (*Crying out.*) How can we get rid of this scoundrel? Let's go—let's go anywhere—to the woods—to the desert— anywhere you like.

KAPILA: You'll have to kill me before you'll really escape me. You could. I don't have the strength to resist Kapila.

PADMINI: (*Using a new argument.*) But I gave you life—

KAPILA: That was no favour. If you hadn't, you would have been a widow now. Actually he should be grateful to me because my wife saved his life. Instead, he's trying to snatch you away.

(*Padmini moans in agony.*)

DEVADATTA: This way we won't get anywhere, Kapila . . .

KAPILA: Call me Devadatta . . .

DEVADATTA: Whatever you are, this is no way to solve the problem.

KAPILA: Of course not. If marriage were a contract it would be. But how can Padmini's fancy be taken as the solution?

DEVADATTA: Then what is the solution to this problem?

(*They all freeze.*)

BHAGAVATA: What? What indeed is the solution to this problem, which holds the entire future of these three unfortunate beings in a balance? Must their fate remain a mystery? And if so shall we not be insulting our audience by tying a question-mark round its neck and bidding it good-bye? We have to face the problem. But it's a deep one and the answer must be sought with the greatest caution. Haste would be disastrous. So there's a break of ten minutes now. Please have some tea, ponder over

this situation and come back with your own solutions. We shall
then continue with our enquiry.

(*The stage-hands hold a white curtain in front of the frozen
threesome, while the Bhagavata and others relax and sip tea.*)

# Act Two

*(The white curtain is removed.)*

BHAGAVATA:  What? What indeed is the solution to this problem, which holds the entire future of these three unfortunate beings in a balance?

Way back in the ages, when King Vikrama was ruling the world, shining in glory like the earth's challenge to the sun, he was asked the same question by the demon Vetala. And the king offered a solution even without, as it were, batting an eyelid. But will his rational, logical answer backed by the Sacred Texts appeal to our audience?

*(Sings.)*

> The future pointed out by the tongue
> safe inside the skull is not acceptable to us.
> We must read the forehead which Brahma
> has disconnected from the entrails.
> We must unravel the net on the palm
> disclaimed by the brain.
> We must plumb the hidden depths of the
> rivers running under our veins.

Yes, that would be the right thing to do.

So our three unfortunate friends went to a great *rishi* in search of a solution to their problem. And the *rishi*—remembering perhaps what King Vikrama had said—gave the solution:

*(In a loud, sonorous voice.)*

As the heavenly Kalpa Vriksha is supreme among trees, so is the head among human limbs. Therefore the man with Devadatta's head is indeed Devadatta and he is the rightful husband of Padmini.

*(The three spring to life. Devadatta and Padmini scream with joy and move to one corner of the stage laughing and dancing. Kapila, brokenhearted, drags his feet to the other corner.)*

DEVADATTA:  *(Embracing Padmini.)* My Padmini . . . my lovely Padmini . . .

PADMINI:   My King—My Master . . .

DEVADATTA:   My little lightning . . .

PADMINI:   The light of my joy . . .

DEVADATTA:   The flower of my palm . . .

PADMINI:   My celestial-bodied Gandharva . . . My sun-faced Indra . . .

DEVADATTA:   My Queen of Indra's Court . . .

PADMINI:   (*Caressing his shoulders.*) Come. Let's go. Let's go quickly. Where the earth is soft and the green grass plays the swing.

DEVADATTA:   Let us. Where the banyan spreads a canopy and curtains off the skies . . .

PADMINI:   What a wide chest. What other canopy do I need?

DEVADATTA:   My soft, swaying Padmini. What other swing do I want?

PADMINI:   My Devadatta comes likes a bridegroom with the ornament of a new body . . .

DEVADATTA:   (*A manly laugh.*) And who should wear the ornaments but the eager bride . . .

PADMINI:   Let's go. (*Pause.*) Wait. (*She runs to Kapila.*) Don't be sad, Kapila. We shall meet again, shan't we? (*In a low voice, so Devadatta can't hear.*) It's my duty to go with Devadatta. But remember I'm going with your body. Let that cheer you up. (*Goes back to Devadatta.*) Good-bye, Kapila.

DEVADATTA:   Good-bye.

> (*They go out, laughing, rubbing against each other. Kapila stands mute for a while. Then moves.*)

BHAGAVATA:   Kapila—Kapila . . (*No reply.*) Don't grieve. It's fate, Kapila, and . . .

KAPILA:   Kapila? What? Me? Why am I Kapila?
(*Exit.*)

BHAGAVATA:   So the roads diverged. Kapila went into the forest and disappeared. He never saw Dharmapura again. In fact he never felt the wind of any city again. As for Devadatta and Padmini, they returned to Dharmapura and plunged into the joys of married life.

> (*Padmini enters and sits. She is stitching clothes, Devadatta comes. He is carrying in his hands two large dolls—which could be played by two children. The dolls are dressed in a way which makes it impossible to decide their sex.*

*Devadatta comes in quietly and stands behind Padmini.*)

DEVADATTA:  Hey!

PADMINI:  (*Startled.*) Oh! Really, Devadatta. You frightened me. The needle pricked me! Look, my finger's bleeding.

DEVADATTA:  Tut-Tut! Is it really? Put it in my mouth—I'll suck it.

PADMINI:  No, thanks. I'll suck it myself. (*Sees the dolls.*) How pretty! Whose are these?

DEVADATTA:  Whose? Ours, of course! The guest is arriving soon— he must have playmates.

PADMINI:  But the guest won't be coming for months yet, silly, and . . .

DEVADATTA:  I know he isn't, but you can't get dolls like these any time you like! These are special dolls from the Ujjain fair . . .

PADMINI:  They are lovely! (*Hugs the dolls.*) They look almost alive —such shining eyes—such delicate cheeks . . . (*Kisses them.*) Now sit down and tell me everything that happened at the fair. You wouldn't take me with you . . .

DEVADATTA:  How could I—in your condition? I went only because you insisted you wanted to keep your word. But I'm glad I went. A very funny thing happened—there was a wrestling pit and a wrestler from Gandhara was challenging people to fight him. I don't know what got into me—Before I'd even realized it, I had stripped, put on the pants given by his assistant and jumped into the pit.

PADMINI:  (*Fondling the dolls.*) You didn't! You've never wrestled before . . .

DEVADATTA:  Didn't think of anything. I felt—'inspired'! Within a couple of minutes, I had pinned him to the ground.

PADMINI:  (*Laughs out.*) What would your father say if he heard of this?

DEVADATTA:  My few acquaintances there were quite amazed.

PADMINI:  (*Caressing his arm.*) That day in the gymnasium you defeated the champion in a sword-fight. Now this! Don't overdo it—people may start suspecting.

DEVADATTA:  Of course they won't. I was standing there bare-bodied and not a soul suspected. A friend even asked me if I'd learnt it from Kapila.

PADMINI:  You have, after all!

(*They laugh.*)

DEVADATTA: You know, I'd always thought one had to use one's brains while wrestling or fencing or swimming. But this body just doesn't wait for thoughts—it acts!

PADMINI: Fabulous body—fabulous brain—fabulous Devadatta.

DEVADATTA: I have been running around all these days without even proper sleep—and yet I don't feel a bit tired. (*Jumps up.*) Come on, we'll have a picnic by the lake. I feel like a good, long swim.

PADMINI: (*Mocking.*) In my condition?

DEVADATTA: I didn't ask you to swim. You sit there and enjoy the scenery. Once our son's born, I'll teach you to swim too . . .

PADMINI: You go on about its being a son. What if it's a daughter?

DEVADATTA: If she's a daughter like you, I'll teach the two of you together.

PADMINI: Ready!

(*He pulls her to him.*)

Now—now—what about the picnic?

DEVADATTA: Quite right. First things first.

PADMINI: (*Pause.*) Devadatta . . .

DEVADATTA: Yes?

PADMINI: Why do you—have to apply that sandal oil on your body?

DEVADATTA: I like it.

PADMINI: I know, but . . .

DEVADATTA: What?

PADMINI: (*Hesitating.*) Your body had that strong, male smell before—I liked it . . .

DEVADATTA: But I've been using sandal oil since I was a child!

PADMINI: I don't mean that. But—when we came back from the temple of Kali—you used to smell so manly . . .

DEVADATTA: You mean that unwashed, sweaty smell Kapila had? (*Incredulous.*) You liked that?

PADMINI: (*Pause. Then lightly.*) It was just a suggestion. Come on, let's start. We'll be late.

(*They go out. A long silence.*)

DOLL I: Not a bad house, I would say.

DOLL II: Could have been worse. I was a little worried.

DOLL I: This is the least we deserved. Actually we should have got a palace. A real palace!

DOLL II:  And a prince to play with. A real prince!

DOLL I:  How the children looked at us at the fair! How their eyes glowed!

DOLL II:  How their mothers stared at us! How their mouths watered!

DOLL I:  Only those beastly men turned up their noses! 'Expensive! Too Expensive!'

DOLL II:  Presuming to judge us! Who do they think they are!

DOLL I:  Only a prince would be worthy of us.

DOLL II:  We should be dusted every day . . .

DOLL I:  . . . dressed in silk . . .

DOLL II:  . . . seated on a cushioned shelf . . .

DOLL I:  . . . given new clothes every week.

DOLL II:  If the doll-maker had any sense, he'd never have sold us.

DOLL I:  If he had any brains, he should never have . . . given us to this man . . .

DOLL II  . . . with his rough labourer's hands.

DOLL I:  Palms like wood . . .

DOLL II:  A grip like a vice . . .

DOLL I:  My arms are still aching . . .

DOLL II:  He doesn't deserve us, the peasant.

(*Devadatta comes running in, tosses the dolls in the air, catches them and kisses them.*)

DEVADATTA:  My dolls, your prince has arrived! The prince has come!

DOLL I:  (*In agony.*) Brute! An absolute brute!

DOLL II:  (*In agony.*) Beast! A complete beast!

DEVADATTA:  (*Runs to the Bhagavata.*) Here, Bhagavata Sir, take these sweets. You must come to the feast tomorrow at our house.

BHAGAVATA:  What's it for?

DEVADATTA:  Haven't you heard? I've got a son like a gem—a son like a rose—Yippeee . . .

(*He goes out dancing some Lezim steps. A long silence.*)

DOLL I:  Is that little satan asleep yet?

DOLL II:  Think so. God! It's killing me . . .

DOLL I:  . . . crying, all day . . .

DOLL II  . . . making a mess every fifteen minutes.

DOLL I:  What have we come to! One should never trust God . . .

DOLL II: It's our fault. We should have been wary from the moment we saw that child in her dreams . . .

DOLL I: We should have noticed she was bloating day by day.

DOLL II: We should have suspected foul play then.

DOLL I: It wasn't our fault. How could we know she was hiding this thing inside her?

DOLL II: How she was swelling! Day by day! Week by week! As though someone were blowing air into her . . .

DOLL I: How ugly she looked . . .

DOLL II. . . . not to her husband, though!

DOLL I: When they were alone, he would place his hand on her belly and say, 'Is he kicking now?'

DOLL II: (*Seriously.*) We should have been on our guard.

DOLL I: (*Dispirited.*) We should.

DOLL II: And then comes this son of a satan . . .

DOLL I: . . . this lump of flesh . . .

DOLL II: He doesn't even have proper eyes or ears . . .

DOLL I . . . but he gets all the attention.

DOLL II: (*In disgust.*) Ugh . . .

DOLL I: (*Sick.*) Awk . . .

(*Devadatta and Padmini enter with the child—for which a wooden doll may be used. They walk across the stage, engrossed in talking to and about the child, and go out.*)

DOLL I: A spider's built its web on my shoulders.

DOLL II: Yesterday a mouse nibbled at my toe.

DOLL I: The other day a cockroach ate my left eye.

DOLL II: Six months—and not a soul has come near us.

DOLL I: Six months—and not a hand has touched us.

DOLL II: Six months and we reach this state. What'll happen in a year's time?

(*Padmini and Devadatta enter.*)

PADMINI: Listen . . .

DEVADATTA: Yes.

PADMINI: You mustn't say 'no'—at least this time.

DEVADATTA: To what?

PADMINI: We'll take him to the lake.

DEVADATTA: In this cold?

PADMINI: What if it's cold? He's older now. There's no need to mollycoddle him. I grew up running around in heat and cold and rain—and nothing happened to me. I'm all right . . .

DEVADATTA: No, it's unnecessary trouble for everyone.

PADMINI: What do you mean trouble? What's happened to you these days? You sit at home all day. Never go out. You've forgotten all your swimming and sports . . .

DEVADATTA: I'm a Brahmin, Padmini, My duty . . .

PADMINI: I've heard all that!

DEVADATTA: It was fun the first few days because it was new. All that muscle and strength. But how long can one go on like that? I have the family tradition to maintain—the daily reading, writing and studies . . .

PADMINI: I don't know.

DEVADATTA: (*Affectionate.*) Now look here, Padmini . . .
(*Puts his hand round her shoulder. She suddenly shudders.*)
Why? What happened?

PADMINI: Nothing—I don't know why—I suddenly had goose flesh.
(*Pause.*)

DEVADATTA: (*Withdrawing his hand.*) Do you know where I've kept the copy of *Dharma Sindhu?* I've been looking for it.

PADMINI: I think I saw it on the shelf. Must be there . . . (*Devadatta goes to Doll I, moves it aside and picks up the book. Doll I shudders.*)

DOLL II: Why? What happened?

DOLL I: He touched me, and . . .

DOLL II: Yes?

DOLL I: His palms! They were so rough, when he first brought us here. Like a labourer's. But now they are soft—sickly soft—like a young girl's.

DOLL II: I know. I've noticed something too.

DOLL I: What?

DOLL II: His stomach. It was so tight and muscular. Now . . .

DOLL I: I know. It's loose . . .

DOLL II: Do you think it'll swell up too?
(*They laugh.*)

DOLL I: (*Holding its hands in front of its stomach to suggest a swollen belly.*) It'll swell a little . . .

DOLL II: (*Holding its hands a little farther in front.*) —then more . . .

DOLL I: (*Even further.*) —more and . . .

DOLL II:   (*Even further.*) —and more until . . .
DOLL I:   . . . if it's a woman . . .
DOLL II:   . . . there'll be a child . . .
DOLL I:   . . . and if it's a man . . .
DOLL II:   BANG!

(*They roll with laughter. Padmini comes in with the child. She sings a lullaby.*)

PADMINI:   Here comes a rider!
           From what land does he come?
           On his head a turban
           with a long pearly tail.
           Round his neck a garland
           of virgin-white jasmines.
           In his fist a sword
           with a diamond-studded hilt.
           The white-clad rider
           rides a white charger
           which spreads its tossing mane
           against the western sky,
           spreads its mane like breakers
           against the western sky.
           Sleep now my baby
           and see smiling dreams.
           There he comes—here he is!
           From which land does he come?
           But why are the jasmines on his chest
           red O so red?
           What shine in his open eyes?
           Pebbles O pebbles.
           Why is his young body
           cold O so cold?
           The white horse gallops
           across hills, streams and fields.
           To what land does he gallop?
           Nowhere O nowhere.

(*Half-way through the lullaby, Devadatta comes in and sits by Padmini's side, reading. They don't look at each other. At the end of the lullaby, they fall asleep.*)

DOLL I:   (*In a hushed voice.*) Hey . . .

DOLL II: Yes . . .

DOLL I: Look . . .

DOLL II: Where . . .

DOLL I: Behind her eyelids. She is dreaming.

DOLL II: I don't see anything.

DOLL I: It's still hazy—hasn't started yet . . . Do you see it now?

DOLL II: (*Eagerly.*) Yes, yes.
   (*They stare at her.*)

DOLL I: A man . . .

DOLL II: But not her husband.

DOLL I: No, someone else.

DOLL II: Is this the one who came last night?

DOLL I: Yes—the same. But I couldn't see his face then.

DOLL II: You can now. Not very nice—rough. Like a labourer's. But he's got a nice body—looks soft.

DOLL I: Who do you think it is?

DOLL II: I—It's fading. (*Urgently.*) Remember the face!

DOLL I: It's fading—Oh! It's gone!

DOLL II: And she won't even remember it tomorrow.
   (*Padmini and Devadatta sit up.*)

PADMINI: Are you ill?

DEVADATTA: Why?

PADMINI: You were moaning in your sleep last night.

DEVADATTA: Was I?

PADMINI: Aren't you feeling well?

DEVADATTA: Who? Me? I'm fine . . .
   (*Gets up energetically to show how well he feels. Suddenly grabs his shoulder with a groan.*)

PADMINI: What's wrong? Tell me . . .

DEVADATTA: (*Avoiding her eyes.*) Nothing. I went to the gymnasium yesterday morning. Then went swimming . . .

PADMINI: To the gymnasium? After all these years? But why?

DEVADATTA: I just felt like it. That's all. Don't go on about it.

PADMINI: (*Without irony.*) Are you going again today?

DEVADATTA: (*Flares up.*) No, I'm not. And there's no need to laugh. I know I've made a fool of myself by going there. I won't again.
   (*Goes out. Long pause.*)

PADMINI: What are you afraid of, Devadatta? What does it matter that you are going soft again, that you are losing your muscles?

I'm not going to be stupid again. Kapila's gone out of my life—forever. I won't let him come back again. (*Pause.*) Kapila? What could he be doing now? Where could he be? Could his body be fair still, and his face dark? (*Long pause.*) Devadatta changes. Kapila changes. And me?

(*Closes her eyes.*)

DOLL I: There he is again.

DOLL II: In the middle of the day?

DOLL I: (*Doubtful.*) I'm not sure this is the usual visitor. This one looks rougher and darker.

DOLL II: It's him all right. Look at his face.

DOLL I: He goes to her . . .

DOLL II: . . . very near her . . .

DOLL I: (*In a whisper.*) What's he going to do now?

DOLL II: (*Even more anxious.*) What?

(*They watch.*)

DOLL I: (*Baffled.*) But he's climbing a tree!

DOLL II: (*Almost a wail of disappointment.*) He's dived into a river!

DOLL I: Is that all he came for?

DOLL II: It's going . . .

DOLL I: . . . going . . .

DOLL II: Gone! Wretched dreams—They just tickle and fade away.

(*Padmini wakes up and mimes putting the crying child to sleep.*)

PADMINI: (*Suddenly vicious.*) Change! Change! Change! Change! Change! The sand trickles. The water fills the pot. And the moon goes on swinging, swinging, swinging, from light to darkness to light.

(*Devadatta comes in. He is now completely changed to his original self—that is, the slender actor who came as Devadatta at the beginning of the play comes back again with the Devadatta mask on.*)

DEVADATTA: A pundit's coming to see me. He wants me to explain some verses to him. Can you keep some sweets and lime-juice ready?

PADMINI: Yes. (*Pause.*) Did you hear . . . ? The maid was telling me . . .

DEVADATTA: What?

PADMINI: Kapila's mother died this morning. (*Pause.*) Poor thing! She'd been bed-ridden all these years, ever since . . .

DEVADATTA:    (*Snapping at her.*) What did you expect me to do about
      it? (*Then embarrassed*). Get the lime-juice ready soon.
          (*They go out.*)
DOLL  I:    Each one to his fate!
DOLL  II:    Each one to her problems!
DOLL  I:    As the doll-maker used to say, 'What are things com-
      ing to!'
DOLL  II:    Especially last night—I mean—that dream . . .
DOLL  I:    Tut-tut—One shouldn't talk about such things!
DOLL  II:    It was so shameless . . .
DOLL  I:    I said be quiet . . .
DOLL  II:    Honestly! The way they . . .
DOLL  I:    Look, if we must talk about it, let me.
DOLL  II:    You didn't want to talk about it. So . . .
DOLL  I:    You don't understand a thing. They . . .
DOLL  II:    What do you know? Last night . . .
DOLL  I:    Let me! In dream . . .
DOLL  II:    I'm . . .
DOLL  I:    Shut up!
DOLL  II:    You shut up!
          (*They start arguing, then fighting. They roll on the ground, on top
          of each other, biting, scratching, hitting each other. They shout,
          scream and giggle. As they fight, the giggles become louder and more
          frantic. Their clothes get torn. At last they lie side by side panting,
          bursting with little giggles. Then they sit up. Padmini enters, looks
          at them.*)
PADMINI:    Just look at the dolls! The baby's really torn them to
      pieces—how long can we go on with them! (*Calls.*) Listen . . .
DEVADATTA:    (*Entering.*) Yes.
PADMINI:    We must get new dolls for our baby. These are in tatters.
DEVADATTA:    You're right. I hadn't noticed.
PADMINI:    The Ujjain fair is to be held in another four days. Why
      don't you go and get new dolls there? If you start today you'll
      be there in time for it. It's unlucky to keep torn dolls at
      home . . .
DOLL  I:    (*To Doll II.*) Did you hear that? She wants to throw us
      out . . .
DOLL  II:    She wants new dolls.
DOLL  I:    The whore.

DOLL II:  The bitch.

DOLL I:  May her house burn down.

DOLL II:  May her teeth fall out.

DEVADATTA:  (*To Padmini.*) All right.

  (*He picks them up by their collars.*)

DOLL I:  See how he picks us up. Like stray puppies.

DOLL II:  That ball of flesh will remain here. But it's the dung-heap for us . . .

DEVADATTA:  (*To Padmini.*) It'll take me more than a week to go to Ujjain and come back. Shall I ask one of the neighbours to get them for us?

DOLL I:  (*To Devadatta.*) You wretch—before you throw us out watch out for yourself.

DOLL II:  Cover your wife before you start worrying about our rags.

PADMINI:  (*To Devadatta.*) Who knows what sort of dolls they'll get for us? We must bring things ourselves for our baby . . .

DEVADATTA:  But . . .

PADMINI:  If you don't want to go, say so. Don't . . .

DEVADATTA:  Shall I ask one of the servants to come and sleep here at night?

PADMINI:  No need. We are not in the middle of a forest.

DOLL I:  (*To Devadatta.*) Watch out, you fool . . .

DOLL II:  Refuse, you idiot . . .

DEVADATTA:  All right. I'll start at once. Take care of yourself.

  (*He drags the dolls out.*)

DOLL I:  Villain . . .

DOLL II:  Rascal . . .

DOLL I:  Swine . . .

DOLL II:  Bastard . . .

  (*One can hear them screaming curses as he takes them out. Padmini stands watching him go. Then to the child in her arms.*)

PADMINI:  My poor child, you haven't yet seen the witching fair of the dark forest, have you? Let's go and see it. How can I describe it to you? There's so much. Long before the sun rises, the shadows of twigs draw *alpanas* on the floor. The stars raise *arati* and go. Then the day dawns and the fun begins. The circus in the tree-tops and the cock-fights in a shower of feathers. And the dances! The tiger-dance, and the peacock-dance, and the dance of the sun's little feet with silver anklets on the river. In the heart of the forest stands the stately chariot of the shield-bearer. It's made of pure gold—rows of birds pull it down the street, and rows of flames of the forest salute it with torches. Then the night comes, and our poor baby is tired—so we blow gently and out goes the moon. But before we leave there's one more thing to do. Right outside the fair, watching it from a distance, stands the tree of the Fortunate Lady. It's an old tree, a close friend of ours. We have to say 'hello' to it. All right?

(*She goes out with the child. A long silence. Kapila enters. He too is as he was at the beginning of the play—tough and muscular.*)

BHAGAVATA: Who? Kapila?

KAPILA: Yes.

BHAGAVATA: It's such a long time since we met.

KAPILA: Yes.

BHAGAVATA: Where are you now?

KAPILA: Here.

BHAGAVATA: Here? In this jungle? It's difficult to believe any man could live here.

KAPILA: Beasts do. Why not men?

BHAGAVATA: What do you do?

KAPILA: Live.

BHAGAVATA: Have you had any news from the city?

KAPILA: Long ago. Father sent word asking me to come back. I said, 'I won't come. No need for you to come here either!' That's all.

BHAGAVATA: You mean—you don't know your father died last year?—Also your mother . . .

KAPILA: (*Expressionless.*) No.

BHAGAVATA: And Padmini has a son.

KAPILA: I see.

BHAGAVATA: Why this anger, Kapila?

KAPILA: What anger?

BHAGAVATA: It shows in the way you stand, you move.

KAPILA: All that is your poetry.

(*Moves on.*)

BHAGAVATA: Kapila! Kapila!

(*Kapila goes round the stage once. He mimes picking up an axe*

*and felling a tree. A long silence. Only the soundless image of*
*Kapila cutting the tree.*
*Padmini enters, child in arms. She is scared and walks in rapidly.*
*She sees Kapila and stands transfixed. Kapila doesn't see her for*
*a while and when he does stands paralysed. A long silence.)*

KAPILA:  *(Slowly.)* You?

PADMINI:  Yes.

KAPILA:  Here?

PADMINI:  My son had never laughed with the river or shivered in
the wind or felt the thorn cut his feet. So I brought him out.
I lost my way in the woods.

KAPILA:  You shouldn't have lost it this far.

PADMINI:  The wrong road stuck to my feet—wouldn't let go.

KAPILA:  You shouldn't have lost it this far. Wild beasts—robbers—
pathless paths—all sorts of dangers.

PADMINI:  I asked the villagers . . . And the pilgrims. And the
hunters. And the tribesmen. When there wasn't anyone any
more, I asked myself. Everyone saw to it that I didn't lose the
wrong road.
*(Pause.)*

KAPILA:  Is that your son?

PADMINI:  Yes. And yours.

KAPILA:  Mine?

PADMINI:  Your body gave him to me.

KAPILA:  Mine? *(Erupting.)* Not mine. I'm Kapila, Padmini. I didn't
accept it that day. But I accept it now, I'm Kapila.

PADMINI:  *(Softly.)* And how's Kapila?
*(The Bhagavata sings. The following is a prose rendering of the*
*song.)*

BHAGAVATA:  I spread my wings, and kicked away the earth and
flew up. I covered the seven continents, the ten shores and
measured the sky.
Now because you have a child at your breast, a husband on
your thighs, the red of rust on the lips of your late-opening
mouth, I pick a picture here, and there a card of fate, and live
for the grace of a grain—an astrologer's bird.

KAPILA:  Can I look at him?

PADMINI:  That's why I brought him.
*(Kapila looks at the child.)*

KAPILA: What's wrong with me? You've come so far and I haven't even asked you to sit down. Why don't you go in and take a little rest?

> (*She goes in with the child. He stands as in a daze. She comes out without the child.*)

KAPILA: Why . . .

PADMINI: I don't need any rest.

> (*Long silence.*)

KAPILA: How are you?

PADMINI: I'm well. No illness, problems or difficulties.

KAPILA: Your son looks exactly like you.

PADMINI: (*A slight pause.*) And you.

> (*Kapila doesn't reply.*)

He has the same mole on his shoulder.

KAPILA: What mole?

> (*She comes to him and points out the mole on his shoulder.*)

PADMINI: This one. Which other could it be? That's the only one you have on your shoulder.

KAPILA: Oh! I hadn't seen it. I don't much look at this body.

PADMINI: (*Quietly.*) Do you despise it that much?

> (*No reply.*)

Why have you tortured it so?

> (*Takes his hand in hers.*)

When this went to you, it was so soft, like a prince's. These arms were so slender and fair. Look at them now. Why have you done this to yourself?

KAPILA: When this body came to me, it was like a corpse hanging by my head. It was a Brahmin's body after all—not made for the woods. I couldn't lift an axe without my elbows moaning. Couldn't run a length without my knees howling. I had no use for it. The moment it came to me, a war started between us.

PADMINI: And who won?

KAPILA: I did.

PADMINI: The head always wins, doesn't it?

KAPILA: Fortunately, yes. Now I can run ten miles and not stop for breath. I can swim through the monsoon floods and fell a banyan. The stomach used to rebel once—Now it digests what I give. If I don't, it doesn't complain.

PADMINI: Must the head always win?

KAPILA:    That's why I am Kapila now. Kapila! Kapila with a face which fits his body.

PADMINI:    What a good mix—
No more tricks—
Is this one that
Or that one this?
Do you remember the song we sang in the Kali temple?

KAPILA:    So?

PADMINI:    Nothing. I often remember it. It's almost my autobiography now, Kapila! Devadatta! Kapila with Devadatta's body! Devadatta with Kapila's body! Four men in one lifetime.

KAPILA:    (*Suddenly.*) Why have you come away from him?

PADMINI:    What do you want me to say?
(*They freeze.*)

BHAGAVATA:    How could I make you understand? If Devadatta had changed overnight and had gone back to his original form, I would have forgotten you completely. But that's not how it happened. He changed day by day. Inch by inch. Hair by hair. Like the trickling sand. Like the water filling the pot. And as I saw him change—I couldn't get rid of you. That's what Padmini must tell Kapila. She should say more, without concealing anything, 'Kapila, if that *rishi* had given me to you, would I have gone back to Devadatta some day exactly like this?' But she doesn't say anything. She remains quiet.

KAPILA:    (*To Padmini.*) Why have you come here?

PADMINI:    I had to see you.

KAPILA:    Why? (*No reply.*) Why? Why did you have to come just when I thought I'd won this long and weary battle? Why did you have to pursue me just when I had succeeded in uprooting these memories? I am Kapila now. The rough and violent Kapila. Kapila without a crack between his head and his shoulders. What do you want now? Another head? Another suicide?—Listen to me. Do me a favour. Go back. Back to Devadatta. He is your husband—the father of this child. Devadatta and Padmini! Devadatta and Padmini! A pair coupled with the holy fire as the witness. I have no place there, no peace, no salvation—So go. I beg of you. Go.
(*A long silence.*)

PADMINI:    I will. If you want me to.

KAPILA: (*Almost a moan.*) Oh God!

PADMINI: Why?

KAPILA: Nothing. Another memory—when I too was asked to go—Yes, go back. Now.

PADMINI: I will. But can I ask a little favour? My son's tired. He's asleep. He has been in my arms for several days now. Let him rest a while. As soon as he gets up I'll go. (*Laughs.*) Yes, you won, Kapila. Devadatta won too. But I—the better half of two bodies—I neither win nor lose. No, don't say anything. I know what you'll say and I've told myself that a thousand times. It's my fault. I mixed the heads up. I must suffer for it. I will. I'm sorry I came—I didn't think before I started—Couldn't. But at least until my child wakes up, may I sit here and look at you? Have my fill for the rest of my life? I won't speak a word.

(*Long pause.*)

KAPILA: What does it matter now whether you stay or go? You've done the damage. I had buried all those faceless memories in my skin. Now you've dug them up with your claws.

PADMINI: Why should one bury anything?

KAPILA: Why shouldn't one? Why should one tolerate this mad dance of incompleteness?

PADMINI: Whose incompleteness? Yours?

KAPILA: Yes, mine. One beats the body into shape, but one can't beat away the memories in it. Isn't that surprising? That the body should have its own ghosts—its own memories? Memories of touch—memories of *a* touch—memories of a body swaying in these arms, of a warm skin against this palm—memories which one cannot recognize, cannot understand, cannot even name because this head wasn't there when they happened . . .

PADMINI: Kapila . . .

KAPILA: (*Without anger.*) Why did you come? You came. You touched me. You held my hand—and my body recognized your touch. I have never touched you, but this body, this appendage, laughed and flowered out in a festival of memories to which I'm an outcaste . . .

PADMINI: Poor Kapila!

KAPILA: Don't pity me.

PADMINI: Be quiet, stupid. Your body bathed in a river, swam and danced in it. Shouldn't your head know what river it was, what swim? Your head too must submerge in that river—the flow must rumple your hair, run its tongue in your ears and press your head to its bosom. Until that's done, you'll continue to be incomplete.

(*Kapila raises his head and looks at her. She caresses his face, like a blind person trying to imprint it on her finger-tips. Then she rests her head on his chest.*)

My Kapila! My poor, poor Kapila! How needlessly you've tortured yourself.

(*Kapila lifts her up and takes her in.*)

BHAGAVATA:   You cannot engrave on water
                   nor wound it with a knife,
                   which is why
                   the river
                   has no fear
                   of memories.

FEMALE CHORUS:   The river only feels the
                   pull of the waterfall.
                   She giggles, and tickles the rushes
                   on the banks, then turns
                   a top of dry leaves
                   in the navel of the whirlpool, weaves
                   a water-snake in the net of silver strands
                   in the green depths, frightens the frog
                   on the rug of moss, sticks and bamboo leaves,
                   sings, tosses, leaps and
                   sweeps on in a rush—

BHAGAVATA:   While the scarecrow on the bank
                   has a face fading
                   on its mudpot head
                   and a body torn
                   with memories.

(*Devadatta enters. He is holding a sword in one hand, and in the other, two dolls, made of cloth.*)

BHAGAVATA:  Who! Devadatta?
DEVADATTA:  Where does Kapila live here?
BHAGAVATA:  Uhm—well—Anyway, how are . . . you . . .
DEVADATTA:  If you don't want to tell me, don't. I can find out for myself.

BHAGAVATA:   There. Behind those trees.

DEVADATTA:   How long has Padmini been here?

BHAGAVATA:   About four or five days.

DEVADATTA:   Amazing! Even a man like me found the road hard.
But how quickly she covered it—and with a child in her arms.

BHAGAVATA:   Devadatta . . .

*(Devadatta moves on.)*

Devadatta moves on. There are only two words which make
sense to him now—Kapila and Padmini! Kapila and Padmini!
The words carry him along like a flood to the doorstep of
Kapila's hut. But suddenly he stops. Until this moment he has
been yearning to taste the blood of Kapila. But now he is still
and calm.

*(Kapila comes out.)*

KAPILA:   Come, Devadatta. I was waiting for you. I've been ex-
pecting you since yesterday. I have been coming out every half
an hour to see if you'd arrived. Not from fear. Only eager.

*(Padmini comes out and stands watching them.)*

KAPILA:   *(To Devadatta.)* You look exactly the same.

DEVADATTA:   *(Laughs.)* You too.

KAPILA:   *(Points to the sword.)* What's that?

DEVADATTA:   *(Extending the hand which holds the dolls.)* Dolls. For
the child. I came home from the fair. There was no one there.
So I came here.

*(Padmini steps forward and takes the dolls. But neither speaks.
Padmini goes back to her place and stands clutching the dolls to her
bosom.)*

KAPILA:   Come in and rest a while. There'll always be time to talk
later.

*(Devadatta shakes his head.)*

Why? Are you angry?

DEVADATTA:   Not any more. *(Pause.)* Did my body bother you too
much?

KAPILA:   It wasn't made for this life. It resisted. It also had its
revenge.

DEVADATTA:   Did it?

KAPILA:   Do you remember how I once used to envy you your
poetry, your ability to imagine things? For me the sky was sky,
and the tree only a tree. Your body gave me new feelings, new

words—I felt awake as I'd never before—even started—writing poems. Very bad ones, I'm afraid.

(*They laugh.*)

There were times when I hated it for what it gave me.

DEVADATTA: I wanted your power but not your wildness. You lived in hate—I in fear.

KAPILA: No, I was the one who was afraid.

DEVADATTA: What a good mix—No more tricks.

(*They laugh.*)

Tell me one thing. Do you really love Padmini?

KAPILA: Yes.

DEVADATTA: So do I.

KAPILA: I know.

(*Silence.*)

Devadatta, couldn't we all three live together—like the Pandavas and Draupadi?

DEVADATTA: What do you think?

(*Silence. Padmini looks at them but doesn't say anything.*)

KAPILA: (*Laughs.*) No, it can't be done.

DEVADATTA: That's why I brought this. (*Shows the sword.*) What won't end has to be cut.

KAPILA: I got your body—but not your wisdom.

DEVADATTA: Where's your sword then?

KAPILA: A moment.

(*Goes in. Padmini stands looking at Devadatta. But he looks somewhere far away.*)

BHAGAVATA:  After sharing with Indra
his wine
his food
his jokes
I returned to the earth
and saw from far—
a crack had appeared
in the earth's face—
exactly
like Indra's smile.

(*Kapila returns with his sword. They take up positions.*)

KAPILA: Are you still in practice?

DEVADATTA: Of course not. But you'd learned well. And you?

KAPILA:   I learnt again. But one's older now—slower at learning.

DEVADATTA:   (*Pause.*) You realize it's immaterial who's better with a sword now, don't you?

KAPILA:   Yes, I do.

DEVADATTA:   There's only one solution to this.

KAPILA:   We must both die.

DEVADATTA:   We must both die.

KAPILA:   With what confidence we chopped off our heads in that temple! Now whose head—whose body—suicide or murder—nothing's clear.

DEVADATTA:   No grounds for friendship now. No question of mercy. We must fight like lions and kill like cobras.

KAPILA:   Let our heads roll to the very hands which cut them in the temple of Kali!

> (*Music starts. The fight is stylized like a dance. Their swords don't touch. Even Padmini's reaction is like a dance.*)

BHAGAVATA:   (*Sings.*) Like cocks in a pit

> we dance—he and I . . .
> foot woven with foot
> eye soldered to eye.
> He knows and I know
> all there's to be known
> the witch's burning thirst
> burns for blood alone.
> Hence this frozen smile,
> which cracks and drips to earth,
> and claw-knives, digging flesh
> for piecemeal death.
> The *rishi* who said 'Knowledge gives rise to
> forgiveness' had no knowledge of death.

> (*Kapila wounds Devadatta who falls to his feet and fights. He stabs Kapila. Both fight on their knees, fall and die.*

> *A long silence. Padmini slowly comes and sits between the bodies.*)

PADMINI:   They burned, lived, fought, embraced and died. I stood silent. If I'd said, 'Yes, I'll live with you both', perhaps they would have been alive yet. But I couldn't say it. I couldn't say, 'Yes'. No, Kapila, no, Devadatta—I know it in my blood you couldn't have lived together. You would've had to share not only me but your bodies as well. Because you knew death you died in each other's arms. You could only have lived ripping each other to pieces. I had to drive you to death. You forgave each other, but again—left me out.

BHAGAVATA: (*Without leaving his seat.*) What is this? It's a sight to freeze the blood in one's veins. What happened, child? Can we help you?

PADMINI: (*Without looking at him.*) Yes, please. My son is sleeping in the hut. Take him under your care. Give him to the hunters who live in this forest and tell them it's Kapila's son. They loved Kapila and will bring the child up. Let the child grow up in the forest with the rivers and the trees. When he's five take him to the Revered Brahmin Vidyasagara of Dharmapura. Tell him it's Devadatta's son.

BHAGAVATA: And you?

PADMINI: Make me a large funeral pyre. We are three.

BHAGAVATA: You mean you are performing *sati*? But why, child?

PADMINI: (*Puts the dolls on the ground.*) Give these dolls to my son. I won't see him . . . He may tempt me away from my path.

(*At a sign from the Bhagavata, two stage-hands come and place a curtain in front of Padmini.*)

Kali, Mother of all Nature, you must have your joke even now. Other women can die praying that they should get the same husband in all the lives to come. You haven't left me even that little consolation.

(*Does* namaskara. *The stage-hands lift the curtain, slowly, very slowly, very slowly, as the song goes on. The curtain has a blazing fire painted on it. And as it is lifted, the flames seem to leap up. The female musicians sing a song. The following is a prose rendering of it.*)

FEMALE CHORUS: Our sister is leaving in a palanquin of sandal-wood. Her mattress is studded with rubies which burn and glow. She is decked in flowers which blossom on tinder-wood and whose petals are made of molten gold. How the garlands leap and cover her, aflame with love.

The Fortunate Lady's procession goes up the street of laburnums, while the *makarandas* tie the pennants and the *jacarandas* hold the lights.

Good-bye, dear Sister. Go you without fear. The Lord of Death will be pleased with the offering of three coconuts.

BHAGAVATA:   (*Picks up the dolls and comes downstage.*) Thus Padmini
    became a *sati*. India is known for its *pativratas*—wives who
    dedicated their whole existence to the service of their hus-
    bands—but it would not be an exaggeration to say that no
    *pativrata* went in the way Padmini did. And yet no one knows
    the spot where she went *sati*. If you ask the hunting tribes who
    dwell in these forests, they only point to a full-blossomed tree
    of the Fortunate Lady. They say that even now on full moon
    and on new moon nights a song rises from the roots of the tree
    and fills the whole forest like a fragrance.

FEMALE CHORUS:   (*Sings.*) Why should love stick to the sap of a
    single body? When the stem is drunk with the thick yearning
    of the many-petalled, many-flowered lantana, why should it be
    tied down to the relation of a single flower?

    A head for each breast. A pupil for each eye. A side for each
    arm. I have neither regret nor shame. The blood pours into the
    earth and a song branches out in the sky.

    (*When the song ends, the Bhagavata does a* namaskara *to the
    audience. The audience should get a definite feeling that the play
    has ended when a scream is heard in the wings.*)

BHAGAVATA:   What's that? Oh! Nata, our Actor!

    (*Actor II comes rushing out. He doesn't even see the Bhagavata in
    his desperate hurry.*)

    Why is he running? Where's the National Anthem?

    (*Actor II suddenly stops in his tracks.*)

ACTOR II:   The National Anthem!

BHAGAVATA:   What?

ACTOR II:   How did you know?

BHAGAVATA:   Know what?

ACTOR II:   Please, Bhagavata Sir, how did you know . . .

BHAGAVATA:   Know what?

ACTOR II:   About the National Anthem.

BHAGAVATA:   What do you mean?

ACTOR II:   Please, Sir, I beg of you. I implore you. Don't make
    fun of me. How did you know it was the National Anthem . . .

BHAGAVATA:   Why? Haven't you seen an audience . . .

ACTOR II:   (*Relieved.*) Phew! *That!* Ram Ram!

BHAGAVATA:   Why? What happened?

ACTOR II:   What happened? Sree Hari! Look . . .

(*Lifts his hand. It's trembling.*)

BHAGAVATA:   Why? What . . .

ACTOR II:   I almost died of fright . . .

BHAGAVATA:   Really?

ACTOR II:   I was coming down the road—when I heard someone
singing at a distance—at the top of his voice. He was singing,
*Jhanda Ooncha Rahe Hamara* (May our flag fly high!) He started
on *Sare Jahan se Acchha Hindostan Hamara* (Our India is better
than the whole world). Then *Rise, Rise my Kannada Land.* Then
*Vande Mataram* . . .

BHAGAVATA:   Then?

ACTOR II:   I was baffled . . . A true patriot at this time of night? I
had to find out who it was. A house—a big, thick fence around
with not a gap in it—But I managed to find a hole to crawl
through. I was just half-way in when I saw . . .

BHAGAVATA:   What?

(*The Actor wipes his brow.*)

Come on . . . what did you see?

ACTOR II:   A horse!

BHAGAVATA:   (*Eager.*) A horse?

ACTOR II:   Yes. It turned to me and in a deep, sonorous voice said,
'Friend, I'm now going to sing the National Anthem. So please
to stand up to attention!'

BHAGAVATA:   Listen, Nata, are you sure . . .

ACTOR II:   I swear . . .

BHAGAVATA:   No, no, what I mean is . . .

(*Commotion in the wings.*)

What's that now?

(*Actor I enters with a boy of about five. The boy is very
serious—even sulky. There's not a trace of laughter on his face. He
is holding the two cloth dolls which we have already seen—but the
dolls are dirtier now. The commotion comes from Actor I, who is
so busy trying to make the child laugh—making faces at him,
clowning, capering and shouting—he doesn't notice the Bhagavata.*)

BHAGAVATA:   (*Delighted.*) Oh! Nata! You again!

ACTOR I:   (*Turns round and sees the Bhagavata.*) Oh, sir, it's you!

BHAGAVATA:   Well well, you'll live to be a hundred.

ACTOR I:   Why? What have I done?

BHAGAVATA:   I was just thinking of you and you turned up. Just now this Nata (*Pointing to Actor II.*) was saying he saw a horse-headed man and I wondered if it was Hayavadana. So I remembered you.

ACTOR II: Bhagavata Sir . . .

ACTOR I: (*Ignoring Actor II.*) There's an actor's fate in a nutshell for you. Always remembered for someone else . . .

BHAGAVATA: Where's Hayavadana now? Has he come back?

ACTOR I: I don't know, sir. He chased me away the moment we reached the Kali temple. Wouldn't let me stay there a minute longer . . .

BHAGAVATA: Oh! I very much hope the goddess granted him what he wanted. (*Sees the child.*) Who's this child?

ACTOR I: Him? Well? (*To the child.*) Go on, tell him.

(*The child remains silent. Doesn't answer any questions.*)

BHAGAVATA: Who are you, child?—What's your name?—Where are your parents?

ACTOR I: You see? Not a word. Children of his age should be outtalking a dictionary, but this one doesn't speak a word. Doesn't laugh, doesn't cry, doesn't even smile. The same long face all twenty-four hours. There's obviously something wrong with him . . .

(*Bends before the child and clowns a bit.*)

See? No response—no reactions. When he grows up he should make a good theatre critic.

ACTOR II: (*Restless.*) Bhagavata Sir . . .

BHAGAVATA: (*To Actor I.*) Where did you find him?

ACTOR I: In a tribal village of hunters. On my way back I had to stay a night there and a tribal woman brought him to me. Said, 'This is not our child. It's from the city. Take it back'.

BHAGAVATA: A child of this city? (*Actor I nods.*) How strange! (*Notices the dolls.*) But—but—these dolls . . .

(*Tries to touch the dolls. The child reacts violently and moves away angry, terrified.*)

ACTOR I: I was about to warn you! Whatever you do don't touch his dolls! At other times he'll starve and freeze to death rather than say a word. But touch the dolls and he'll bare his fangs. He almost bit off my finger once . . .

ACTOR II: Bhagavata Sir . . .

BHAGAVATA: (*To Actor I.*) But Nata—(*Pause.*) Child, let me see
your shoulder . . .
(*The child moves back.*)
No, no, I won't touch the dolls. I promise you. Just your
shoulder . . .
(*Inspects his shoulder. Then with a cry of triumph . . .*) Nata . . .

ACTOR II:  Bhagavata Sir . . .

ACTOR I:  Yes . . .

BHAGAVATA:  Look, the mole. It's Padmini's son . . . there's no
doubt about it . . .

ACTOR I:  Padmini? Which . . .

ACTOR II:  (*Shouting at the top of his voice.*) Bhagavata Sir!
(*Actor I and the Bhagavata react.*)

BHAGAVATA:  Yes? Why are you shouting?

ACTOR II:  I have been calling you for the last half-an-hour . . .

BHAGAVATA:  Yes, yes. What's it?

ACTOR II:  You said I'd seen a horse-headed man. I didn't. What
I saw was a complete, perfect, proper . . .
(*A voice is heard off-stage singing the third stanza of 'Jana Gana
Mana'.*)
There it is!
(*All stare in the direction of the song. A horse enters the stage
singing.*)

HORSE:  *Tava Karunaruna Rage*
*Nidrita Bharata Jage*
*Tava Charane Nata Matha*
*Jaya Jaya Jaya He Jaya Rajeshwara . . .*
(*Comes and stands in front of them.*)
Hohoo! What's this? Mr Bhagavata Sir! My Actor Friend! Well,
well, well! What a pleasant surprise! Delightful! How are you,
Sir, how are you?

BHAGAVATA:  It's not—not Hayavadana, is it?

HAYAVADANA:  Your most obedient servant, Sir . . .

BHAGAVATA:  But what . . .

ACTOR II:  You mean you know this horse?

BHAGAVATA:  (*Bursts into a guffaw.*) We're old friends.

ACTOR I:  (*Laughing.*) Fellow-pilgrims!

HAYAVADANA:  But not fellow-travellers. What?
(*They roar with laughter. Suddenly the boy too starts laughing.*

Doubles up with laughter. The dolls fall out of his hand as he claps
his hands.)

THE BOY: (*Clapping his hands.*) The horse is laughing! The horse is
laughing!

ACTOR I: (*Jumping with delight.*) The boy is laughing!

HAYAVADANA: (*Goes to the boy.*) Why, my little friend, you may
laugh—but I may not?

(*The boy is in hysterics.*)

BHAGAVATA: That's Padmini's son, Hayavadana . . .

HAYAVADANA: Padmini? I am not aware of . . .

BHAGAVATA: You don't know her. But this poor child—he hadn't
laughed, or cried, or talked in all these years. Now you have
made him laugh . . .

HAYAVADANA: Delighted. Delighted.

BHAGAVATA: But tell me—you went to the goddess to become a
complete man, didn't you? What happened?

HAYAVADANA: Ah! That's a long story. I went there, picked up a
sword which was lying around—very unsafe, I tell you—put
it on my neck and said: 'Mother of all Nature, if you don't help
me I'll chop off my head!'

ACTOR I: Then?

HAYAVADANA: The goddess appeared. Very prompt. But looked
rather put out. She said—rather peevishly, I thought—'Why
don't you people go somewhere else if you want to chop off
your stupid heads? Why do you have to come to me?' I fell at
her feet and said, 'Mother, make me complete'. She said 'So be
it' and disappeared—even before I could say 'Make me a
complete man!' I became a horse.

ACTOR I: I am sorry to hear that . . .

HAYAVADANA: Sorry? Whatever for? The goddess knew what she
was doing. I can tell you that. Ha Ha! Being a horse has its
points . . . (*Pause.*) I have only one sorrow . . .

BHAGAVATA: Yes?

HAYAVADANA: I have become a complete horse—but not a complete being! This human voice—this cursed human voice—it's
still there! How can I call myself complete? If I only could.
What should I do, Bhagavata Sir? How can I get rid of this
human voice?

BHAGAVATA: I don't know what to tell you, Hayavadana.

HAYAVADANA:   That's why I sing all these patriotic songs—and the National Anthem! That particularly! I have noticed that the people singing the National Anthem always seem to have ruined their voices—so I try. But—but—it—it doesn't seem to work . . . What should I do?
>    (*He starts to sob.*)

BOY:   Don't cry, horse. Don't cry. Stop it now . . .

HAYAVADANA:   No, I won't cry. The boy's right. What's the point of shedding tears?

BOY:   Don't cry—you look nice when you laugh . . .

HAYAVADANA:   No, I won't cry. I won't give up trying either. Come, little friend, let's sing the National Anthem together.

BOY:   What is that?

BHAGAVATA:   How could he? He has been brought up in a forest . . .

HAYAVADANA:   Then sing some other song. Look, if you sing a song, I'll take you round on my back.

BOY:   (*Excited.*) Yes—please . . .

HAYAVADANA:   Well, then, what are we waiting for? Get on my back. Quick.
>    (*The Bhagavata seats the child on the horse's back.*)

BOY:   Hiyah—Hiyah—

HAYAVADANA:   No, no. You sing first. Then we start.

BHAGAVATA:   Sing, son.
>    (*The boy sings and the horse goes around in a slow trot.*)
>    Here comes a rider.
>    From what land O what land?
>    On his head a turban.
>    Sleep now, sleep now.
>    Why his chest
>    Red O red?
>    Why his eyes
>    Pebbles O pebbles?
>    Why his body
>    Cold O cold?
>    Where goes the horse?
>    Nowhere O nowhere.
>    (*As the song ends, the horse comes and stands in front of the Bhagavata.*)

HAYAVADANA:   Mr Bhagavata Sir . . .

BHAGAVATA:   Yes.

HAYAVADANA:   It seems to me the rider described in the song is dead. I am right?

BHAGAVATA:   Er—I think so—yes.

HAYAVADANA:   Who could have taught this child such a tragic song?

BOY:   Mother . . .

BHAGAVATA:   What's there in a song, Hayavadana? The real beauty lies in the child's laughter—in the innocent joy of that laughter. No tragedy can touch it.

HAYAVADANA:   Is that so?

BHAGAVATA:   Indeed. What can match a child's laughter in its purity?

HAYAVADANA:   To be honest, Mr Bhagavata Sir, I have my doubts about this theory. I believe—in fact I may go so far as to say I firmly believe—that it's this sort of sentimentality which has been the bane of our literature and national life. It has kept us from accepting Reality and encouraged escapism. Still, if you say so, I won't argue. Come, child, let's have another song.

BOY:   I don't know . . .

HAYAVADANA:   Then sing the same song again.

BOY:   You laugh first.

HAYAVADANA:   Laugh again?—Let me try (*Tries to laugh.*) Ha Ha Ha! No, it's not easy to laugh—just like that . . .

BOY:   (*Mimes whipping.*) Laugh—laugh . . .

HAYAVADANA:   All right. All right. I'll try again. Ha! Ha! Ha! Ha!—Huhhuh . . . Heahhh . . .

(*His laughter ends up as a proper neigh.*)

ALL:   What's that?

BHAGAVATA:   Hayavadana—Hayavadana . . .

HAYAVADANA:   Heahhh . . .

(*His human voice is gone now. He can only neigh and leaps around with great joy.*)

BHAGAVATA:   Careful—careful. Don't drop the child . . .

(*But the horse is too happy to listen. It prances around, neighing gleefully. The boy is also enjoying himself, singing bits of the song and urging the horse on.*)

BHAGAVATA:   So at long last Hayavadana has become complete. (*To the Actors.*) You two go and tell the Revered Brahmin Vidyasagar that his grandson is returning home in triumph, riding a big, white charger . . .

ACTOR II:   And the dolls?

BHAGAVATA:   Throw them away. There's no further need for them . . .

(*The Actors go out with the dolls.*)

Unfathomable indeed is the mercy of the elephant-headed Ganesha. He fulfils the desires of all—a grandson to a grandfather, a smile to a child, a neigh to a horse. How indeed can one describe his glory in our poor, disabled words?

Come, Hayavadana, come. Enough of this dancing. Our play is over and it's time we all prayed and thanked the Lord for having ensured the completion and success of our play.

(*Hayavadana comes and stands by the Bhagavata. The Bhagavata helps the child down. At this point the curtain, with the fire painted on it,—which has been there all the time—is dropped and Padmini, Kapila and Devadatta step forward and join the Bhagavata in prayer.*)

Grant us, O Lord, good rains, good crop,

Prosperity in poetry, science, industry and other affairs.

Give the rulers of our country success in all endeavours, and along with it, a little bit of sense.

# *Tughlaq*

# Note to Tughlaq

This play was originally written in Kannada in 1964. I was persuaded to translate it into English by Alyque Padamsee, who later produced it for the Theatre Group, Bombay. This translation was first staged at the Bhulabhai Auditorium, Bombay, in August 1970.

I should like to express here my thanks to Alyque Padamsee and the Theatre Group for the care and imagination with which they produced the play. My special thanks are also due to S. Gopalie, Madras, for his invaluable help with the translation.

This play is dedicated to Krishna Basrur with affection and admiration.

Dharwar, 1971                                                    G.K.

# Introduction to *Tughlaq*

*Tughlaq*, which was published in Kannada in 1964, is Girish Karnad's second play. His first play, *Yayati*, was a self-consciously existentialist drama on the theme of responsibility. And those of us writing in the Kannada *Navya* movement of the time can still remember the excitement when we first read it in 1961. His interpretation of the familiar old myth on the exchange of ages between father and son baffled and angered many conventional critics but, for others, who were trying to root their contemporary concerns in old myths, Karnad's unheroic hero, Puru, was a great experience.

*Tughlaq* was an immediate success on the stage. It was first produced in Kannada in 1965 and was also done, about the same time, in Hindi by the National School of Drama. Bengali and Marathi productions followed, and in 1970 there was an English production in Bombay which was a major success.

It is not hard to account for the immediate response the play has received from Kannada as well as other audiences. One can enjoy the play on the stage without paying much attention to its rich and complex symbolism and the subtle weaving of its different motifs. The play has an interesting story, an intricate plot, scope for spectacle, and uses dramatic conventions like the comic pair, Aziz and Aazam (the *Akara and Makara of Natak* performances), to which theatre audiences respond readily.

Another reason for *Tughlaq's* appeal to Indian audiences is that it is a play of the sixties, and reflects as no other play perhaps does the political mood of disillusionment which followed the Nehru era of idealism in the country. Karnad himself has commented (*Enact*, June 1971) on this:

What struck me absolutely about Tughlaq's history was that it was contemporary. The fact that here was the most idealistic, the most intelligent king ever to come on the throne of Delhi . . . and one of the greatest failures also. And within a span of twenty years this tremendously capable man had gone to pieces. This seemed to be both due to his idealism as well as the shortcomings within him, such as his impatience, his cruelty, his feeling that he had the only correct answer. And I felt in the early sixties India had also come very far in the same direction—the twenty-year period seemed to me very much a striking parallel.

But the play is more than a political allegory. It has an irreducible, puzzling quality which comes from the ambiguities of Tughlaq's character, the dominating figure in the play. All the other characters are dramatized aspects of his complex personality, yet they also exist in their own right. Kannada critics have made detailed analyses of the play, paying special attention to the symbolism of the game of chess, the theme of disguise, the ironic success of Aziz whose amazing story runs parallel to Tughlaq's, and the dualism of the man and the hero in Tughlaq, which is the source of the entire tragedy. Yet no critical examination of the play can easily exhaust its total meaning for the reader, because the play has, finally, an elusive and haunting quality which it gets from the character of Tughlaq who has been realized in great psychological depth. But it would be unjust to say that the play is about an 'interesting' character, for the play relates the character of Tughlaq to philosophical questions on the nature of man and the destiny of a whole kingdom which a dreamer like him controls.

Although the theme of the play is from history—there are many such plays in Kannada—Karnad's treatment of the theme is not historical. Take, for instance, the use Karnad makes of the leitmotiv of the play, 'prayer', in the scene where the Muslim chieftains along with Sheik Shams-ud-din, a pacifist priest, conspire to murder Tughlaq while at prayer. The use of prayer for murder is reminiscent of what Tughlaq himself did to kill his father. That prayer, which is most dear to Tughlaq, is vitiated by him as well as his enemies, is symbolic of the fact that his life is corrupted at its very source. The whole episode is ironic. It involves Shihab-ud-din, an idealist who has put great trust in Tughlaq's rule, and is himself ultimately betrayed by Ratansingh who masterminds the entire plan of murder for his own ends. The intrigue here not only enhances the theatrical interest of the play, but is a dramatized projection of Tughlaq's tortured, divided self. Thus, the external action throughout enacts the inner drama of Tughlaq. Both Tughlaq and his enemies initially appear to be idealists; yet, in the pursuit of the ideal, they perpetrate its opposite. The whole play is structured on these opposites: the ideal and the real; the divine aspiration and the deft intrigue. Tughlaq is what he is in spite of his self-knowledge and an intense desire for divine grace. He is aware of the irony of his life when Aziz, the only character in the play who has skilfully used all the schemes of Tughlaq for his own designs, kills Ghiyas-ud-din and comes in his guise as a holy messenger of peace to purify the land and revive the banned prayer. The irony is deeply tragic. In the end Tughlaq and his kingdom are one in their chaos, and he knows it.

There are some good single plays in Kannada like Masti's *Kakana Kote* and the plays of Adya Rangacharya who has kept the tradition of serious play-writing in Kannada alive; yet there is, perhaps, no play in Kannada comparable to *Tughlaq* in its depth and range. It is likely to become a classic in Kannada literature. The present translation, which has been ably done by Karnad himself, will be warmly welcomed by readers eager to know what is happening in the Indian languages.

It may not be out of place to mention here that many teachers of English in India have felt and still feel the need for English translations of literature in the Indian languages. Teachers like myself have often wished that along with Indian writing in English which we prescribe to our students, we should also be able to teach English translations of classics in the Indian languages which will engage our student's attention fully and meaningfully. Karnad's *Tughlaq* should be as rewarding an experience to teach and to study, as it has been to see on the stage all over India.

Mysore                                    U.R. Anantha Murthy
September, 1971

# *Characters*

*(In the order of their appearance)*

ANNOUNCER
SULTAN MUHAMMAD TUGHLAQ
AAZAM
AZIZ
STEP-MOTHER
VIZIER MUHAMMAD NAJIB
ZIA-UD-DIN BARANI
SHEIKH IMAM-UD-DIN
SHIHAB-UD-DIN
SARDAR RATANSINGH
SHEIKH SHAMS-UD-DIN TAJUDDARFIM
GHIYAS-UD-DIN ABBASID

CROWD OF CITIZENS KAZI-I-MUMALIK AND RETINUE GUARD DOOR-
KEEPER SERVANT AMIRS SAYYID MUZZIN SOLDIERS HINDU WOMAN
REFUGEE FAMILY WATCHMEN KARIM

*The action of the play takes place first of all in Delhi in the year 1327,
then on the road from Delhi to Daulatabad, and lastly in and around the
fort in Daulatabad five years later.*

# Scene One

## AD 1327

*The yard in front of the Chief Court of Justice in Delhi. A crowd of citizens—mostly Muslims, with a few Hindus here and there.*

OLD MAN:   God, what's this country coming to!

YOUNG MAN:   What are you worried about, grandfather? The country's in perfectly safe hands—safer than any you've seen before.

OLD MAN:   I don't know. I've been alive a long time, seen many Sultans, but I never thought I would live to see a thing like this.

YOUNG MAN:   Your days are over, old man. What's the use of Sultans who didn't allow a subject within a mile's distance? This King now, he isn't afraid to be human—

THIRD MAN:   But does he have to make such a fuss about being human? Announce his mistakes to the whole world—invite the entire capital?

OLD MAN:   And get kicked by an infidel too. It's an insult to Islam.

YOUNG MAN:   That's good that! Insult to Islam! So you want to teach him Islam, do you? Tell me, how often did you pray before he came to the throne?

THIRD MAN:   That isn't the point.

YOUNG MAN:   That's precisely the point. Not even once a week, I bet. Now you pray five times a day because that's the law and if you break it, you'll have the officers on your neck. Can you mention one earlier Sultan in whose time people read the Koran in the streets like now? Just one?

OLD MAN:   What's the use? One must act according to it . . .

THIRD MAN:   All this about the Hindus not paying the jiziya tax. That's against the Koran, you know. A Mowlvi told me that—

HINDU:   Now, now, don't look at *me* when you say that. We didn't want an exemption! Look, when a Sultan kicks me in the teeth and says, 'Pay up, you Hindu dog', I'm happy. I know I'm safe.

But the moment a man comes along and says, 'I know you are a Hindu, but you are also a human being'—well, that makes me nervous.

YOUNG MAN:   Ungrateful wretch!

OLD MAN:   But this wretch is our best friend, Jamal. Beware of the Hindu who embraces you. Before you know what, he'll turn Islam into another caste and call the Prophet an incarnation of his god . . .

(*The Public Announcer comes out and beats his drum. Silence.*)

ANNOUNCER:   Attention! Attention! In the name of Allah it is hereby announced that Vishnu Prasad, a Brahmin of Shiknar, had filed a suit against His Merciful Majesty, that his land had been seized illegally by the officers of the State and that he should be given just compensation for the loss of the land and the privation resulting therefrom. The Kazi-i-Mumalik having considered this matter carefully and in full detail has declared . . .

(*He pauses for effect. The audience is tense and the Announcer looks pleased.*)

. . . has declared that the Brahmin's claim is just . . .

(*Commotion in the crowd. The Announcer silences them with a couple of drum beats and continues.*)

. . . that the Brahmin's claim is just and that His Merciful Majesty is guilty of illegal appropriation of land. The Kazi-i-Mumalik has further declared that in return for the land and in compensation of the privation resulting from its loss the said Vishnu Prasad should receive a grant of five hundred silver dinars from the State Treasury.

(*Renewed commotion. But the Announcer isn't finished yet.*)

His Merciful Majesty has accepted the decision of the Kazi-i-Mumalik as just and in addition to the grant of five hundred silver dinars has offered the said Vishnu Prasad a post in the Civil Service to ensure him a regular and adequate income.

(*Beats the drums again and retires.*)

OLD MAN:   What folly is this! May Heaven guide our Sultan.

HINDU:   I don't believe a word of it. There's something more to this, that much is obvious—

(*The Announcer comes out followed by Muhammad, the Kazi and the retinue.*)

ANNOUNCER:   Attention! Attention! The Warrior in the Path of

God, the Defender of the Word of the Prophet, the Friend of
the Khalif, the Just, His Merciful Majesty, Sultan Muhammad
Tughlaq.

CROWD: Victory—to the King.

MUHAMMAD: My beloved people, you have heard the judgement
of the Kazi and seen for yourselves how justice works in my
kingdom—without any consideration of might or weakness,
religion or creed. May this moment burn bright and light up
our path towards greater justice, equality, progress and peace—
not just peace but a more purposeful life.

And to achieve this end I am taking a new step in which I hope
I shall have your support and cooperation. Later this year the
capital of my empire will be moved from Delhi to Daulatabad.

(*The crowd reacts in bewilderment. Muhammad smiles.*)

Your surprise is natural, but I beg you to realize that this is no
mad whim of a tyrant. My ministers and I took this decision
after careful thought and discussion. My empire is large now
and embraces the South and I need a capital which is at its heart.
Delhi is too near the border and as you well know its peace is
never free from the fear of invaders. But for me the most
important factor is that Daulatabad is a city of the Hindus and
as the capital it will symbolize the bond between Muslims and
Hindus which I wish to develop and strengthen in my kingdom.
I invite you all to accompany me to Daulatabad. This is only
an invitation and not an order. Only those who have faith in
me may come with me. With their help I shall build an empire
which will be the envy of the world.

(*Exits with the retinue.*)

OLD MAN: You can go to the Kazi-i-Mumalik for small offences.
But who do you appeal to against such madness?

THIRD MAN: This is tyranny! Sheer tyranny! Move the capital to
Daulatabad! Such things never happened in his father's days—
may his soul rest in peace. Now he's got his father's throne.
He isn't happy with that and—

YOUNG MAN: What do you mean?

THIRD MAN: What?

YOUNG MAN: What did you mean by that—when you said he had
got his father's throne?

THIRD MAN:   Don't try to threaten me, boy. The whole capital saw it.

YOUNG MAN:   Saw what?

THIRD MAN:   You know what.

YOUNG MAN:   Were you there?

THIRD MAN:   There were others—my friends—

YOUNG MAN:   Hang your friends! Were you there?

THIRD MAN:   No!

YOUNG MAN:   Well, I was. And I tell you it was an accident.

THIRD MAN:   I see.

YOUNG MAN:   It was. The elephant suddenly went wild. The crowds must have frightened it. It just ran and dashed against the wooden pandal. And the pandal collapsed.

OLD MAN:   Very convenient.

THIRD MAN:   And to think the procession had been arranged by the father in his honour!

YOUNG MAN:   But the Sultan had gone to the mosque to pray! The old Sultan should never have had the procession at prayer time—You all know it was prayer time and the Sultan never misses a prayer!

HINDU:   Yes, yes, we know that. But tell me. How did the elephant know it was time for prayer?
         (*Laughter.*)

THIRD MAN:   All right, don't trust my word. But do you think a man like Sheikh Imam-ud-din would lie? Well, he said in clear loud words that it was murder. And he said it publicly—I was there!

OLD MAN:   (*Eagerly.*) You've seen the Sheikh?

THIRD MAN:   Why, of course. Only a week ago. In Kanpur. What a man! What a voice! The audience was spell-bound. And he said the Sultan's guilty of killing his father and brother, he said. He said so many other things too—about Islam and what's happening to it. It was the most inspiring speech I've ever heard. The audience went wild and burnt down half of Kanpur. You think he would talk like that if he wasn't sure?

OLD MAN:   They say he looks like the Sultan.

THIRD MAN:   No—not very much. People exaggerate, you know. But he has a certain resemblance—some gestures, you know, some mannerisms—

HINDU:   Perhaps that's where he gets his habit of making speeches.

THIRD MAN:   Watch your words, infidel. Don't you dare mock a
saint like him.

*(The Guard come out of the Court. )*

GUARD:   All right, all right. Go home! What are you waiting for?
The show's over! Go home—

*(The crowd disperses. Only Aazam remains, hanging around.)*

Well, what do you want?

AAZAM:   Nothing, I just wanted to see the Brahmin. He hasn't
come out yet, has he?

GUARD:   Oh, get away. Wants to see the Brahmin, if you please.
Be off—

*(Aazam retreats. The Guard looks into the Court and shouts.)*

Come out—come out. Don't be scared, Your Highness.

*(The Brahmin comes out.)*

Perhaps Your Highness will want an escort to see you safely
home! Complaining against the Sultan! Bloody Infidel! Get
going, I'm already late.

BRAHMIN:   Yes, yes. Certainly. Good-bye.

GUARD:   Good-bye.

*(Goes in and shuts the door. The Brahmin starts to go. Aazam
follows him and then slowly taps him on the shoulder.)*

AAZAM:   Ho . . . ooo . . .

*(The Brahmin whirls round and pulls out a dagger as he turns.
Aazam jumps back.)*

AAZAM:   Oops . . .

*(They watch each other. Aazam's jaw falls in surprise.)*

AAZAM:   Who? Not . . . not . . .

BRAHMIN:   Aazam?

AAZAM:   Aziz? What on earth . . .

*(Gives a shout of joy, lifts Aziz up and whirls him round and
round ecstatically.)*

AZIZ:   Let me down—let me down—

*(Aazam lets him down.)*

And hold your tongue. If they find out, I'm finished, man.

AAZAM:   But—I don't see you for years and then—this—this?

AZIZ:   Shut up!

*(They move off and sit under a tree.)*

AAZAM:   I thought something was funny. I mean a man wins a case

against the King himself—you would expect him to come out victoriously—I mean holding his head high? Not hide inside! Listen, Brahmins don't carry daggers around like that.
(*Aziz quickly hides the dagger.*)

AZIZ: What are you doing here?

AAZAM: I am where there is a crowd. Look, today's earnings. And you won't believe me if I tell you where they hide their money—

AZIZ: So your bad habits continue, do they?

AAZAM: Not habit. Occupation. Anyway, I'm just a common pickpocket. But you are up to no good either, I can see that. A Muslim dhobi can't become a Brahmin that easily.

AZIZ: For God's sake, keep your voice down. Now look, if I tell you the truth, will you keep it to yourself?

AAZAM: Depends on what I get out of it—all right, you're an old friend. I'll keep quiet for nothing. So?

AZIZ: Did you hear the royal proclamation the other day?

AAZAM: Which one? There are so many.

AZIZ: You know, the one on the second anniversary of his coronation. (*Mimicking a public announcer.*)
'Henceforth people may file a suit against the Sultan himself for the misbehaviour of his officers . . . No one need have any fear . . . Justice will be done . . .' Et cetera. Well, I was at the end of my tether then. There's no future in being a dhobi these days. So I did a bit of thinking. There's a Brahmin called Vishnu Prasad whose land had been confiscated recently. I shaved my head and went to him. I said I would buy the land.

AAZAM: Please a little slowly. I—you know I'm not very bright. But what's the point? I mean the land was confiscated, wasn't it?

AZIZ: Exactly, that's what he said too. But I said, 'Never mind about that'. So he sold me the land—backdating the contract. And I filed my suit. Well, here I am. Five hundred silver dinars for nothing, and a job in His Merciful Majesty's own Civil Service.

AZIZ: But what if he had cut off your head instead?
(*Aziz laughs.*)
Anyway, why did you have to dress up in these ungodly clothes? Couldn't you have come like a proper Muslim?

AZIZ: (*Scandalized.*) But then what would happen to the King's impartial justice? A Muslim plaintiff against a Muslim king? I mean, where's the question of justice there? Where's the equality between Hindus and Muslims? If on the other hand the plaintiff's a Hindu . . . well, you saw the crowds.

AAZAM: Complicated!

AZIZ: It's a bit too subtle for you. Anyway here's my offer. From tomorrow I join the Civil Service. Why don't you come along too? I'll get you a job under me. You know, a Brahmin with a Muslim friend—the Sultan will like that.

AAZAM: No thanks, I'm quite happy—

AZIZ: Come along. It won't be for long. I didn't intend to be a Brahmin all my life! There's money here and we'll make a pile by the time we reach Daulatabad.

AAZAM: And then?

AZIZ: How should I know?

## Scene Two

*(A room in the palace. Muhammad is bent over a chess-board, smiling with suppressed excitement. The Step-Mother enters.)*

STEP-MOTHER: Muhammad—

MUHAMMAD: Ah, there you are! Absolutely at the right moment. If you had come a minute earlier, the world would have been so much poorer.

STEP-MOTHER: Really? That sounds very important.

MUHAMMAD: But it is. I have just solved the most famous problem in chess. Even al-Adli and as-Sarakhi said it was insoluble. And it's so simple—

STEP-MOTHER: Who were they?

MUHAMMAD: Mother! How can you ask? They were the greatest chess players the world's ever seen.

STEP-MOTHER: What do I know about your chess? You'd better write to Ain-ul-Mulk about it. He'll love it!

MUHAMMAD: Funny you should mention him. I was just thinking of him—but not with reference to chess. You see, my dear friend Ain-ul-Mulk, the companion of my childhood, my fellow champion in chess, is at this very moment marching on Delhi.

STEP-MOTHER: What? What do you mean?

MUHAMMAD: Exactly what I said. He is marching on Delhi with an army of thirty thousand.

STEP-MOTHER: But why, Muhammad?

MUHAMMAD: I don't know. The last letter I wrote to him asked him to be the Governor of the Deccan. I need a strong man there and I thought he would like it.

STEP-MOTHER: But there must be some other reason! *(No reply.)* What are you going to do now?

MUHAMMAD: Do the best I can. But I don't even have six thousand soldiers—Look, I was so happy about this problem and now you've ruined it all. Anyway, you came for something?

STEP-MOTHER: It doesn't matter any more.

MUHAMMAD: But it does, certainly.

STEP-MOTHER: I was worried about your late nights. These days you never seem to go to bed at all. I just wanted to know why.

MUHAMMAD: (*Smiles.*) And you think you've found the answer? Look, if I was that worried about Ain-ul-Mulk why would I waste my time on this?

(*Points to the chess-board.*)

STEP-MOTHER: Then what do you do all night?

MUHAMMAD: (*Theatrical.*) I pray to the Almighty to save me from sleep. All day long I have to worry about tomorrow but it's only when the night falls that I can step beyond all that. I look at the Pleiades and I think of Ibn-ul-Mottazz who thought it was an ostrich egg and Dur-rumma who thought it was a swallow. And then I want to go back to their poetry and sink myself in their words. Then again I want to climb up, up to the top of the tallest tree in the world, and call out to my people: 'Come, my people, I am waiting for you. Confide in me your worries. Let me share your joys. Let's laugh and cry together and then, let's pray. Let's pray till our bodies melt and flow and our blood turns into air. History is ours to play with—ours now! Let's be the light and cover the earth with greenery. Let's be darkness and cover up the boundaries of nations. Come! I am waiting to embrace you all!'

But then how can I spread my branches in the stars while the roots have yet to find their hold in the earth? I wish I could believe in recurring births like the Hindu but I have only one life, one body, and my hopes, my people, my God are all fighting for it. Tell me, how dare I waste my time by sleeping? And don't tell me to go and get married and breed a family because I won't sleep.

STEP-MOTHER: (*Bursts into laughter.*) I don't know what to do with you. I can't ask a simple question without your giving a royal performance. Even Ain-ul-Mulk doesn't seem to stop you—

MUHAMMAD: Mother, suppose I die fighting Ain-ul-Mulk—

STEP-MOTHER: Stop it!

MUHAMMAD: No, really. Suppose I die in the battle. What of it? Why should I waste my last few days worrying? I am not worried about my enemies. I'm only worried about my people.

STEP-MOTHER: Pompous ass! As though other kings didn't do that.

MUHAMMAD: No, they didn't. Look at the past Sultans of Delhi.

They couldn't bear the weight of their crown. They couldn't leave it aside. So they died senile in their youth or were murdered.

STEP-MOTHER: (*Sharply.*) Please, Muhammad—

MUHAMMAD: What?

STEP-MOTHER: Nothing—I can't bear to see you joking about murder.

MUHAMMAD: Why not?

STEP-MOTHER: I can't. That's all.

(*Silence. They are both tense now.*)

MUHAMMAD: So you too believe that piece of gossip!

STEP-MOTHER: What gossip?

MUHAMMAD: (*Mocking.*) What gossip? What scandal? You know perfectly well what I mean.

STEP-MOTHER: Don't be silly. I didn't mean anything of that kind.

MUHAMMAD: But you do believe it? And why shouldn't you? After all my own mother believes it. The whole court believes it. My Amirs believe it. Why shouldn't my step-mother believe it?

STEP-MOTHER: (*Flaring up.*) Shut up, fool! I've told you I won't have you calling me that!

MUHAMMAD: (*Suddenly calm, but with deliberate viciousness.*) I know. But you *are* my step-mother!

(*Silence. Enter the Door-Keeper.*)

DOOR-KEEPER: In the name of Allah. Vizier Muhammad Najib and Zia-ud-din Barani to see you, Your Majesty

MUHAMMAD: Send them in.

(*The Door-Keeper goes out. The Step-Mother lowers the veil on her face. Najib and Barani enter.*)

NAJIB, BARANI: In the name of Allah.

MUHAMMAD: Come in, come in. I was just saying to Mother . . .

STEP-MOTHER: Muhammad, why don't you tell them about your chess?

MUHAMMAD: Because they aren't interested. Barani is a historian— he's only interested in playing chess with the shadows of the dead. And Najib's a politician—he wants pawns of flesh and blood. He doesn't have the patience to breathe life into these bones. One needs Ain-ul-Mulk for that. So Najib, how far have we reached?

NAJIB: I'm doing my best, Your Majesty. But I don't think we'll get more than six thousand. The odds against us are very heavy . . .

BARANI:   May I know what odds, Your Majesty?

NAJIB:   . . . but another equally important problem has come up, Your Majesty. Sheikh Imam-ud-din is in Delhi.

MUHAMMAD:   Aha! Then we should take his blessings before we leave.

NAJIB:   Yes, Your Majesty, and get rid of him.

BARANI:   What a terrible thing to say about a holy man like that!

MUHAMMAD:   (*Smiles to the Step-Mother, explaining.*) Najib is upset because the Sheikh criticizes me publicly—demands that I abdicate. The Sheikh thinks I'm incompetent.

NAJIB:   It's worse than that. He has become a backbone of the rebels. As for what else he says, you may ask Barani.

MUHAMMAD:   So you've heard him, Barani. What's he like? Is it true he looks like me?

BARANI:   (*Flustered.*) A little, Your Majesty. But—how did Najib know I had heard the Sheikh? Forgive me, Your Majesty, but I don't like being spied upon.

NAJIB:   It's my job to know. That's why I asked you to come here with me now.

MUHAMMAD:   Surely a historian doesn't need an invitation to watch history take shape! Come, Barani, what does he say?

BARANI:   It's as Your Majesty said . . . He says the Sultan is a disgrace to Islam.

MUHAMMAD:   That's all? I could find worse faults in me. What else? (*Silence.*)

NAJIB:   He says Your Majesty has forfeited the right to rule, by murdering your father and brother at prayer time.
(*The Step-Mother and Barani react sharply, but Muhammad is still. A short pause.*)

MUHAMMAD:   (*Quietly.*) Did he say that?

BARANI:   (*Almost in a whisper.*) Yes, Your Majesty.

MUHAMMAD:   So now they talk about it openly, do they?

BARANI:   He said it in the heat of the moment, Your Majesty. I'm sure he didn't mean it. Your Majesty must ignore these little things.

MUHAMMAD:   Do you really think parricide is a little thing? And fratricide? And the pollution of prayer? It's not what people say,

Barani, it's their crooked minds that horrify me. Look at my own mother—she won't talk to me now—not because father died but because my brother died in that accident. He was more amenable to her whims and he would have made a better king for her. So she believes I killed them. Do you know, I've just found out that even this step-mother of mine thinks I am a murderer.

(*Silence.*)

NAJIB: (*Quietly.*) What about the Sheikh, Your Majesty?

MUHAMMAD: (*In a tired voice.*) Let him babble. He is a saint, it's his privilege.

NAJIB: But we must do something. In Kanpur, they're still rioting and he started it. Now he's here—in the capital.

BARANI: But His Majesty is right. The people have been told that they have a right to criticize the Sultan, to voice their grievances openly. Surely this is the time to show that the Sultan means it—that they were not empty words. The people will surely respond to His Majesty's courage, honesty and justice . . .

NAJIB: (*Groans.*) Courage, honesty and justice! My dear Barani, we are dealing with a political problem!

BARANI: I know and that's where they count most. Because that's where the Kingdom of Islam which the Prophet has gifted us must blossom. Oh! You won't understand it. Your Hindu childhood has twisted your attitudes beyond repair.

NAJIB: Do you know why I gave up Hinduism? Because it didn't speak of the salvation of society. It only talked of the soul—my individual soul—while a poor, frenzied world screamed in agony around. So I became a Muslim. Islam is worried about this world, I said, it'll bring the Kingdom of Heaven on earth. But I know now—it won't work. There's only the present moment and we must grasp it firmly.

MUHAMMAD: (*Ironic but affectionate.*) So what does the present moment demand now?

BARANI: It's obvious, Your Majesty. He wants the Sheikh dead.

NAJIB: Nonsense! That'll make him a martyr. You can't kill the dead. If we kill him now, we're finished. We might as well surrender to Ain-ul-Mulk.

BARANI: (*Startled.*) Surrender to whom?

MUHAMMAD: Ain-ul-Mulk. He is marching on Delhi.

BARANI:  I don't believe it! (*Silence.*) But you mustn't act hastily, Your Majesty. There's obviously been some misunderstanding. (*Earnestly.*) You know Ain-ul-Mulk. He is a good man and he worships you. He isn't the treacherous type. You know that!

MUHAMMAD:  (*In anguish.*) But why *now*? Can't he see that I've no time for 'misunderstandings' now? He knows how important it is for me to concentrate on moving to Daulatabad.

BARANI:  But there must be some way of finding out why he's doing this. Please send an envoy . . . send me . . . I'll go . . .

NAJIB:  What's the point? We can't waste our time on that. A traitor's a traitor, friend or saint, and he must be crushed.

BARANI:  But don't you want to know why?

NAJIB:  I do know why. It's obvious.
     (*The rest look at him in surprise.*)

MUHAMMAD:  It is?

NAJIB:  Your Majesty, when you came to the throne, there was anarchy in Avadh and you made Ain-ul-Mulk the Governor then. He crushed the rebels, restored law and order, and the people in Avadh think him a God almost. He's happy there, secure. Then suddenly he gets your letter making him the Governor of the Deccan, asking him to leave immediately. Is it surprising he should suspect a knife in his back?
     (*Silence.*)

MUHAMMAD:  God, why didn't I think of that?

BARANI:  But Najib did, Your Majesty, and didn't warn you.

NAJIB:  Would His Majesty have listened to me if I'd warned then? His Majesty loved Ain-ul-Mulk—too much.

BARANI:  And you hate him?

NAJIB:  Dear Barani, not hate, just suspicion. It's my job to be suspicious and I can't exempt anyone from it.

STEP-MOTHER:  No one?

NAJIB:  No, Your Highness.

STEP-MOTHER:  Not even the Sultan?

NAJIB:  (*Senses a trap, but calmly.*) No, not even the Sultan, Your Highness.

STEP-MOTHER:  (*Flaring up.*) Muhammad—
     (*Muhammad silences her with a gesture of impatience.*)

MUHAMMAD:  So, Najib, what do you propose?

NAJIB:   I can't think of anything right now, Your Majesty—except that the Sheikh has a striking resemblance to you.
          (*Muhammad, startled, stares at Najib.*)
BARANI:   What has the Sheikh got to do with this?
MUHAMMAD:   (*Slowly.*) You are a devil, Najib! (*Pause. Then briskly.*) Good. We'll think about that. In the meantime, the army should be ready to march. We'll start for Kanauj the day after tomorrow in the evening.
STEP-MOTHER:   And who'll look after the administration here, Muhammad?
MUHAMMAD:   Najib will be here.
          (*The Step-Mother obviously doesn't like the answer. Najib smiles ironically but not too openly.*)
          Besides I have invited Shihab-ud-din, the Prince of Sampan-shahr, to be here in my absence. You see, the Amir there doesn't like me very much, so I thought inviting his son would be a nice friendly gesture.
BARANI:   What's all this, Your Majesty? I can't follow a thing. But my heart trembles for you.
MUHAMMAD:   Forgive me if I let you down, Barani, but I must play this game my own way. Come, Najib, we must see the Commander-in-Chief. Mother, if you'll excuse us. (*Bows to her.*)
STEP-MOTHER:   Can Barani stay for a while? I want to talk to him.
MUHAMMAD:   Why, yes, certainly.
          (*Muhammad and Najib go out. Silence.*)
STEP-MOTHER:   I don't know what to say, Barani. I mustn't complain against my own son—
BARANI:   Your Highness may place full trust in me.
STEP-MOTHER:   I know, that's why I asked you to stay. I am worried about him. You know what he is like. He is such an intelligent boy and he works so hard for the people. He doesn't even go to bed these days. (*Pause.*) But he is so impulsive—and when he gets into one of his moods I don't know what he'll do next. (*Pause.*) You are a sober man, Barani, level-headed and honest, and he needs friends like you. I just wanted to ask you . . . Oh, God! It all sounds so stupid.
BARANI:   I fully understand Your Highness's feelings.
STEP-MOTHER:   It's not that. It's just that I don't like so many of

his advisers and friends, (*Suddenly.*) Please promise me not to leave him—ever—whatever he does.

BARANI: (*Overwhelmed to the point of tears.*) May God help me to retain such confidence untarnished. I won't leave His Majesty, Your Highness, I promise you. I love him too much to do that.

STEP-MOTHER: Look at him now. He won't show it, but Ain-ul-Mulk has hurt him. And this Sheikh Imam-ud-din—I don't know what he's going to do.

BARANI: It's not for me to advise, Your Highness, but I have to mention it. I am not jealous of Najib and I admire his integrity. But sometimes I am bothered by his influence on the Sultan.

STEP-MOTHER: I know. I am watching. I'll wait for a few days. (*With sudden violence.*) If he goes on like this, I won't wish his fate even on a dog!

(*Barani, driven to tears by her maternal concern, looks up startled by the venom in her voice.*)

*(The Announcer.)*

ANNOUNCER: Attention! Attention! The Slave of the Lord, the Merciful, the ever-Victorious Sultan Muhammad has declared that this evening after the prayer a meeting will be organized in the yard in front of the Big Mosque. Sheikh Imam-ud-din, who is revered all over India as a Saint and as one who stands in the Grace of Allah, will address the meeting. He will analyse His Merciful Majesty's administration and show where His Majesty has inadvertently taken wrong measures—measures harmful to the country and the Faith. His Majesty himself will be present at the meeting to seek direction from the Revered Sheikh, and the citizens of Delhi are requested to attend the meeting in large numbers and do likewise. Attention! Attention!

# Scene Three

(*The yard in front of the Big Mosque. Muhammad and Sheikh Imam-ud-Din and a few odd servants of the palace. No one else. There is a long silence.*)

MUHAMMAD: (*Suddenly.*) I can't bear this any longer!

IMAM-UD-DIN: Why Your Majesty? You should be happy if no one turns up.

MUHAMMAD: Do you think I would have gone to the trouble of arranging this meeting if I didn't want my people to hear you? I don't want my people to be dumb cattle, Sheikhsahib, and I do not claim to be omniscient myself. I am quite willing to learn from you—even eager.

IMAM-UD-DIN: Will you be as eager when you hear me, I wonder? You know I am not the type to sweeten my words because the Sultan himself is present.

MUHAMMAD: Don't I know it? The whole of Delhi has heard of the courage and integrity of Sheikh Imam-ud-din. I would not have taken so much trouble for anyone else.

(*Claps. A Servant enters and bows.*)

Go at once and tell the Vizier I want everyone here—all the Khans, Amirs, Sardars—everyone—and at once!

IMAM-UD-DIN: But Your Majesty, I haven't come here to speak to a collection of courtiers—

MUHAMMAD: And I'm afraid I can't go now from door to door asking people to come. I should have given orders at the Court today. We have been waiting for over half an hour—and not a soul has come yet!

IMAM-UD-DIN: They say we look alike, but we don't think alike, do we? What's the point in my addressing a gang of bootlickers? I want to speak to the people who are willing to act, who are willing to do something for Islam and the country. If no one comes today, well, no matter. I'll go to the market-place tomorrow and speak there.

(*Muhammad signs to the Servant to go. He goes out.*)

MUHAMMAD: Would you believe me if I told you I have never consciously tried to go against the tenets of Islam?

IMAM-UD-DIN: Please, Your Majesty, even you can't believe that! I can quote scores of transgressions. If they weren't wilful, they could only be results of ignorance. But I can't believe that in a scholar of your eminence. Perhaps you are sincere. But if one fails to understand what the Koran says one must ask the Sayyids and the Ulema. Instead you have put the best of them behind bars in the name of justice.

MUHAMMAD: They tried to indulge in politics—I couldn't allow that. I have never denied the word of God, Sheikhsahib, because its my bread and drink. I need it most when the surrounding void pushes itself into my soul and starts putting out every light burning there. But I am alone in my life. My kingdom has millions—Muslims, Hindus, Jains. Yes, there is dirt and sickness in my kingdom. But why should I call on God to clean the dirt deposited by men?

IMAM-UD-DIN: Because only the Voice of God, the Holy Word, can do it. Please listen to me, Your Majesty. The Arabs spread Islam round the world and they struggled and fought for it for seven hundred years. They are tired now, limp and exhausted. But their work must continue and we need someone to take the lead. You could do it. You are one of the most powerful kings on earth today and you could spread the Kingdom of Heaven on earth. God has given you everything—power, learning, intelligence, talent. Now you must repay His debt.

MUHAMMAD: No one can go far on his knees. I have a long way to go. I can't afford to crawl—I have to gallop.

IMAM-UD-DIN: And you will do it without the Koran to guide you? Beware, Sultan, you are trying to become another God. It's a sin worse than parricide.

MUHAMMAD: (*Refusing the bait.*) Only an atheist can try to be God. I am God's most humble slave.

IMAM-UD-DIN: Yes. And slaves have often tried to replace their masters.

MUHAMMAD: My congratulations, Imam-ud-din Sahib. For a saint you are very good at innuendoes—I know all about slaves. My grandfather was one and he became a king. But that was in mundane politics. The analogy doesn't work here.

IMAM-UD-DIN:   Religion! Politics! Take heed, Sultan, one day these verbal distinctions will rip you into two.

MUHAMMAD:   Don't I know it? I still remember the days when I read the Greeks—Sukrat who took poison so he could give the world the drink of gods, Aflatoon who condemned poets and wrote incomparably beautiful poetry himself—and I can still feel the thrill with which I found a new world, a world I had not found in the Arabs or even the Koran. They tore me into shreds. And to be whole now, I shall have to kill the part of me which sang to them. And my kingdom too is what I am—torn into pieces by visions whose validity I can't deny. You are asking me to make myself complete by killing the Greek in me and you propose to unify my people by denying the visions which led Zarathustra or the Buddha. (*Smiles.*) I'm sorry. But it can't be done.

IMAM-UD-DIN:   You are a learned man. You may be able to manage this delicate balance within yourself. But a kingdom needs not one king but a line of rulers. Will they manage this balance? Where are these brilliant successors of yours? Where are these guarantors of your balanced future?

MUHAMMAD:   There is none—yet. But I haven't lost hope. I shall find them and teach them to think like me. They are only cattle yet, but I shall make men out of a few of them. Look, Sheikhsahib, in Kanpur you found so many honest men that they burnt down the whole of Kanpur. They are still on the rampage there and your words inspire them. Now you've come to Delhi and there isn't even a fly to listen to you. They are staying away—at home, safe and secure. They don't want you here. Do you know why?

(*Silence.*)

Because they suspect you now. The moment they heard that I, the Sultan, was organizing a meeting in which you, my severest critic, was going to speak—they became suspicious. Why should the Sultan sponsor his worst critic? They have smelt a trap. And wisely they have stayed away.

IMAM-UD-DIN:   (*Stunned.*) Was this a trap?

MUHAMMAD:   No, I promise you.

IMAM-UD-DIN:   But—you knew this would happen?

MUHAMMAD: I didn't *know*. But I half expected it. I know my people.

IMAM-UD-DIN: So they think I'm your spy—and you knew it when you arranged this meeting!

MUHAMMAD: Believe me, Sheikhsahib, I'm sorry I am not disappointed. Yes, they will now decide you are a spy—they'll greet you as a spy in the market-place tomorrow. But now you do see what I mean, don't you? You are known as a saint and you have risked your life by speaking out against the Sultan. Yet a trick—and they suspect you. It's futile to think of them as members of the *dar-ul-Islam*. Generations of devout Sultans have twisted their minds and I have to mend their minds before I can think of their souls.

(*There is a long silence. Then Sheikh Imam-ud-Din starts to move down slowly.*)

IMAM-UD-DIN: My turn to congratulate you. Your experiment was a brilliant success. Yes, I have learnt my lesson. Thank you—and good-bye.

MUHAMMAD: Good-bye? You are not going?

IMAM-UD-DIN: You have finished my work for me. You don't want me to wait longer, do you? For an audience which won't turn up?

MUHAMMAD: I need your help, Sheikhsahib.

IMAM-UD-DIN: Don't play any more games with me—

MUHAMMAD: There's no time for games. I am desperate. Ain-ul-Mulk of Avadh is marching on Delhi at this very moment.

IMAM-UD-DIN: What? Your intimate friend and confidant? Why? No, I don't wish to know why. That's politics and you know your way there. But why tell me this?

MUHAMMAD: Because I want peace. I am willing to make peace but how can I do it? I don't even know why he has turned against me. He won't even see my official envoys. (*Pause.*) But he will see you.

(*The Sheikh is about to speak. But Muhammad goes on.*)

He respects you as every Muslim in India does. He will trust your word. That's why I'm asking you—will you please go as my envoy and dissuade him from this folly? Please Sheikhsahib, I'm not asking you only for my sake but for all the Muslims who will die at the hands of Muslims if there is a war.

(*Pause.*)

IMAM-UD-DIN:  I don't trust your motives.

MUHAMMAD:  What do my motives matter? You can't deny that this war will mean a slaughter of Muslims at the hands of fellow-Muslims. Isn't that enough for the great Sheikh Imam-ud-din? You have attacked me for inaction. You can't turn away now when you are offered a chance. You can't!

IMAM-UD-DIN:  I know I can't.

MUHAMMAD:  So you agree?

IMAM-UD-DIN:  Do you leave me an alternative?

MUHAMMAD:  (*Slowly.*) I'll never be able to thank you enough for this.

(*Claps his hands. A Servant enters and bows.*)

Bring the robes of honour for the royal envoy. At once!

(*The Servant departs.*)

IMAM-UD-DIN:  You don't mean the robes are ready.

MUHAMMAD:  Forgive me, Sheikhsahib, but I knew you wouldn't refuse.

IMAM-UD-DIN:  But what about Ain-ul-Mulk? Won't he also think of me as your spy? It won't take long before he will know of this. (*Indicates the empty auditorium.*)

MUHAMMAD:  He is not a fool. Besides he won't know. There isn't time. We have to start before nightfall. Ain-ul-Mulk has already started and we must meet him near the plains of Kanauj.

(*The Servant brings the robes of honour and the headdress on a golden plate. Muhammad takes the robe and goes near the Sheikh.*)

IMAM-UD-DIN:  (*Stopping him.*) If you want peace, what does it matter where we meet him?

MUHAMMAD:  I do want peace. But I can't leave anything to chance. If Ain-ul-Mulk refuses, I have to have my army in a safe place. I owe it to my soldiers.

(*Pause.*)

IMAM-UD-DIN:  You know, Sultan, I'm just beginning to understand why they say you are the cleverest man in the world.

MUHAMMAD:  I am an incompetent fool—will you wear the robes now?

IMAM-UD-DIN:  Very well.

(*He puts on the robes. Muhammad places the head-dress on his*

*head. They stand facing each other. The dress makes them look
even more alike.*)
I wish I could be more sure of you . . .

# Scene Four

*The Palace. Shihab-ud-Din is reading a few letters. There is an announcement.*

DOOR-KEEPER: (*Announcing.*) Her Highness the Queen Mother.
(*Shihab-ud-Din leaps up. The Step-Mother enters and he bows to her.*)

SHIHAB-UD-DIN: Welcome, Your Highness. I am most honoured by the visit but, had Your Highness sent for me, I would have come myself.

STEP-MOTHER: I suddenly felt frightened, Shihab-ud-din. I couldn't bear the tension any longer. Has there been any further news?

SHIHAB-UD-DIN: I'm afraid not, Your Highness. The last bulletin was received a week ago. Your Highness knows the contents. There has been nothing since then. I'm sorry but—

STEP-MOTHER: No, no, please don't apologize. I don't know what I should have done without you here. You know when Muhammad said he was inviting you to look after Delhi, I didn't understand him at all. I couldn't see why he had to ask you, rather than a local Amir. I know now—he couldn't have chosen a better man.

SHIHAB-UD-DIN: I am most grateful for Your Highness's trust, But I did very little. The credit should go to Vizier Muhammad Najib.

STEP-MOTHER: Oh! Don't talk to me about him. Thanks to you, I didn't have to deal with him.

SHIHAB-UD-DIN: Your Highness's most humble servant.
(*The Door-Keeper enters.*)

DOOR-KEEPER: In the name of Allah. Sardar Ratansingh.

SHIHAB-UD-DIN: (*Excited.*) He is here? Send him in at once.
(*The Door-Keeper goes out.*)

STEP-MOTHER: Who is that?

SHIHAB-UD-DIN: My adopted brother, Your Highness.

STEP-MOTHER: Him! He'll have news of the front then!

*(Ratansingh enters. Shihab-ud-din goes to him in great excitement and embraces him.)*

SHIHAB-UD-DIN:  Welcome, Ratansingh. What happened?

RATANSINGH:  His Majesty is back in Delhi. We arrived a few minutes ago.

STEP-MOTHER:  Oh, then I must go.

RATANSINGH:  Forgive me, Your Highness, but His Majesty has gone to see the Vizier. He has asked me to inform Your Highness that he will be here any minute.

*(The Step-Mother doesn't like it. But she swallows it.)*

STEP-MOTHER:  But I can't understand it. Why didn't he send word he was coming? Why this secrecy?

RATANSINGH:  *(Hesitates.)* I don't think it was meant to be secret, Your Highness. It's just that His Majesty seems much affected by the death of Sheikh Imam-ud-din.

STEP-MOTHER:  What? Sheikh Imam-ud-din dead?

RATANSINGH:  Yes, Your Highness. He was killed in the battle.

*(Her face goes white.)*

SHIHAB-UD-DIN:  But what was the Sheikh doing in the battle?

DOOR-KEEPER:  *(Off-stage.)* The Warrior in the path of God, the Victorious, the Mighty, His Majesty the Sultan.

*(Muhammad enters with Najib and Barani.)*

SHIHAB-UD-DIN:  *(Bows.)* In the name of Allah. May He shower greater successes on Your Majesty.

MUHAMMAD:  That's no way to welcome, Shihab. Come—

*(They embrace.)*

I am grateful to you for looking after my people in my absence.

SHIHAB-UD-DIN:  Your Majesty's humble slave.

STEP-MOTHER:  Muhammad, what's this about Sheikh Imam-ud-din?

*(Muhammad freezes. Then slowly.)*

MUHAMMAD:  Did you have to mention it now? It was a terrible sight. They brought his body into my tent and I felt—as though it was I who was lying dead there and that he was standing above me looking at me. I should have been there—in his place.

*(Pause.)*

BARANI:  It's a great loss to Islam.

STEP-MOTHER:  And what about Ain-ul-Mulk? I hope he's dead too.

MUHAMMAD:   I let him go.
>    (*General surprise.*)

STEP-MOTHER:   You didn't! You couldn't have!

NAJIB:   I hate to say it on this happy occasion, Your Majesty, but that would be really tossing another torch into the chaos at Avadh.

BARANI:   Your Highness must forgive me, but His Majesty deserves congratulations on his courage. He has shown there are things more valuable then vengeance.

NAJIB:   Not that again!

MUHAMMAD:   I didn't just set him free, Najib. I gave him back the Kingdom of Avadh, *and* I promised not to send him to the Deccan.

NAJIB:   We are helpless if Your Majesty insists on . . . (*Stops.*)

STEP-MOTHER:   Why, Muhammad? Why did he deserve such special treatment?

MUHAMMAD:   I'll tell you what happened. You remember the chess problem I solved the other day? Well, when they brought Ain-ul-Mulk before me, I said: 'Look, I have solved the famous problem set by al-Adli!' He didn't say a word. I drew a sketch on the floor and showed him the solution. He said he liked it, then looked harder for a couple of minutes and said: 'No, there's a flaw here'. And he actually showed me where I had gone wrong! Think of that! I had spent days on that wretched problem and he spots a flaw within half a minute. I had to forgive him.

BARANI:   You are a great man, Your Majesty, . . .

MUHAMMAD:   (*Laughing.*) And you are a good man, Barani, and that's more important. Look at Najib—look at the expression on his face! He can't even believe I can be generous.

NAJIB:   I am suspicious by nature, Your Majesty; fortunately my duty also demands it of me.

MUHAMMAD:   We must go now. Najib, Delhi will observe a day of mourning tomorrow for Sheikh Imam-ud-din. And there will be no festivities to celebrate the victory. When men like him die, it's a sin to be alive. Come, Mother. Good-bye, Shibah-ud-din and many, many thanks.
>    (*All except Shihab-ud-Din and Ratansingh go. A brief silence.*)

RATANSINGH:   I have never seen an honest scoundrel like your

Sultan. He murders a man calmly and then actually enjoys the feeling of guilt.

SHIHAB-UD-DIN:   What are you talking about?

RATANSINGH:   I'm silent!

SHIHAB-UD-DIN:   I'm sorry. But you have never liked the Sultan, I don't know why. After all that he has done for the Hindus—

RATANSINGH:   Yes indeed, who can deny that! He is impartial! Haven't you heard about the Doab? He levied such taxes on the poor farmers that they preferred to starve. Now there's a famine there. And of course Hindus as well as Muslims are dying with absolute impartiality.

SHIHAB-UD-DIN:   What's that got to do with Sheikh Imam-ud-din?

RATANSINGH:   I don't know. But I tell you I'm glad to escape the Sultan's impartiality and be alive.

SHIHAB-UD-DIN:   Must you spin riddles?

RATANSINGH:   And do you really want to know the truth? All right. Because you insisted, I went to fight alongside the Sultan. I went and saw him in Kanauj. He didn't seem too pleased to see me. He actually scowled. A Sultan's scowl is a terrible thing.

SHIHAB-UD-DIN:   So?

RATANSINGH:   Next day I see what the scowl is doing. Sheikh Imam-ud-din is to go and propose peace to Ain-ul-Mulk. A platoon of soldiers is to accompany him. And I am placed in the front rank of the platoon. You know what that means. The front rank never survives a battle.

SHIHAB-UD-DIN:   Go on.

RATANSINGH:   The Sheikh is delighted about being the Sultan's peace emissary. He looks gorgeous—all dressed up in royal robes, a royal turban, even royal slippers, and sitting on the royal elephant. In fact, he looks exactly like the Sultan.

SHIHAB-UD-DIN:   (*Suspicious.*) And the Sultan? What was he doing?

RATANSINGH:   I didn't know it then, but he was hiding behind some hills with the rest of the army. Laying a trap.

SHIHAB-UD-DIN:   A trap?

RATANSINGH:   So we marched towards Ain-ul-Mulk's army, led by the gorgeous Sheikh on the royal elephant. The elephant halted about a hundred yards away from the enemy. The Sheikh stood up on it and tried to say something when a trumpeter on

our side sounded the charge! The battle was on—yes, my dear
Shihab, Ain-ul-Mulk didn't start the battle. We did!

SHIHAB-UD-DIN:   And the Sultan?

RATANSINGH:   I couldn't understand what was happening. Neither
did the Sheikh, obviously. His face was twisted with fear but
he was shouting at the top of his voice asking us to stop. He
didn't stand a chance. Arrows poured into him and within
minutes he looked a gory human porcupine.

SHIHAB-UD-DIN:   And the Sultan? Didn't he do anything?

RATANSINGH:   He did! The Sheikh plunged down from the elephant and over his corpse we fled in confusion. The enemy was
convinced the Sultan was dead and they pursued us. They
walked right into the trap. It was the bloodiest massacre I've
ever seen . . . We won! (*Pause.*) Sheikh Imam-ud-din was
murdered, you know. In cold blood.

SHIHAB-UD-DIN:   Oh my God!

RATANSINGH:   This isn't all. There's a longer history to all this.
(*Pause.*) Do you want to hear it? (*Pause.*) Listen, in a few days
the nobles of the court and the important citizens of Delhi are
going to hold a secret meeting to discuss . . . (*Stops.*)

SHIHAB-UD-DIN:   What?

RATANSINGH:   How should I know? I haven't attended the meeting
yet.

SHIHAB-UD-DIN:   How do you know about it?

RATANSINGH:   Ah! That's Delhi for you! They were looking for
recruits and the moment they realized the Sultan had tried to
kill me off, they discreetly approached me and invited me. They
have asked you too, incidentally. They hope you won't be too
apathetic toward the attempted murder of your adopted brother!

   (*Silence.*)

I have accepted the invitation, of course. Would you like to
come along too?

   (*Silence.*)

Why, Shihab, you look pale!

# Scene Five

*A house in Delhi. A collection of Amirs, Sayyids, etc. Shihab-ud-Din and Ratansingh.*

SHIHAB-UD-DIN:  I'll be plain with you. If you don't like the present administration, that's your problem. I'm an outsider in Delhi. I've nothing to do with it.

AMIR I:  But that's the whole point, don't you see? You're the only man he won't suspect.

SHIHAB-UD-DIN:  I hope that's not a point against him.

AMIR II:  Besides, the people in Delhi never trust each other. It's the climate. They have to have an outsider to lead them!

SHIHAB-UD-DIN:  Lead them in what?

AMIR I:  Just consider this. Why is he taking us to Daulatabad? Have you wondered about that? I'll tell you. He wants to weaken the Amirs. You see, we are strong in Delhi. This is where we belong. But Daulatabad is a Hindu city and we'll be helpless there. We'll have to lick his feet.

AMIR III:  And it's no use his saying stay behind if you like. We have to be in the capital!

AMIR II:  Look at what's happening in Delhi. Just look at it! You can't take a step without paying some tax or another. There's even a tax on gambling. How are we to live? You can't even cheat without having to pay tax for it.

SHIHAB-UD-DIN:  But he has done a lot of good work. Built schools, roads, hospitals. He has made good use of the money.

SAYYID:  Then why can't he get it the right way? The Koran sanctions only four taxes, but . . . (*Looks at* RATANSINGH *and stops.*)

RATANSINGH:  (*Smiles.*) Carry on, sir. Don't mind me. I'm here because Shihab's here; otherwise I am invisible!

SAYYID:  Well . . . uhm, he could tax the Hindus. The jiziya is sanctioned by the Koran. All infidels should pay it. Instead he says the infidels are our brothers . . .

SHIHAB-UD-DIN:  (*Getting up in disgust.*) Come, Ratansingh, let's go.

This is worse than I thought. They don't deserve to kiss the hem of the Sultan's dress.

(*The others are offended and retreat.*)

RATANSINGH: Ah, well . . .

(*Gets up. At this point an old man who has been sitting in a corner all along steps forward.*)

SHEIKH: Shihab-ud-din—

SHIHAB-UD-DIN: I said I am not going to associate . . .

SHEIKH: Shihab-ud-din, I have never asked anything of anyone but Allah. Today I implore you. In the name of Allah, help us.

SHIHAB-UD-DIN: (*Impressed by the old man's age and sincerity.*) Who are you?

SAYYID: (*Contemptuously.*) Don't you know? He is Sheikh Shams-ud-din Tajuddarfim?

SHIHAB-UD-DIN: Sheikh Shams-ud-din? Sir, what is a holy man like you doing in this company?

SHEIKH: Yes, you are right. I should shut myself up in a mosque and devote myself to Allah. I shouldn't get mixed up in the treacherous games of politicians. I know and I had hoped my life would be like that. But Allah isn't only for me, Shihab-ud-din; He's for everyone who believes in him. While tyranny crushes the faithful into dust, how can I continue to hide in my hole? Haven't you heard what's happening to the leaders of Islam today? Sheikh Haidari is in prison. Sheikh Hood in exile . . .

SHIHAB-UD-DIN: I know. But they dabbled in politics.

SHEIKH: Is it so reprehensible to worry about people? Is it a crime to speak out for oneself and one's family? What politics did Sheikh Imam-ud-din indulge in? That he was open, frank and honest?

SHIHAB-UD-DIN: I don't know enough about that. But, to me it seems clear that if the Sultan is to be blamed for that death, so are all the citizens of Delhi. I sometimes feel the Sheikh must have almost wished for death after what happened in Delhi.

AMIR I: What did happen in Delhi?

SHIHAB-UD-DIN: You know that better than me! He came here to speak to the people and not a soul turned up to hear him. Not one of you had the courage to come to the meeting . . . and now you have the cheek to blame the Sultan for his death.

(*The others whisper and chuckle in derision.*)

SHEIKH:   So you don't know what actually happened behind the scenes?

SHIHAB-UD-DIN:   Behind the scenes?

(*More derisive laughter.*)

SHEIKH:   Yes, behind the scenes. It's true the Sultan invited the whole of Delhi to hear the Sheikh. Yet, on that very afternoon, soldiers went from door to door threatening dire consequences if anyone dared to attend the meeting.

(*Silence.*)

SHIHAB-UD-DIN:   (*Slowly.*) Does the Sultan know this?

(*More laughter.*)

SHEIKH:   They were his orders! And do you know, while the Sultan stood in front of the Great Mosque with the Sheikh and got more and more agitated at the empty auditorium, his soldiers were hiding in the streets around stopping those who tried to come? You don't believe it? Look here . . .

(*Unbuttons his shirt and shows a wound on his shoulder.*)

I tried to force my way to the Big Mosque and this is what I got for it. Who else would do this to an old man like me?

RATANSINGH:   There, you see! That explains why he had to invite you from Sampanshahr to look after Delhi in his absence. There's confidence for you!

SHIHAB-UD-DIN:   (*Doggedly.*) Perhaps. But it's done me no harm.

RATANSINGH:   Of course not. Had he meant to harm you, you wouldn't be here to talk about it!

SHEIKH:   Will you only think about yourself, Shihab-ud-din? You are the strong, the powerful in this country. You have the capacity to set things right. Won't you worry a little about the people? The citizens of Delhi don't wish to go to Daulatabad, but they are weak. Will you do nothing for them? How many people like Sheikh Imam-ud-din have to die before you'll be ready to act?

(*No reply.*)

AMIR I:   We have to act now—while the army here is still tired and disorganized. We have to do something while you're here. If you won't join us, will you at least promise not to fight against us?

SHIHAB-UD-DIN:   I know too much now to remain neutral.

RATANSINGH:    (*With a sudden burst of anger.*) Then why not join them? Even my infidel blood boils when I think of Sheikh Imam-ud-din and Sheikh Shams-ud-din here. You accuse the people of Delhi of cowardice and yet you won't raise a finger to correct an obvious wrong. (*Gets up.*) Come, let's go to the palace.

The problem of justice won't bother us there.

AMIR I:    You must help us, Shihab-ud-din.

SHEIKH:    Islam needs your help.

SHIHAB-UD-DIN:    What do you want me to do? You don't need me. You need my father. He is the strong man and even the Sultan is afraid of him. But you're in a hurry. I can only swell your numbers—little else.

RATANSINGH:    Don't be stupid, Shihab. Don't tell me you still think the Amirs want to fight the Sultan in the open.

     (*Shihab-ud-din looks up at him sharply. Ratansingh smiles and turns to the rest.*)

You see what it is. Shihab is a clever young man but he's just too nice! You see his father . . .

SHIHAB-UD-DIN:    Don't, Ratansingh . . .

RATANSINGH:    Come on, every one knows about it! His father is supposed to have killed my father by treachery and usurped the kingdom. Shihab can't forget that. He wants to make up for it. That's why I'm here, as his adopted brother. And that's why he just can't stand the mention of treachery. (*To Shihab-ud-Din.*) Don't overdo it. You'll have to face it some day. After all, what did the Sultan do to Sheikh Imam-ud-din?

SAYYID:    It's not going to be easy. We can't afford to make mistakes.

AMIR II:    I know. I have been trying to think of some way. But it just gives me a headache.

     (*A long silence.*)

RATANSINGH:    I have a plan. It's perfect.

SHIHAB-UD-DIN:    Yes?

RATANSINGH:    Yes. The Sultan, as you know, is a fanatic about prayer. He has made it compulsory for every Muslim to pray five times a day.

SAYYID:    That's his only saving grace.

RATANSINGH:    Quite! Even the soldiers have to pray, and while

they pray they are not allowed to carry arms. Which means that
at the time of prayers, the whole palace is unarmed.
      (*Long pause.*)
AMIR II:   It takes a Hindu to notice that! (*Half terrified by the simplicity
      of it all.*) So?
RATANSINGH:   Next Tuesday the Amirs here will be seeing the
      Sultan for the Durbar-i-Khas. See that you prolong the meeting
      till the prayer hour. Pray with him. You'll only need an extra
      couple of hundred soldiers outside the palace. The muezzin's
      call to prayer will be the signal of attack!
      (*There is an uncomfortable silence.*)
AMIR II:   (*Quietly.*) Fantastic!
SAYYID:   But kill some one during prayer . . .
AMIR I:   And a Muslim too . . .
RATANSINGH:   Where's your Holy Koran? The tyrant doesn't
      deserve to be considered among the faithful. And then, he killed
      his own father during prayer time, after all.
AMIR I:   That's true. But . . .
RATANSINGH:   That's my plan. Think of a better one if you can.
AMIR I:   But we'll have to smuggle arms into the palace.
AMIR II:   That can be arranged.
AMIR I:   You are sure?
AMIR II:   Of course, I'm sure. I think this is a brilliant plan.
AMIR III:   It is simple.
      (*They all talk animatedly.*)
SHEIKH:   No, we can't have it!
      (*Sudden silence as they all turn to Sheikh Shams-ud-Din.*)
SHIHAB-UD-DIN:   Why, pray?
SHEIKH:   You can't pollute the time of prayer. It's a sacred time.
      We can't stain it with the blood of a Mussulman.
AMIR II:   O come, we can always make up later. Do penance for
      it.
SHEIKH:   But prayer isn't penance. Remember we are here to save
      Islam, not to insult it.
AMIR I:   Don't get excited. Islam will benefit in the long run.
SHEIKH:   (*To Shihab-ud-Din, pleading.*) You can't agree to this,
      Shihab-ud-din. You are the only sensible person here. You can't
      agree to this sacrilege. You can't do this to Islam . . .
SHIHAB-UD-DIN:   Does your Islam work only at prayer? You have

persuaded me to do what I had sworn never to do —*you*, Your Holiness. I'm sure the Lord will not mind an interrupted prayer. (*To the others.*) All right, let's get down to the details. We have to work everything out carefully. (*Suddenly.*) Must we do this, Ratan? Must we?

# Scene Six

*The palace. Muhammad, Najib and Barani. Silence for a while. Muhammad is restless and paces up and down.*

BARANI:   Why are you both so quiet?

NAJIB:   Oh, shut up!

MUHAMMAD:   Please, Najib.

*(Silence again. The Door-Keeper enters.)*

DOOR-KEEPER:   In the name of Allah. The Amirs have come for the Durbar-i-Khas.

MUHAMMAD:   Send them in.

*(The Door-Keeper goes out. Barani and Najib stand up. The Amirs enter along with Shihab-ud-Din. They greet each other.)*

AMIR I:   In the name of Allah.

*(Najib smiles to himself.)*

MUHAMMAD:   *(With obvious warmth.)* Come in, come in. Please take your seats. I am glad you have all come on time. I want to finish the Durbar-i-Khas as soon as possible. I have promised the Imam I'll be at the mosque for today's prayer. That doesn't give us much time, I'm afraid. Are there any special problems any of you wish to raise?

*(No reply.)*

Excellent! I have only two topics myself. Not much to discuss there, but naturally I want to inform the Durbar-i-Khas before announcing to the public. First, I am very happy to inform you that Abbasid Ghiyas-ud-din Muhammad has accepted my invitation to visit our capital.

*(Silence.)*

AMIR I:   Who is he, Your Majesty?

AMIR II:   I am afraid I have never heard of that name . . .

MUHAMMAD:   Well, that's nothing to be ashamed of. Abbasid Ghiyas-ud-din Muhammad is not exactly famous. He is a member of the hallowed family of the Abbasid Khalifs.

*(Silence while the Amirs digest this bit of news which obviously makes no sense to them.)*

BARANI:   It's good news that a descendant of the last Khalif is visiting us, Your Majesty.

SHIHAB-UD-DIN:   May I compliment His Majesty on his wisdom?

MUHAMMAD:   Wisdom? What a strange word to use. Why wisdom? A visit by the descendant of the Khalif could show how faithful I am or how religious I am or even perhaps how modest. But why do you say 'wisdom'? Do you think I am inviting him to placate the stupid priests?

SHIHAB-UD-DIN:   I didn't mean to . . .

MUHAMMAD:   You know, since Sheikh Imam-ud-din died I have been asking myself just one question. I am a king. I wear the royal robes. I have honoured myself with the title of Sultan. But what gives me the right to call myself a King?
       (*The Amirs are baffled.*)
    Am I a king only because I am the son of a king? Or is it because I can make the people accept my laws and the army move to my commands? Or can self-confidence alone justify it? I ask you—all of you—what would you have me do to become a real king in your eyes?
       (*Silence.*)

NAJIB:   (*Disapproving.*) Your Majesty—

MUHAMMAD:   You are all silent. The others only tell me what I should not do but not what I should. Until I know what else to do, Shihab-ud-din, I have to go on clutching the sceptre in my fist. But I am not happy and I am turning to tradition and history now and seeking an answer there—in the blessings of the Abbasid Khalif.

AMIR I:   The sins of Delhi will be washed clean by the visit of so great a man.

MUHAMMAD:   You bring tears to my eyes. But the great man isn't coming to Delhi. We shall be in Daulatabad by then.

SHIHAB-UD-DIN:   I implore Your Majesty not to move the capital to Daulatabad. I am not from Delhi myself and have no stake in it. But I know the people of Delhi are very unhappy about the move. I have seen—

MUHAMMAD:   What am I to do, Shihab-ud-din? I have explained every reason to them, shown how my empire cannot flourish with Delhi as its capital. But how can I explain tomorrow to those who haven't even opened their eyes to the light of today?

Let's not waste more time over that. They'll see the point soon. It's getting late and I must tell you the more important news. From next year, we shall have copper currency in our empire along with the silver dinars.

AMIR I: Whatever for? I mean what does one do with a copper coin?

MUHAMMAD: Exchange it for a silver coin! A copper coin will have the same value as a silver dinar.

SHIHAB-UD-DIN: But I don't understand, Your Majesty. How can one accept a copper coin to have the same value as a silver one?

MUHAMMAD: It's a question of confidence. A question of trust! The other day I heard that in China they have paper currency— paper, mind you—and yet it works because the people accept it. They have faith in the Emperor's seal on the pieces of paper.

AMIR I: (*Whispers to the next man.*) I told you he's mad!

MUHAMMAD: What was that?

AMIR I: I was just saying people here won't accept copper currency.

MUHAMMAD: Then why not say it aloud? Because people are afraid, will you mistrust me too? Laugh at me if you like, criticize me, but please don't distrust me. I can order you all to obey me but tell me, how do I gain your full trust? I can only beg for it. (*Pleading.*) I have hopes of building a new future for India and I need your support for that. If you don't understand me, ask me to explain myself and I'll do it. If you don't understand my explanations, bear with me in patience until I can show you the results. But please don't let me down, I beg you. I'll kneel before you if you wish but please don't let go of my hand.

(*He kneels before them. The Amirs almost recoil at this sudden gesture.*)

SHIHAB-UD-DIN: (*Embarrassed.*) But, Your Majesty, it's not for a king to beg. He must command. We are your ever-willing servants.

MUHAMMAD: Is this your voice alone, Shihab-ud-din, or do the rest of the Amirs agree with you?

AMIRS: Of course we all do—no question of it—Your Majesty should trust us . . .

MUHAMMAD: Thank you!

(*Gets up, walks up to the throne, picks up a copy of the Koran lying on it.*)

Will you all then take an oath on the Koran to support me in
my measures?
>    (*A long tense silence.*)
SHIHAB-UD-DIN:    Does His Majesty distrust us so much that he needs
an oath on the Koran from us?
>    (*Muhammad turns to him in a sudden burst of rage, then controls
>    himself and replaces the Koran on the throne. Silence again. The
>    Door-Keeper enters.*)
DOOR-KEEPER:    In the name of Allah. It's the hour of prayer, Your
Majesty.
>    (*Muhammad stands silent for a while. The atmosphere is very tense.*)
MUHAMMAD:    (*Very slowly.*) We'll all pray here.
>    (*The Door-Keeper bows and exits. At the same moment, the
>    Muezzin's voice is heard calling the faithful to the prayer.*)
MUEZZIN:    (*Off-stage.*) Alla-Ho-Akbar! Alla-Ho-Akbar!
Alla-Ho-Akbar! Alla-Ho-Akbar!
Ashahado La Elaha Illilah
Ashahado La Elaha Illilah
Ashahado Anna Muhammadur Rasool Illah
Ashahado Anna Muhammadur Rasool Illah
Haiyah Alis Salaat—Haiyah Alis Salaat
Haiyah Salil Falaa—Haiyah Salil Falaa
Alla-Ho-Akbar! Alla-Ho-Akbar!
La Elaha Illilah . . .
>    (*As soon as the Muezzin's call begins, Muhammad unbuckles his
>    sword and places it on the throne. About a dozen servants enter
>    with pots of water, in which those on the stage wash their hands,
>    faces, heads and feet. Another servant brings about a dozen mats
>    on a plank and takes them round. Each person picks up a mat and
>    spreads it facing west. They start praying. Muhammad leads the
>    prayer. Half-way through the prayer a commotion is heard off-stage.
>    Taking that as a cue, Shihab-ud-Din and the Amirs get up and
>    pull out their daggers.*)
BARANI:    (*Frightened.*) What's this? What's this?
>    (*The Amirs step towards the throne, near which Muhammad is
>    praying. Suddenly from behind the curtain near the throne about
>    twenty Hindu soldiers rush in with spears and surround the Amirs.
>    One or two Amirs try to run out but the soldiers bar their way.
>    The Amirs stand frozen in fear, then slowly throw down their*

*daggers. The soldiers drag them away—all except Shihab-ud-Din.*
*While all this is going on, Muhammad goes on praying unconcerned.*
*Only after finishing the prayer does he step down from the throne.*
*Every one is silent for a while.*)

SHIHAB-UD-DIN:  How did you guess?

MUHAMMAD:  Do you really want to know?

SHIHAB-UD-DIN:  You aren't worried about hurting my feelings, are
you?

MUHAMMAD:  There was a letter in my letter-room today. A strange
letter—strange because, unlike all the others, it didn't abuse me
and it was signed. (*Pause.*)
By Ratansingh.

SHIHAB-UD-DIN:  (*Smiles.*) Do you really think I'll believe that? It's
the oldest trick in the world.

MUHAMMAD:  Why should I lie to a dead man?
(*Takes out the letter from his robe and holds it before Shihab-ud-*
*Din. Shihab-ud-Din looks crushed and frightened.*)

SHIHAB-UD-DIN:  (*Almost to himself.*) But does he say why he is doing
this to me?

NAJIB:  He has disappeared—without a trace!

MUHAMMAD:  Let me ask you something. Why did you go against
me? What wrong have I done you?

SHIHAB-UD-DIN:  What's the point? You won't understand it anyway.

MUHAMMAD:  Won't I? Or could it be that you don't know?

SHIHAB-UD-DIN:  (*Suddenly violent.*) Get on with your killing, Muhammad. Or does your hand refuse to rise against me? Beware!
You won't be able to trap me with your wiles. I am not
Ain-ul-Mulk to live crushed under your kindness.
(*Muhammad slowly takes out his dagger. Shihab-ud-Din is getting*
*more and more frightened. He is almost screaming now as he speaks.*)
You want to solve all problems in the flash of a dagger, don't
you? But you can't stop this uprising now. My father distrusts
you and I've already written to him, about everything here
. . . everything . . .

NAJIB:  Sorry, but Ratansingh has sent those letters to us.

SHIHAB-UD-DIN:  (*Screaming.*) Where will you hide my corpse? How
will you gag my voice? Kill me—but you won't stop this—this
will go on—

MUHAMMAD:   I could have killed you with a word. But I like you
    too much.
    (*Stabs him. Then almost frenzied, goes on stabbing him. Hits out
    at Shihab-ud-Din's dead body with a ferocity that makes even the
    soldiers holding the body turn away in horror.*)
BARANI:   Your Majesty—he's dead!
    (*Muhammad stops, then flings the dagger away in disgust.*)
MUHAMMAD:   (*Anguished.*) Why must this happen, Barani? Are all
    those I trust condemned to go down in history as traitors? What
    is happening? Tell me, Barani, will my reign be nothing more
    than a tortured scream which will stab the night and melt away
    in the silence?
    (*He is trembling all over. At a sign from Najib, the soldiers lay the
    body down on a mat and go away. Muhammad stares at the body.*)
    Najib, see that every man involved in this is caught and
    beheaded. Stuff their bodies with straw and hang them up in
    the palace-yard. Let them hang there for a week. No, send them
    round my kingdom. Let every one of my subjects see them. Let
    every one see what . . . (*Chokes.*)
BARANI:   What will that achieve, Your Majesty? What's the use?
    (*Pause.*)
NAJIB:   We must do something about Shihab-ud-din's father. He
    is a powerful man and he won't like this.
MUHAMMAD:   (*Regaining control of himself.*) Don't worry about him.
    Make a public announcement that there was a rebellion in the
    palace and that the nobles of the court tried to assassinate the
    Sultan during prayer. Say that the Sultan was saved by Shihab-
    ud-din who died a martyr's death defending him. The funeral
    will be held in Delhi and will be a grand affair. Invite his father
    to it and see that he is treated with the respect due to the father
    of a loyal nobleman.
BARANI:   Oh God! Aren't even the dead free from your politics?
NAJIB:   Your Majesty, if this incident is to be kept a secret, I'm
    afraid we'll have to hang everyone who was here—even the
    Hindu guards. They remained loyal to Your Majesty but they
    have seen it all and are bound to talk. It does mean more corpses.
    But then that'll only make the show more impressive.
MUHAMMAD:   Najib, I want Delhi vacated immediately. Every
    living soul in Delhi will leave for Daulatabad within a fortnight.

I was too soft, I can see that now. They'll only understand the whip. Everyone must leave. Not a light should be seen in the windows of Delhi. Not a wisp of smoke should rise from its chimneys. Nothing but an empty graveyard of Delhi will satisfy me now.

BARANI:			May Heaven protect us!

MUHAMMAD:			Call on Heaven while you can, Barani—you may not get another chance. What hopes I had built up when I came to the throne! I had wanted every act in my kingdom to become a prayer, every prayer to become a further step in knowledge, every step to lead us nearer to God. But our prayers too are ridden with disease, and must be exiled. There will be no more praying in the kingdom, Najib. Anyone caught praying will be severely punished. Henceforth let the moment of prayer walk my streets in silence and leave without a trace.

NAJIB:			But that would only be playing into the hands of the Ulema, Your Majesty. I suggest we say there'll be no more prayers till Ghiyas-ud-din Abbasid, the descendant of the Khalif, visits us. God alone knows when he'll come. Besides, it'll make such a beautiful little paradox!

			(*Muhammad does not reply. Najib goes out. Barani sobs. Muhammad stands staring at Shihab-ud-Din's corpse. Barani gets up, takes the silken cloth from the throne and starts spreading it on the corpse. But Muhammad casts the cloth aside.*)

MUHAMMAD:			Don't cover him, Barani. I want my people to see his wounds.

ANNOUNCER: Attention! Attention! The Merciful Sultan Muhammad has declared—that within the next month every citizen of Delhi must leave for Daulatabad. No one should remain behind in Delhi. Anyone who attempts to stay behind or to go elsewhere will be severely punished. All arrangements have been made to ensure the comfort of citizens on the way to Daulatabad. All the needs of the citizens, regarding food, clothing or medicine, will be catered to by the State. It is hoped that every citizen will use these amenities to the full and be in Daulatabad as soon as possible. Attention! Attention!

# Scene Seven

*A Camp on the Delhi-Daulatabad route. Aziz still dressed as a Brahmin, and Aazam. A Hindu Woman is kneeling in front of Aziz.*

HINDU WOMAN: Please let me go, sir . . . My child . . . please have mercy on it . . . only for a day, sir . . .

AZIZ: I told you I can't. No one can be allowed out of sight until we reach Daulatabad. I'm sorry, but I have my orders.

HINDU WOMAN: But I'll return tomorrow . . . I swear by my child I will . . . It's dying, Your Excellency, I have to take it to a doctor . . .

AZIZ: But what can I do? There's the hakim's tent. Go to him. He'll give you some medicine. (*In a low voice.*) I've told you what you can do. I could try and bribe my senior officials, but you'll have to pay for it.

HINDU WOMAN: But I haven't got a paisa on me, Your Excellency. And what will I give the doctor? My husband's also ill, sir, please, I hold your feet—please let me go.

AZIZ: I can't waste any more time on you. There's a lot of work here. Stop screaming and get back to your tent—I said, get back to your tent!

(*The Hindu Woman goes out weeping.*)

AAZAM: Poor thing! Why don't you let her go? The doctor may help her.

AZIZ: Have you seen the child? No witch-doctor can save it now. My niece had that illness and went out like a light. It's a waste of good money and she's going to need every paisa of it. I'm doing her a favour! And watch out for paise, Aazam; they're going to cost a lot soon.

(*Footsteps are heard off-stage. Aziz buries his head into his books. A family comes in. A man with a woman and six kids. They come and stand. Aziz continues to read. Aazam, embarrassed, wanders around without looking at them. The family waits patiently.*)

Three more families! They must be walking on their knees. (*Looks up and stares at the man.*) So you've come at last, have

you? Perhaps you went to visit your in-laws on the way. Don't
you know the orders? You were supposed to be here well before
sunset.

MAN:   What was I to do, Your Excellency? There were two corpses
there on the road. Poor things! They must have walked till their
hearts gave out. I thought, sinner that I am, I would at least
give them a decent burial, Your Excellency.

AAZAM:   Poor souls. From which camp were they, do you think?

AZIZ:   I hope you checked whether they were Muslims before
burying them.

MAN:   Who's to do all that, Your Excellency? I did what I could.

AZIZ:   And what if they were Hindus, pray? You know they don't
bury their dead. You'll be in trouble if some one finds out.
Actually I ought to send you back to dig them up again. It's
against the orders to insult or cause harm to Hinduism—

MAN:   I just didn't think of it, Your Excellency. Sinner that I am,
I thought I would lighten the burden of my sins by giving them
a resting place.

AZIZ:   Leave the corpses alone in future. What did you do in Delhi,
sinner that you are?

MAN:   I am a Kafir, Your Excellency. I have to guard the dead
bodies in the palace yard—those executed by the Sultan, you
know. I have to guard them for a week, ten at a time, sir, and
then carry them to the canal outside the city. There again I have
to guard them against thieves.

AAZAM:   Thieves? Ugh!

MAN:   Isn't it terrible, Your Excellency? But there it is. That's what
men have come to. The relatives of the dead have to pay us a
fine before taking the bodies. Well, if the orders had been
obeyed I would have built a house by now. But no, they won't
pay—even for the dead! They come at night and steal them.
Not just the poor. Even the rich folk—the most respectable
people of Delhi! I could tell you a name or two and you
wouldn't believe it. It is terrible. People won't stop at anything
once they get into the habit of thieving, that's certain.

   (*Aziz looks at Aazam and laughs. Aazam grimaces.*)

AZIZ:   So this is your family. All eight here?

MAN:   Yes, Sir.

AZIZ:   Get on with you there. There's a tent kept for you. Yes!

Whatever happens to the others, people like you mustn't die.
The Sultan will need a lot more like you soon. So what are you
going to do till the Sultan arrives in Daulatabad? Another couple
of children?

MAN:  Well, we have decided to get married first, Your Excellency.

AAZAM:  (*In disgust.*) Oh God!

MAN:  (*Apologetic.*) Couldn't find time for it in Delhi, sir.

AAZAM:  Go away. Go away!

(*The family goes off.*)
God, what a dirty man! I am feeling sick.

AZIZ:  I like such people. They are the real stoics.

AAZAM:  I just keep thinking of that poor woman. Why don't you
let her see the doctor? I'm sure she'll come back. Look, if you
want money, tell me. There are enough rich men in this camp.
I'll get some in to time.

AZIZ:  Don't you do anything of the kind! You'll ruin us both if
they catch you.

AAZAM:  We'll be ruined anyway ultimately. If not today, then
tomorrow. What other future's there for us? One day my fingers
will slow down. I'll get caught. Then, no arms! No legs! A torn
mat and a begging bowl, that's all.

AZIZ:  You are a hopeless case, you know. Pathetic! You've been
in Delhi for so many years and you're as stupid as ever. Look
at me. Only a few months in Delhi and I have discovered a
whole new world—politics! My dear fellow, that's where our
future is—politics! It's a beautiful world—wealth, success, position, power—and yet it's full of brainless people, people with
not an idea in their head. When I think of all the tricks I used
in our village to pinch a few torn clothes from people—if one
uses half that intelligence here, one can get robes of power. And
not have to pinch them either—get them! It's a fantastic world!

(*The Hindu Woman is heard wailing.*)

AAZAM:  That's that Hindu woman. Her child's dead. She'll complain against you now. If you go on like this, Aziz, we'll soon
keep the Kafir company in Daulatabad.

AZIZ:  Don't call me Aziz. I've told you. As for her, I've only
obeyed my orders. Besides I'm a Brahmin and she won't
complain against a Brahmin to a Muslim officer. That'll send
her straight to hell. In any case—and listen to this carefully—we

won't stay in the Sultan's service for long. I heard some rumours in Delhi. The Sultan's going to introduce copper coins soon. And a copper coin will have the same value as a silver dinar. What do you say to that?

AAZAM: (*Making a face.*) Eyah! There's no fun in stealing copper coins.

AZIZ: Shut up! Just listen to what I'm telling you—you are not going to pinch any coins, you are going to make them. Make counterfeit coins, you understand? If your fingers are getting restless, use them there. (*Noise off-stage.*) Ha! There's the next lot!

(*Buries his head in his books.*)

# Scene Eight

AD 1332. Five years later

*The fort at Daulatabad. Two watchmen—one young, the other past his middle-age. Night.*

YOUNG MAN:   What time do you think it is, grandfather?

OLD MAN:   Must be just past midnight.

YOUNG MAN:   Only that? Good God! When I was in the army, less than two seconds seemed to divide the lamp-lighting hour from the daybreak. Now the night scarcely moves.

OLD MAN:   It's only when you wait for the morning that the night stands still. A good sentry must forget that morning even exists.

YOUNG MAN:   (*Looking down the side of the fort.*) What a fantastic fort! I have a good head but even my head goes round when I look down. And isn't that long white thing the road from Daulatabad to Delhi?

OLD MAN:   Yes.

YOUNG MAN:   They say it's the widest road in the world. But it looks no bigger than a thin snake from here.

OLD MAN:   And four years ago that snake bit a whole city to death.

YOUNG MAN:   What a fort! What a magnificent thing! I met a foreign visitor the other day and he said he has been round the world and not seen any fort as strong as this anywhere. No army could take this.

OLD MAN:   No, if this fort ever falls, it will crumble from the inside.

YOUNG MAN:   You don't love this fort very much, do you, grandfather?

OLD MAN:   I am a man of the plains, son. I find it hard to breathe in this eagle nest.

YOUNG MAN:   You are from Delhi?

OLD MAN:   Yes.

YOUNG MAN:   Was it hard, coming from Delhi to here?

OLD MAN:   I survived. But my family was more fortunate. They all died on the way.

YOUNG MAN: (*Sympathetically.*) I am sorry. The arrangements must have been very bad.

OLD MAN: Oh no. The merciful Sultan had made perfect arrangements. But do you know, you can love a city like a woman? My old father had lived in Delhi all his life. He died of a broken heart. Then my son Ismail. He was six years old—would have been ten now! The fine dust that hung in the air, fine as silk, it covered him like a silken shroud. After him, his mother.

(*Silence. The Young Man is embarrassed.*)

YOUNG MAN: Tell me more about this fort, grandfather. Is it true there is a strange and frightening passage within this fort? Dark, they say, like the new moon night.

OLD MAN: Yes, it's a long passage, a big passage, coiled like an enormous hollow python inside the belly of the fort. And we shall be far, far happier when that python breaks out and swallows everything in sight—every man, woman, child, and beast.

(*Footsteps off-stage.*)

YOUNG MAN: (*Raising his spear.*) Who is that?

MUHAMMAD: Muhammad.

YOUNG MAN: Muhammad? What Muhammad?

OLD MAN: Shut up, fool. It's the Sultan.

(*Muhammad walks in—almost in a trance.*)

BOTH: In the name of Allah!

MUHAMMAD: (*To the old man.*) Go and tell Barani I want to see him.

(*The Old Man bows and retires.*)

YOUNG MAN: I beg your Majesty's pardon for my impertinence. I didn't realize . . .

MUHAMMAD: Don't worry. You were doing your duty.

(*Goes to the edge of the wall and looks down.*)

YOUNG MAN: Your Majesty must forgive my impudence, but I beg Your Majesty not to go too near the edge of the fort. It's a very steep fall.

MUHAMMAD: (*Smiles.*) You are new here, aren't you?

YOUNG MAN: Yes, I am, Your Majesty. I was in the army all these years. They sent me here yesterday. I am very sorry if I've said anything wrong, Your Majesty.

MUHAMMAD: Don't apologize at every word. If you stay here long

enough you'll anyway learn to ooze spittle before everyone. Be
yourself at least until then. How old are you?

YOUNG MAN:   Nineteen, Your Majesty.

MUHAMMAD:   Nineteen. Nice age! An age when you think you
can clasp the whole world in your palm like a rare diamond. I
was twenty-one when I came to Daulatabad first, and built this
fort. I supervised the placing of every brick in it and I said to
myself, one day I shall build my own history like this, brick by
brick.

One night I was standing on the ramparts of the old fort
here. There was a torch near me flapping its wild wings and
scattering golden feathers on everything in sight. There was a
half-built gate nearby trying to contain the sky within its cleft.
Suddenly something happened—as though some one had cast
a spell. The torch, the gate, the fort and the sky—all melted
and merged and flowed in my blood-stream with the darkness
of the night. The moment shed its symbols, its questions and
answers, and stood naked and calm where the stars throbbed in
my veins. I was the earth, was the grass, was the smoke, was
the sky. Suddenly a sentry called from far: 'Attention! Attention!'
And to that challenge the half-burnt torch and the half-built
gate fell apart.

No, young man, I don't envy you your youth. All that you
have to face and suffer is still ahead of you. Look at me. I have
searched for that moment since then and here I am still searching
for it. But in the last four years, I have seen only the woods
clinging to the earth, heard only the howl of wild wolves and
the answering bay of street dogs. Another twenty years and
you'll be as old as me. I might be lying under those woods
there. Do you think you'll remember me then?

(*No answer.*)

Come, why are you silent?

YOUNG MAN:   (*Scared.*) Your Majesty must forgive me, Your Majesty. But I don't understand what Your Majesty is saying.

MUHAMMAD:   (*Incensed.*) You don't understand! You don't understand! Why do you live? Why do you corrupt the air with your
diseased breath? (*Suddenly calm.*) I'm sorry. It's my turn to
apologize. It isn't your fault. You are also one of them.

(*Uncomfortable silence. Barani enters.*)

BARANI:  In the name of Allah. Your Majesty sent for me?
.      (*Muhammad waves the sentries away.*)
MUHAMMAD:  I couldn't bear the walls any more. When I came
here I felt I needed an audience—someone to confess my
self-pity to. You were asleep?
BARANI:  No, Your Majesty. I was reading a book by Imam Abu
Hanifa.
MUHAMMAD:  Fortunate! You can read when you don't feel sleepy.
I can't sleep. I can't read. Even Rumi, who once used to
transport me, has become simply a web of words. Do you know,
five years ago I actually used to pray to God not to send me
any sleep? I can't believe it now.
BARANI:  Why don't you see a hakim, Your Majesty?
MUHAMMAD:  What can a hakim do? You are a historian, Barani,
you are the man to prescribe remedies for this. Have you heard
the latest news? Fakr-ud-din has risen against me in Bengal.
BARANI:  Oh, I'm . . .
MUHAMMAD:  Yes. And there's been another uprising in the Deccan. In Ma'bar Ehsanshah has declared himself independent.
Bahal-ud-din Gashtasp is collecting an army against me. The
drought in Doab is spreading from town to town—burning up
the country. Only one industry flourishes in my kingdom, only
one—and that's of making counterfeit copper coins. Every
Hindu home has become a domestic mint; the traders are just
waiting for me to close my eyes; and in my whole kingdom
there are only two people I can trust—Ain-ul-Mulk and
Shihab-ud-din's father. What should I do, Barani? What would
you prescribe for this honeycomb of diseases? I have tried
everything. But what cures one disease just worsens another.
BARANI:  I am a humble historian, Your Majesty: It's not for me
to prescribe. But since Your Majesty has done me the honour
of confiding in me, may I make a suggestion? It is a difficult
thing to suggest to a king and I beg you to forgive me if it hurts.
But you are a learned man, Your Majesty, you are known the
world over for your knowledge of philosophy and poetry.
History is not made only in statecraft; its lasting results are
produced in the ranks of learned men. That's where you belong,
Your Majesty, in the company of learned men. Not in the
market of corpses.

MUHAMMAD:   You want me to retire from my throne? (*Laughs.*)
   Barani, if you were capable of irony, I would have thought you .
   were laughing at me. But as usual you mean it, which makes it
   harder. I wish it was as easy as that. I have often thought of that
   myself—to give up this futile see-saw struggle and go to Mecca.
   Sit there by the Kaaba and search for the peace which Daulatabad
   hasn't given me. What bliss! But it isn't that easy. It isn't as easy
   as leaving the patient in the wilderness because there's no cure
   for his disease. Don't you see—this patient, racked by fever and
   crazed by the fear of the enveloping vultures, can't be separated
   from me? Don't you see that the only way I can abdicate is by
   killing myself? I could have done something if the vultures
   weren't so close. I could have crawled forward on my knees
   and elbows. But what can you do when every moment you
   expect a beak to dig into you and tear a muscle out? What can
   you do? Barani, what vengeance is driving these shapes after
   me?
BARANI:   Your Majesty . . .
MUHAMMAD:   You know what my beloved subjects call me? Mad
   Muhammad! Mad Muhammad! (*Suddenly pleading.*) How can I
   become wise again, Barani?
BARANI:   Your Majesty, there was a time when you believed in
   love, in peace, in God. What has happened to those ideals? You
   won't let your subjects pray. You torture them for the smallest
   offence. Hang them on suspicion. Why this bloodshed? Please
   stop it, and I promise Your Majesty something better will
   emerge out of it.
MUHAMMAD:   But for that I'll have to admit I've been wrong all
   these years. And I know I haven't. I have something to give,
   something to teach, which may open the eyes of history but I
   have to do it within this life. I've got to make them listen to
   me before I lose even that!
   (*The Old Man comes in running.*)
OLD MAN:   In the name of Allah—a calamity, Your Majesty—the
   Nayab Vizier has sent word—
MUHAMMAD:   What is it?
OLD MAN:   Vizier Muhammad Najib is dead. His body was found
   in his bed. The Nayab Vizier says it is murder . . .

# Scene Nine

*A hide-out in the hills. Aziz and Aazam are stretched out on the floor.*

AAZAM: It's so hot—I'm fed up, I'm fed up of life, I'm fed up of
the whole bloody world.

AZIZ: Why don't you just go and commit suicide?

AAZAM: Tried once. Went and jumped into a well. But the cold
water cheered me up so much that I had a good swim and went
back home. I don't think I could try again.

AZIZ: You'll never learn to do a thing properly.

AAZAM: But how come I steal properly? I have never made a
mistake while stealing. Why am I a thief, Aziz? Why aren't we
like other people? Have a nice home, till a farm and live happily?

AZIZ: How many happy people have you met? Besides, a man must
commit a crime at least once in his life-time. Only then will
his virtue be recognized!

AAZAM: Aw, shut up!

AZIZ: No, truly. Listen. If you remain virtuous throughout your
life no one will say a good thing about you because they won't
need to. But start stealing—and they'll say: 'What a nice boy
he was! But he's ruined now . . . ' Then kill and they will beat
their breasts and say: 'Heavens! He was only a petty thief all
these days. Never hurt anyone. But alas!' Then rape a woman
and the chorus will go into hallelujahs: 'He was a saint, a real
saint and look at him now . . . '

AAZAM: Well, you have robbed and killed. Now all you have to
do to become a saint is rape.

AZIZ: Presently, presently. No hurry. What's the point in raping
for sheer lust? That's a mug's game. First one must have
power—the authority to rape! Then everything takes on meaning.

AAZAM: (*Giggles.*) So you want power, do you? What do you want
to be, a Sultan?

AZIZ: Laugh away, stupid. You'll soon see. It all depends on
whether Karim will bring the goods.

AAZAM: (*Seriously.*) But no, Aziz, why are you so dissatisfied? We have such a nice establishment here. We take enough money from travellers and the other robbers are scared to death of you. There's no limit to what we can make here.

AZIZ: I am bored stiff with all this running and hiding. You rob a man, you run, and hide. It's all so pointless. One should be able to rob a man and then stay there to punish him for getting robbed. That's called 'class'—that's being a real king!

AAZAM: May Allah shower His blessings on Your Majesty! Is there a post for your humble slave at the court?

AZIZ: Oh, yes! You are brainless. So you'll make a good noble-man—an Amir.

AAZAM: (*In disgust.*) Eah! I don't like that. I don't think I could be anything but a common pickpocket. What about a court thief?
(*Aziz bursts into laughter.*)

AZIZ: That's beautiful, Aazam! A court thief! I'd never thought of that. It opens up all sorts of possibilities . . . There's Karim now!
(*Karim comes in with a man, bound and gagged.*)
You are late. Are you sure this is the right man?

KARIM: No need to worry.

AZIZ: Excellent. Here you are. (*Gives him a purse.*) I'll send for you if there's any more work.
(*Karim salaams and exits.*)

AAZAM: Who is this animal?

AZIZ: Wait and see. Untie him first.
(*Aazam unties the man. Aziz stares at him and an expression of horror spreads on his face.*)
My God! I'll kill that ass Karim! He's brought the wrong man!

MAN: I told him so. I told him who I was. I told him clearly. The rascal wouldn't listen. Tied me up. Me! Let the Sultan hear of this outrage. He'll whip you to death.

AZIZ, AAZAM: The Sultan?

AZIZ: We beg your pardon, Sir. There's been a mistake. Karim was supposed to bring some one else—a Turk merchant. But—may we know who you are?

MAN: You'll soon know, you scoundrels. I am Ghiyas-ud-din Abbasid. The descendant of Khalif Abbasid. I am the Guest of Honour of His Majesty.

AAZAM: Ya Allah!

(*Aziz and Aazam prostrate themselves in front of him.*)

GHIYAS-UD-DIN:   You'll pay for this! I've come all the way from Arabia and not a soul dared touch me. They trembled at the mention of my name. And now this outrage! You'll hear more about this—

AZIZ:   Forgive us, Your Worship. It was a mistake. There's been a slip somewhere. It's just that you are alone—I mean the Sultan's Guest of Honour—from the Holy Family of the Khalifs—

GHIYAS-UD-DIN:   Mind your own business, slave. I'll soon have an entourage, as soon as the Sultan knows I've arrived. He is sending a special entourage from Daulatabad.

AZIZ:   Then perhaps Your Worship will allow us to make amends for this sacrilege by following you? We'll be your slaves till you reach Daulatabad.

GHIYAS-UD-DIN:   Hm! You may redeem yourself that way. Get up. No need to prostrate yourself so long. Yes, I do need guides. It's an unfamiliar country and the people here are treacherous. The moment they know you are a foreigner they're out to rob you. Yes, you'll do till the entourage arrives.

AZIZ:   But haven't you been here before, Your Worship? Haven't you see the Sultan?

GHIYAS-UD-DIN:   I haven't. But I shall soon.

(*In the meantime, Aazam has spread a mat on which Ghiyas-ud-Din sits imperially. Aazam offers him some fruits to eat.*)

AZIZ:   Forgive me if I am talking beyond my station, Your Worship. But I must warn you that the Sultan is in a suspicious frame of mind, we hear. There have been a lot of deaths since he came to Daulatabad.

GHIYAS-UD-DIN:   Yes, I've heard all that. I'm not worried.

AZIZ:   Recently he flogged a man to death, had his body filled with straw and strung up in the market place—all because the man claimed to be a descendant of the Prophet.

GHIYAS-UD-DIN:   For a common thief you talk too much. What's your name?

AZIZ:   Aziz, Your Worship and this is Aazam. I realize I sound impertinent, Your Worship. We are happy to follow you to Daulatabad, be your slaves to make up for our sacrilege. But Your Worship will forgive us for being worried about our necks—

GHIYAS-UD-DIN:   You don't need to worry. I have got the Sultan's
   letters with me—and the ring he sent as a mark of recognition.
   (*Shows the ring.*) I know there are no precious stones in it. But
   that would have attracted too much attention.

AZIZ:   The Sultan is a wise man. But Your Worship has no friends
   or acquaintances in Daulatabad?

GHIYAS-UD-DIN:   (*Irritated.*) You ask too many questions for a slave.
   No, no friends there. You just hold your tongue and follow
   me.

        (*Aziz laughs. Ghiyas-ud-Din looks at him, suddenly suspicious.*
        *Aziz bursts into loud laughter and jumps up.*)

AZIZ:   Caught him, Aazam! He fell into my trap like a mouse. This
   is the goods, Aazam, this is it! I had heard he was here—without
   a paisa on him but boasting of his good fortune—

GHIYAS-UD-DIN:   What do you mean?

AZIZ:   In five minutes, you won't need to know any meanings.

AAZAM:   (*Frightened.*) Don't kill him, Aziz, please don't! He's the
   Khalif's grandson—

GHIYAS-UD-DIN:   (*Frightened.*) Kill me? But why? What'll you gain
   by killing me? I've nothing—you know that—I'll get nothing
   till I reach Daulatabad—I'm a poor man. Why kill me?

AAZAM:   He is right, Aziz.

GHIYAS-UD-DIN:   It's the truth, I swear. That's how I've come here
   alive—no one could get anything out of me. What do you want
   from me? Look, if you come with me to Daulatabad, I'll see
   you'll get something too—

AZIZ:   I am not going with you. I am going in your place.

AAZAM:   Aziz, listen—

AZIZ:   Shut up! Don't waste your breath! We'll never get an
   opportunity like this again. Arabia must be full of the Khalif's
   descendants. They were a fertile lot, the Khalifs. Now the
   Sultan's picked this rat up from the gutters for some game of
   his own. Who will worry about this fool when people are dying
   without food in Daulatabad? Get out now. Get out. You'll just
   make things worse.

        (*Aazam goes out.*)

GHIYAS-UD-DIN:   Don't kill me, please. I'll kiss your feet. Take
   everything—my ring, letters, everything. I'll go back. I'll go

back to my village. I won't bother you. Please don't kill me. I'll kiss your feet. Please let me go. (*Embraces his legs.*)

AZIZ:   No!

GHIYAS-UD-DIN:   No? No! No! I knew it. I knew something like this would happen. It was too good to be true—to grow up in filth, live in filth—and then a letter from nowhere. A hope—a ray of light. Now my fate will change, I thought, now I'll be happy. Now things will start afresh. So I started. But I knew it was too good—good things don't come like that—they don't stay—

　　　(*He gives Aziz a sudden push. Aziz falls down on the floor. Ghiyas-ud-Din runs out.*)

AZIZ:   (*Shouts without getting up.*) Stop him, Aazam. Stop him.

　　　(*Jumps up and runs out. Noise of a scuffle.*)

AZIZ:   (*Off-stage.*) That's it, Aazam! Bravo!

GHIYAS-UD-DIN:   (*Off-stage.*) Don't kill me, please.

　　　(*A scream. Then silence. Aazam comes in running. He is covered with blood. He is sweating, trembling and weeping. After a while Aziz comes in, with Ghiyas-ud-Din's turban on his head.*)

AZIZ:   Why are you crying, you clown?

AAZAM:   Don't talk to me—God! God! Why did I stop him? Why didn't I let him go?

　　　(*Aziz opens Ghiyas-ud-Din's bundle.*)

AZIZ:   You are a funny creature. You have seen enough corpses to last you seven lives. You have stuffed them with straw, practised obscenities on them. And still you can't see a man die. (*Takes out a robe and puts it on.*) How do I look, eh? The great-grandson of the Khalif!

　　　(*Aazam looks away. Aziz slaps him on the back.*)

Laugh, you fool, laugh. Celebrate! What are you crying for? Look, look at the palace doors. They are opening for us. Dance, dance, you son of an ass—

　　　(*Sings.*)

Grandson of the Khalif! Great-grandson of the Khalif! Great-great-great-grandson of the Khalif!

　　　(*Sings and dances in a circle, clapping his hands. Aziz looks at him angrily. Then slowly his face breaks into a smile and soon he is laughing.*)

# Scene Ten

*The Palace. Muhammad is looking out of the window. The Step-Mother comes in.*

STEP-MOTHER: Muhammad, do you know what's happening outside?

MUHAMMAD: Yes.

STEP-MOTHER: Why are you doing it?

MUHAMMAD: What else can I do? I said the new copper coins would have the same value as the silver dinars. Now I can't go against my own orders.

STEP-MOTHER: But this is sheer folly! The Vizier says there are five hundred carts out there and they are all full of counterfeit coins. Are you going to exchange them all for silver?

MUHAMMAD: There's nothing else for it. I should have expected this but didn't—that was my fault. If I don't withdraw the coins now, the whole economy will be in shambles. It's in a bad enough state already.

STEP-MOTHER: Five hundred carts on the first day! And what about tomorrow and the day after? You are just legalizing robbery—

MUHAMMAD: It's all their wealth. I can't let my whim ruin them.

STEP-MOTHER: And how is a treasury full of counterfeit coins going to help them? Will that revive your economy?

MUHAMMAD: Don't worry, Mother. The coins aren't going into the treasury. They'll all be heaped in the new rose garden.

STEP-MOTHER: What's wrong with you? You spent years planning that rose garden and now—

MUHAMMAD: Now I don't need a rose garden. I built it because I wanted to make for myself an image of Sadi's poems. I wanted every rose in it to be a poem. I wanted every thorn in it to prick and quicken the senses. But I don't need these airy trappings now; a funeral has no need for a separate symbol.

STEP-MOTHER: Then why don't you stop the funeral? Why this unending line of corpses? Muhammad, I have been hearing rumours lately. The Amirs and Khans are apparently getting upset because you are hounding them about Najib.

MUHAMMAD: I am not hounding them. I merely want to find out who murdered Najib.

STEP-MOTHER: Is it true five of them have fled?

MUHAMMAD: Not five—four. The fifth committed suicide. Amir Jalal-ud-din.

STEP-MOTHER: Oh God!

MUHAMMAD: He told his wife he knew who had killed Najib. One of his servants overheard the conversation.

STEP-MOTHER: (*Alarmed.*) Please, don't go on like this. Please. Najib's dead. Finished. You can't drive the nobles to rebellion for his sake?

MUHAMMAD: Don't you think it strange that an Amir like Jalal-ud-din should kill himself to save the murderer? It must be someone very special.

STEP-MOTHER: I'm glad Najib's dead. He was leading you astray. It's because you wouldn't trust anyone as much as him that the kingdom's in this state! The Ulema are against you; the noble-men are against you; the people hate you. It's all his work. I'm glad he's dead, He should have died a long time ago.

MUHAMMAD: Najib wasn't loyal to me; he was loyal to the throne. The day he turned against me I would have known I'd made a mistake.

STEP-MOTHER: Why not forget him? What good is it to the throne—

MUHAMMAD: I must know who killed him and why.

STEP-MOTHER: Muhammad, how long are you going to torture yourself like this?

MUHAMMAD: Not for long. The Amirs will return. If they don't, I'll be sorry for their families.

STEP-MOTHER: You frighten me, Muhammad, you really do. Please stop this. Muhammad—please—for my sake.

(*No reply.*)

Won't you? I appeal to you.

(*No reply.*)

All right. I killed him. I had him murdered.

MUHAMMAD: (*Exploding.*) For God's sake, don't joke about it! And don't try to be noble and save me from the moronic Amirs and Khans. This isn't a small thing.

STEP-MOTHER: I am perfectly serious. I had him poisoned.

MUHAMMAD: Stop it! Why are you torturing me now? Don't you see how you're burning out my guts with your infantile jokes?

STEP-MOTHER: Why shouldn't I have killed him? It was easier than killing one's father or brother. It was better than killing Sheikh Imam-ud-din.

MUHAMMAD: I killed them—yes—but I killed them for an ideal. Don't I know its results? Don't you think I've suffered from the curse? My mother won't speak to me—I can't even look into a mirror for fear of seeing their faces in it. I had only three friends in the world—you, Najib and Barani. And now you want me to believe you killed Najib. Why are you doing this to me?

STEP-MOTHER: It's only seven years ago that you came to the throne. How glorious you were then, how idealistic, how full of hopes. Look at your kingdom now. It's become a kitchen of death—all because of him. I couldn't bear it any longer.

MUHAMMAD: But you don't know that for the past few months he had been advising me against violence, do you? He wanted me to hold back my sword for the stability of the throne.

STEP-MOTHER: Then why didn't you?

MUHAMMAD: Because I couldn't. Not now. Remember Shihab-ud-din of Sampanshahr? He was the first man I killed with my own hands. And I had a glimmer then of what now I know only too well. Not words but the sword—that's all I have to keep my faith in my mission. Why should Najib be sacrificed for that?

STEP-MOTHER: You had your share of futile deaths. I have mine now.

MUHAMMAD: (*Shouting.*) No, they were not futile. They gave me what I wanted—power, strength to shape my thoughts, strength to act, strength to recognize myself. What did your little murder give you?

(*Suddenly freezes. Stares at her. Then quietly.*)

Woman, woman, so you are also one of them! So that's what you too wanted! Mother is annoyed she can't control me. And now you too are trying the same game, aren't you? Get rid of Najib, so you could control me?

STEP-MOTHER: I want nothing for myself. You are my life, Muhammad. You know that. If I had wanted power, I wouldn't have confessed.

MUHAMMAD: You needn't have confessed. I would have found out on my own. Or else, the Amirs would have rebelled. And then, what power? Clever you. You thought I wouldn't punish you, didn't you? Because I love you more than I have loved anyone in my life. That was the price of your love, wasn't it? (*Suddenly in agony.*) Why did you have to do it?

STEP-MOTHER: (*Puts her hand on his shoulder.*) Listen to me—

MUHAMMAD: Don't touch me! There's only one punishment for treachery—death!
(*Claps twice.*)

STEP-MOTHER: Don't be a fool, Muhammad. I'm telling you for your own sake. My death won't make you happy. You have enough ghosts to haunt you. Don't add mine to it.

MUHAMMAD: The others died unjustly. You deserve to die—
(*Two soldiers enter.*)
You are worse than an adulteress. But I can't think of a worse punishment for you. Take her to prison.
(*The Step-Mother stands petrified. The soldiers are also baffled.*)
(*Screaming.*) Take her away!
(*The soldiers hold her. She tries to break away.*)
Tell the Nayab Vizier I want her stoned to death publicly tomorrow morning.

STEP-MOTHER: (*Finding her voice.*) Not that, Muhammad, don't do that to me—please.

MUHAMMAD: That's how an adulteress dies. Take her away.

STEP-MOTHER: Muhammad, please—
(*She is dragged away. Muhammad stands looking stunned. Then suddenly he falls to his knees and clutches his hands to his breast.*)

MUHAMMAD: God, God in Heaven, please help me. Please don't let go of my hand. My skin drips with blood and I don't know how much of it is mine and how much of others. I started in Your path, Lord, why am I wandering naked in this desert now? I started in search of You. Why am I become a pig rolling in this gory mud? Raise me. Clean me. Cover me with Your Infinite Mercy. I can only clutch at the hem of Your cloak with my bloody fingers and plead. I can only beg—have pity on me.

I have no one but You now. Only You. Only You . . .
You . . . You . . . You . . .
(*Enter Barani.*)

BARANI: In the name . . .
(*Stops. Muhammad raises his head.*)

MUHAMMAD: Come in, Barani. You've come at the right moment.
You have saved me from treachery, you know. I was trying to
pray! Think of that—no one in my kingdom is allowed to pray
and I was praying. Against my own orders! But what else could
I do, Barani? My legs couldn't hold me up any longer.

BARANI: (*Smiles.*) You needn't worry, Your Majesty. I'm here
because I insisted on bringing the joyful tidings myself—

MUHAMMAD: Joy? It's such a long time since I heard that word.

BARANI: We have just received a letter from your Governor.
Ghiyas-ud-din Abbasid, the descendant of the Khalif's is arriving
here—within the next month or so. We can all pray now, Your
Majesty.

MUHAMMAD: What's the use? I was trying to pray—but I could
only find words learnt by rote which left no echo in the heart.
I am teetering on the brink of madness, Barani, but the madness
of God still eludes me. (*Shouting.*) And why should I deserve
that madness? I have condemned my mother to death and I'm
not even sure she was guilty of the crime . . .

(*The Announcer.*)


ANNOUNCER: Attention! Attention! Muhammad Tughlaq who
craves only for the mercy of Allah and for the blessings of the
Khalifs, hereby announces that His Worship Ghiyas-ud-din
Muhammad, son of His Worship Abdul Kahir, grandson of His
Worship Yusuf, great-grandson of His Worship Abdul Aziz,
great-great-grandson of His Imperial Holiness Abbasid Al-Mustansir, the Khalif of Baghdad, will bless and purify Daulatabad
by arriving here tomorrow afternoon. And Muhammad is sure
that the citizens of this city will collect in large numbers to
welcome this Saviour.

This is a holy day for us—a day of joy! And its glory will
be crowned by the fact that the Public Prayer, which has been
mute in our land these five years, will be started again from next
Friday. Henceforth every Muslim will pray five times a day as
enjoined by the Holy Koran and declare himself a Faithful Slave
of the Lord. Attention! Attention!

# Scene Eleven

*A plain outside the fort of Daulatabad. Crowds of citizens.*

FIRST MAN: Prayer! Prayer! Who wants prayers now?

SECOND MAN: Ask them to give us some food.

FIRST MAN: There's no food. Food's only in the palace. It's prayers for us.

SECOND MAN: The Amirs have food.

FIRST MAN: We starve and they want us to pray. They want to save our souls.

THIRD MAN: Is it true the Sultan has opened up his granary?

SECOND MAN: There was not a grain in it! Not a skin of paddy.

FIRST MAN: And they want us to pray.

THIRD MAN: The other day my younger brother came here from our village. He says it's much worse there. We are better off here, he says. They have to pay twenty grains of silver for a fistful of wheat. And the scenes he saw on his way here! Ugh!

SECOND MAN: (*Getting annoyed.*) Hm . . .

THIRD MAN: He says the roads are lined with skeletons. A man starved to death right in front of his eyes. In Doab, people are eating barks off the trees, he says. Yes, and women have to make do with skins of dead horses.

SECOND MAN: Shut up.

THIRD MAN: In Baran—that's wnere Barani, the Sultan's friend, comes from you know—they have to eat burnt strips of skin, he says. No one knows what animals—

SECOND MAN: Why don't you shut up?

(*The crowd listens, tensely.*)

THIRD MAN: He says we are much better off here. Not them. On his way here he saw people crowding round a butcher's shop. You know why? To catch the blood spurting from the slaughtered breasts and drink it!

SECOND MAN: Shut up, you butcher—

(*He attacks the Third Man. There's a fight. The Second Man throws the Third Man down, sits on his chest and beats him. He is crying even as he beats. The others watch.*)

FIRST MAN:   Why do they need prayer?

(*Music and the announcers are heard from the two sides of the stage.*)

ANNOUNCER I:   Attention! Attention! The Slave of the Lord, the Upholder of the Word of the Prophet, the Friend of the Khalif, the Faithful, Sultan Muhammad Tughlaq—

ANNOUNCER II:   Attention! Attention! The Protector of the Faith, the Descendant of the Holy Khalif al-Mustansir, Amir-ul-Mominin Ghiyas-ud-din Muhammad—

(*Aziz, Aazam and their entourage enter from one side. Exactly at the same moment, Muhammad and his entourage step down from the fort. There is tense silence. Muhammad stares at Aziz as though he is not quite sure what is happening. The Hindu Woman of Scene Seven steps out of the crowd and stares at Aziz. Her husband pulls her back. Muhammad steps forward and embraces Aziz.*)

MUHAMMAD:   Welcome to our city, Your Holiness, welcome to our poor land. My kingdom rejoices at the arrival of your gracious presence. We have waited for years for this joyful moment. Our streets have waited in silence for the moment when the call to the holy prayer will ring in them again. And each year has been a century. We have waited long, Your Holiness, and our sins have become shadows that entwine round our feet. They have become our dumbness and deprived us of prayer. They have become the fiery sun and burnt up our crops. Now the moment has come for me and my people to rejoice. Only you can save me now, Your Holiness, only the dust of your feet on my head can save me now—

(*Falls to his feet. The crowd gasps. Then everyone kneels.*)

AZIZ:   Amen.

(*Muhammad gets up. They embrace again. They depart to the accompaniment of the announcements.*)

HINDU WOMAN:   It's him! It's him—

THIRD MAN:   Who?

HINDU WOMAN:   He killed my child! Those eyes—I'll never forget them—he killed my child . . . (*Screams.*) He killed my child . . . (*Keeps on screaming.*)

FIRST MAN:   What's it?

SECOND MAN:   I didn't hear. Something about a child—

ANOTHER: She says someone killed her child—

FIRST MAN: Who killed the child?

SECOND MAN: I didn't hear properly. Probably the Sultan—

FIRST MAN: Who else will kill her child?

THIRD MAN: It's murder, that's what it is. To ask us to live without food. My daughter died without food. She was murdered.

FIRST MAN: How long are we going to starve like this?

SECOND MAN: Just a fistful of rice—a piece of meat would be enough—

FIRST MAN: We don't want any prayer. We want food—

SEVERAL VOICES: Yes, food—we want food—not prayer—

A SOLDIER: Quiet! Quiet!

FIRST MAN: (*Shouting.*) Kill us, kills us. Don't starve us to death. Kill us quickly . . .

SECOND MAN: They'll kill us, will they? Let's see who kills whom? Bring them down.

ALL: Bring him down—let's see—so they'll give us poison instead of food, will they—kill him—kill him—show him what we can do—

(*Confusion. Some of them mob the Soldier and beat him. A group of soldiers arrives and starts beating them, ordering them to keep quiet. The riots begin.*)

# Scene Twelve

(*The Palace. Aziz is eating some fruit. Aazam enters.*)

AAZAM: Aziz—

AZIZ: Shut up! I've told you not to call me by that name.

AAZAM: I'm fed up of these games, Aziz, I'm going.

AZIZ: Going? Where?

AAZAM: I don't know. But I've bribed two servants of the palace. They are to bring two horses. They'll be here with the horses inside of half an hour. So hurry up.

AZIZ: Fool, now you've probably made them suspicious. I've told you a hundred times nothing can happen to us here. You're asking for the butcher's block.

AAZAM: Have you seen the city? The people are like mad dogs. They have been screaming, burning houses, killing people for a whole week now. Have you ever stepped out of the palace?

AZIZ: Of course not.

AAZAM: I have. Twice.

AZIZ: Twice! Is your skull filled with dung? Twice! How did you go out?

AAZAM: There's a secret passage. I discovered it the day we came here. I have been through it. Twice. And do you know what the city is like? In the northern part, the houses are like forts and the streets are like little fingers. And they are full of dead bodies. Corpses and flies. It stank so much I almost fainted—I can't stand it any longer, Aziz. Today the people are a little quieter. They are tired; besides, they have to dispose of the bodies. Tomorrow they'll start again . . .

AZIZ: Now look. Why don't you think? Just once—once in your lifetime? How do you know the servants won't betray you? Listen to me. Stay in the palace. It's the safest place now.

AAZAM: Safe? This palace? Ha! The Sultan's mad. How can you trust him? Don't you know how he can slaughter people? How can you trust this lord of skins? It's better to trust servants. Listen.

You know there are those heaps of counterfeit coins in the garden outside my window?

AZIZ:  I hope they haven't scared you. After all, quite a lot of them are our handiwork.

AAZAM:  On the night we came here, I was so nervous I couldn't sleep. So I was standing by the window, looking at those heaps. They looked like giant ant-hills in the moonlight. Suddenly I saw a shadow moving among them. I stared. It was a man wandering alone in the garden. He went to a heap, stood there for half an hour, still as a rock. Then he dug into the heaps with his fists, raised his fists and let the coins trickle out. It was frightening. And you know who it was? Your Sultan. He does that every night—every single night—it's like witchcraft—

AZIZ:  So you are running away because the Sultan has insomnia? What about all that you were hoping to get? And what happens to me if you go? How will Ghiyas-ud-din Abbasid explain the disappearance of his disciple?

AAZAM:  You come with me too, Aziz. I can't go alone. I've tied all our presents in a bundle. It's a huge bundle. Will last us for ever. You are a clever man, Aziz. I know I am a fool. I can't survive without you . . . It's time. The horses will probably have come. Let's go. Come on . . .

AZIZ:  I order you to stay, Aazam.

AAZAM:  I can't. I can't. I'll die of fright here.

AZIZ:  All right then. Go. Get out, you traitor.

AAZAM:  What else can I do? I wish you would come too. Look. We'll forget all this wealth, these courts, this luxury and live in peace. Please come . . . please, Aziz, I'll kiss your feet—
    (*No reply.*)
    I'm going, Aziz . . .
    (*No reply.*)
    Good-bye.
    (*Goes out.*)

AZIZ:  Idiot!

# Scene Thirteen

*Another part of the Palace. Muhammad and Barani.*

MUHAMMAD:   May I know why, Barani?

BARANI:   It's as I said. Your Majesty, I have just received a letter from Baran and it says my mother's dead. I couldn't be by her side in the last moments of her life. I must be there at least for her funeral.

MUHAMMAD:   What did she die of, do you know?

BARANI:   I don't know, Your Majesty. The letter didn't say anything more.

MUHAMMAD:   I see. (*Pause.*) And you will return to the court after the funeral, won't you?

BARANI:   (*Frightened.*) I don't know, Your Majesty.

MUHAMMAD:   If you are only going for the funeral, why shouldn't you be able to come back?

BARANI:   (*Desperately.*) I don't know.

MUHAMMAD:   Don't you? Because I do. She died in the riots, didn't she, when my soldiers butchered everyone in sight—old men, women, children, everyone? So you see, even I know what is happening in my kingdom. I may be responsible for that massacre, I accept. But have I really fallen so low that even you have to lie to me?

BARANI:   (*Almost crying.*) I don't know. I don't know. Please don't ask me. I beg of you.

(*Silence. A Soldier enters running.*)

SOLDIER:   In the name of Allah. A terrible thing—Your Majesty, I don't know how to—

MUHAMMAD:   What is it now?

SOLDIER:   Your Majesty, Aazam Jahan, the friend of His Holiness Ghiyas-ud-din Abbasid, is dead.

BARANI:   Dead?

SOLDIER:   Murdered, Your Majesty. I was on sentry duty at the mouth of the secret tunnel from the palace. I heard a scream. I ran to the spot. It was Aazam Jahan. He was lying in a pool of blood.

BARANI: Heaven have mercy on us!

MUHAMMAD: Was anyone else there?

SOLDIER: Two horsemen, Your Majesty. They had a big bundle with them. But before I could even shout, they were gone. I didn't even see their faces—

MUHAMMAD: Did he say anything before he died?

SOLDIER: No, Your Majesty. He was alive for a while. When I went near I thought—I thought—

MUHAMMAD: Yes?

SOLDIER: I thought he was laughing—giggling. But of course it could be just—his dying breath—

(*There is a long silence. Muhammad stares at the Soldier, stunned and incredulous.*)

MUHAMMAD: Not a word of this to anyone. Not even to His Holiness Ghiyas-ud-din Abbasid. No one in the palace must know. You understand?

SOLDIER: Yes, Your Majesty.

MUHAMMAD: Go back to your place. And ask the doorman to fetch His Holiness—at once.

SOLDIER: Yes, Your Majesty.

(*Goes out.*)

MUHAMMAD: (*Almost to himself.*) Don't you think it ironic that a man who has just come from Arabia should prefer the bloody streets to the palace?

BARANI: But I don't understand, Your Majesty, I can't understand how—

MUHAMMAD: You wanted to see history formed in front of your eyes, didn't you? Just wait a few moments, and you'll see not just the form but the coiled intestines of it.

BARANI: (*Wounded.*) Your Majesty is a learned man and has every right to laugh at a poor fool like me. But I implore Your Majesty to understand I am not going because my life here has been futile. I have spent seven years here and the greatest historians of the world would have given half their lives to see a year in it. Your Majesty has given me a gift—

MUHAMMAD: Must there be a farewell speech before you go? You want to go. Go. That's all there is to it.

(*Silence.*)

BARANI: (*Suddenly remembering.*) But the public prayer! It' to start within half-an-hour! It wouldn't be right to start it when the palace is in mourning. Your Majesty must—

MUHAMMAD: No, no, no! This is the first public prayer in my kingdom after a silence of five years! We are praying because a holy man like Ghiyas-ud-din Abbasid has come to our land and blessed us! We can't let anything stop that! (*Laughs.*) Oh Barani, Najib should have been here now. He would have loved this farce.

(*Aziz enters with soldiers. Barani and Muhammad bow. The soldiers bow and retire.*)

AZIZ: (*Blessing them.*) May Heaven guide Your Majesty.

MUHAMMAD: I hope Your Holiness is well.

AZIZ: Who would have grounds for complaint when the generosity of Your Majesty looks after him?

MUHAMMAD: I hope Your Holiness has not been too inconvenienced by the riots. I was busy and couldn't attend to your needs personally. And now that I see you, I stand a bearer of evil tidings. We have just received some tragic news. (*Pause.*) Aazam Jahan's body has been found outside the palace. He was murdered.

AZIZ: May Allah save our souls. What's happening to this world? What's man coming to if even an innocent like Aazam Jahan isn't to be spared the sword?

MUHAMMAD: Who are you?

(*Silence. For a moment no one speaks. Aziz is obviously frightened.*) Who are you? How long did you hope to go on fooling us with your masquerade?

BARANI: But your Majesty—

MUHAMMAD: Answer me. Don't make me lose my temper.

AZIZ: I am a dhobi from Shiknar. My first name was Aziz. There have been many others since then.

BARANI: But—what about His Holiness?

MUHAMMAD: Do you know the punishment for killing a saint like Ghiyas-ud-din Abbasid? And for deceiving me and my subjects?

AZIZ: (*Bolder.*) No, Your Majesty, though I have never underestimated Your Majesty's powers of imagination. But it would be a grave injustice if I were punished, Your Majesty.

BARANI: What's happening here?

AZIZ: 'Saint' is a word meant for people like Sheikh Imam-ud-din. I doubt if your Majesty would have used it for Ghiyas-ud-din. I know I am a dhobi and he was a descendant of the Khalif. But surely Your Majesty has never associated greatness with pedigree.

MUHAMMAD: Be careful, dhobi. Don't overreach yourself.

AZIZ: I daren't. But since Your Majesty came to the throne, I have been your most devout servant. I have studied every order, followed every instruction, considered every measure of Your Majesty's with the greatest attention. I insist I am Your Majesty's true disciple.

MUHAMMAD: Don't try to flatter me. I am accustomed to it.

AZIZ: It's hardly flattering you, Your Majesty, to say I am your disciple. But I have watched Your Majesty try to explain your ideas and acts to the people. And I have seen with regret how few have understood them.

BARANI: (*Who is just beginning to comprehend.*) Your Majesty, this scoundrel is trying to spread a net of words around you. It's dangerous even to talk to him. He must be punished at once.

AZIZ: Come, sir, let's be sensible. You know His Majesty will never do that to me.

MUHAMMAD: Won't I?

AZIZ: Forgive me. But Your Majesty has publicly welcomed me as a saint, started the public prayers after a lapse of five years in my honour, called me a Saviour. Your Majesty has even—forgive me for pointing it out, I wasn't responsible for it—fallen at my feet, publicly.

BARANI: Villain—

AZIZ: But I am not a common blackmailer, Your Majesty. I stand here on the strength of my convictions and my loyalty to you.

MUHAMMAD: What do you want to say?

AZIZ: I was a poor starving dhobi, when Your Majesty came to the throne and declared the brotherhood of all religions. Does the Sultan remember the Brahmin who brought a case against him and won? I was that Brahmin.

MUHAMMAD: Was the disguise necessary?

AZIZ: I think so. (*Pause.*) Soon after that Your Majesty introduced the new copper currency. I succumbed to its temptation.

BARANI:  God . . . God . . .

AZIZ:  There was enough money in that business, but too much competition. Soon it became unprofitable, so we took the silver dinars and went to Doab and bought some land there for farming.

BARANI:  But this is nonsense! There has been famine there for five years . . .

MUHAMMAD:  That's exactly his point. They got the land dirt-cheap and collected the State subsidy for farmers. When they were discovered, they ran into the hills and became robbers. (*With mock humility to Aziz.*) Am I right?

AZIZ:  Dare I contradict what the whole world knows about His Majesty's wisdom? But Your Majesty missed out an important stage in my life. Your officers track down criminals with the zest of a tribe of hunters and there was only one way to escape them. We joined them as servants. We had to shift the corpses of all the rebels executed by the State and hang them up for exhibition.

  Such famous kings, warriors and leaders of men passed through our hands then! Beautiful strong bodies and bodies eaten-up by corruption—all, all were stuffed with straw and went to the top of the poles.

  One day, suddenly I had a revelation. This was all human life was worth, I said. This was the real meaning of the mystery of death—straw and skin! With that enlightenment I found peace. We left the camp and headed for the hills.

MUHAMMAD:  Yes, that was a rather important stage.

AZIZ:  One day I heard about a beggar who claimed to be Ghiyas-ud-din Abbasid and was on his way to the capital—I couldn't resist the temptation of seeing my master in person. I admit I killed Ghiyas-ud-din and cheated you. Yet I am Your Majesty's true disciple. I ask you, Your Majesty, which other man in India has spent five years of his life fitting every act, deed and thought to Your Majesty's words?

BARANI:  This man should be buried alive this minute!

AZIZ:  I only acted according to His Majesty's edicts.

MUHAMMAD:  (*Exploding.*) Hold your tongue, fool! You dare pass judgement on me? You think your tongue is so light and swift that you can trap me by your stupid clowning? Let's see how

well it wags when hanging from the top of a pole. I haven't
cared for the bravest and wisest of men—you think I would
succumb to you, a dhobi, masquerading as a saint?

AZIZ:     (*Quietly.*) What if I am a dhobi, Your Majesty? When it
comes to washing away filth, no saint is a match for a dhobi.
(*Muhammad suddenly bursts into a guffaw. There is a slight
hysterical tinge to the laughter.*)

MUHAMMAD:     (*Laughing.*) Checkmate! Checkmate! I don't think I
have ever seen such insolence. This man's a genius—all right,
tell me. What punishment should I give you for your crimes?

AZIZ:     Make me an officer of your State, Your Majesty.

MUHAMMAD:     That would be punishing myself—not you.

AZIZ:     All these years I have been a beggar wasting my life and I'm
not proud of that. I beg Your Majesty to give me a chance to
show my loyalty. I'm ready to die for my Sultan.

MUHAMMAD:     I don't know why I am acting like a fool. Yet perhaps
a State office really would be the best punishment for you.
You'll have to return to Arabia after Aazam Jahan's funeral, and
disappear on the way. Can you do it?

AZIZ:     It certainly won't be the first time I've done that.

MUHAMMAD:     Good, Then go to the Deccan. I'll give you a letter
for Khusrau Malik appointing you as an officer in his army.
He'll look after you.

AZIZ:     What can I say? How can I express my gratitude? In the
name of the Prophet, I swear—

MUHAMMAD:     Don't overdo it. It's time for the prayer. Remember,
you are still His Holiness Ghiyas-ud-din Abbasid and you have
to be there to lead the prayer. Be off now.

AZIZ:     Your Majesty's most faithful servant.
(*Bows and retires. Muhammad slowly moves to the throne. He
looks tired, dispirited. There is silence for a while. Barani can't
contain himself any longer.*)

BARANI:     But why? Why?

MUHAMMAD:     All your life you wait for someone who understands
you. And then—you meet him—punishment for wanting too
much! . . . As he said, 'One day suddenly I had a revelation'.

BARANI:     By all the history I know, I swear he'll stab you in the
back. This is sheer folly. He is a thief and a murderer and Your
Majesty knows he won't keep trust. Once he has power in the

Deccan, his ambition will know no barriers. He is bound to find unlimited scope for his villainy there. He is bound to rebel against the Sultan. How can you not see that, Your Majesty?

MUHAMMAD: I forgave Ain-ul-Mulk once, and you were on my side then.

BARANI: But how can one mention Ain-ul-Mulk in the same breath as this rascal?

MUHAMMAD: Last week I received a letter from Ain-ul-Mulk. He has invited me and my subjects to his capital to stay there until the famine here subsides.

BARANI: He is a great man, a great friend of yours—

MUHAMMAD: A friend? How are you so sure it's his friendship that invites us to his capital? You know that, since the day he killed Sheikh Imam-ud-din, he has lost his hold on people. His maulvis won't support him, his people don't trust him. He needs my support now. How do you know he isn't inviting me to strengthen himself?

BARANI: Then . . . Your Majesty isn't accepting the invitation?

MUHAMMAD: There is only one place to go back to now. Delhi. Back to Delhi, Barani, I have to get back to Delhi with my people.

BARANI: But why—why are you doing this to yourself and your people? Your subjects starve for you—struggle for you—die for you—and you honour this murderer? What's the logic in it? It's criminals like him that deserve to die. Death would be too simple a punishment for him. It wouldn't be enough if you flogged the skin off his back. It wouldn't be enough if you had his tongue pulled out. It wouldn't even be enough if you had him put in a sack and tied to a running horse—

MUHAMMAD: Bravo! I doubt if even that dhobi could have thought of so many tortures—

(*Barani shudders as though he were slapped in the face.*)

If justice was as simple as you think or logic as beautiful as I had hopes, life would have been so much clearer. I have been chasing these words now for five years and now I don't know if I am pursuing a mirage or fleeing a shadow. Anyway what do all these subtle distinctions matter in the blinding madness of the day? Sweep your logic away into a corner, Barani, all I need now is myself and my madness—madness to prance in a field eaten bare by the scarecrow violence. But I am not alone, Barani. Thank Heaven! For once I am not alone. I have a Companion to share my madness now—the Omnipotent God! (*Tired.*) When you pass your final judgement on me, don't forget Him.

BARANI:   Who am I to pass judgement on you, Your Majesty? I have to judge myself now and that's why I must go and go immediately. I am terrified when I think of all the tortures I recommended only a moment ago. I am a weak man, Your Majesty. I don't have your strength to play with violence and yet not be sucked in by it. Your Majesty warned me when I slipped and I am grateful for that. I ask Your Majesty's permission to go while I'm still safe.

*(Waits for an answer. There's no answer. Muhammad is sitting on the throne with his eyes closed.)*

Your Majesty—

*(No answer.)*

Your Majesty—

MUHAMMAD:   (*Opening his eyes.*) Yes?

BARANI:   Is Your Majesty not feeling well?

MUHAMMAD:   I am suddenly feeling tired. And sleepy. For five years sleep has avoided me and now suddenly it's coming back. Go, Barani. But before you go—pray for us.

*(Closes his eyes again. Barani bows and exits, obviously in tears. There is silence on the stage for a while, and then a Servant comes in.)*

SERVANT:   In the name of . . .

*(He sees that Muhammad is asleep and goes out. Muhammad's head falls forward on his chest in deep sleep. The Servant re-enters with a shawl which he carefully wraps round the Sultan. He is about to go out when the Muezzin's call to prayer is heard. The Servant turns to wake the Sultan, then after a pause goes out without doing so.)*

MUEZZIN:   (*Off-stage.*) Alla-Ho-Akbar! Alla-Ho-Akbar!
Alla-Ho-Akbar! Alla-Ho-Akbar!
Ashahado La Elaha Illilah
Ashahado La Elaha Illilah
Ashahado Anna Muhammadur Rasool Illah
Ashahado Anna Muhammadur Rasool Illah

Haiyah Alis Salaat—Haiyah Alis Salaat
Haiyah Salil Falaa—Haiyah Salil Falaa
Alla-Ho-Akbar! Alla-Ho-Akbar!
La Elaha Illilah . . .

> (*As the Muezzin's call fades away, Muhammad suddenly opens his eyes. He looks around, dazed and frightened, as though he can't comprehend where he is.* )